Identity, Territories, and Sustainability

Identity, Territories, and Sustainability: Challenges and Opportunities for Achieving the UN Sustainable Development Goals

BY

SALVATORE MONACO

Free University of Bozen-Bolzano, Italy

United Kingdom – North America – Japan – India – Malaysia – China

Emerald Publishing Limited
Emerald Publishing, Floor 5, Northspring, 21-23 Wellington Street, Leeds LS1 4DL.

First edition 2024

Copyright © 2024 Salvatore Monaco.
Published under exclusive licence by Emerald Publishing Limited.

Reprints and permissions service
Contact: www.copyright.com

No part of this book may be reproduced, stored in a retrieval system, transmitted in any form or by any means electronic, mechanical, photocopying, recording or otherwise without either the prior written permission of the publisher or a licence permitting restricted copying issued in the UK by The Copyright Licensing Agency and in the USA by The Copyright Clearance Center. Any opinions expressed in the chapters are those of the authors. Whilst Emerald makes every effort to ensure the quality and accuracy of its content, Emerald makes no representation implied or otherwise, as to the chapters' suitability and application and disclaims any warranties, express or implied, to their use.

British Library Cataloguing in Publication Data
A catalogue record for this book is available from the British Library

ISBN: 978-1-83797-550-1 (Print)
ISBN: 978-1-83797-549-5 (Online)
ISBN: 978-1-83797-551-8 (Epub)

INVESTOR IN PEOPLE

Contents

Foreword *vii*

Introduction: Integrating Territorial Identity into SDGs *1*

Chapter 1 SDG 1. End Poverty in All Its Forms Everywhere *15*

Chapter 2 SDG 2. End Hunger, Achieve Food Security and Improved Nutrition and Promote Sustainable Agriculture *25*

Chapter 3 SDG 3. Ensure Healthy Lives and Promote Well-Being for All at All Ages *33*

Chapter 4 SDG 4. Ensure Inclusive and Equitable Quality Education and Promote Lifelong Learning Opportunities for All *43*

Chapter 5 SDG 5. Achieve Gender Equality and Empower All Women and Girls *51*

Chapter 6 SDG 6. Ensure Availability and Sustainable Management of Water and Sanitation for All *63*

Chapter 7 SDG 7. Ensure Access to Affordable, Reliable, Sustainable, and Modern Energy for All *71*

Chapter 8 SDG 8. Promote Sustained, Inclusive and Sustainable Economic Growth, Full and Productive Employment, and Decent Work for All *81*

Chapter 9 SDG 9. Build Resilient Infrastructure, Promote Inclusive and Sustainable Industrialization, and Foster Innovation *87*

Chapter 10 SDG 10. Reduce Inequality Within and Among Countries *95*

Chapter 11 SDG 11. Make Cities and Human Settlements Inclusive, Safe, Resilient, and Sustainable 107

Chapter 12 SDG 12. Ensure Sustainable Consumption and Production Patterns 117

Chapter 13 SDG 13. Take Urgent Action to Combat Climate Change and Its Impacts 129

Chapter 14 SDG 14. Conserve and Sustainably Use the Oceans, Seas, and Marine Resources for Sustainable Development 137

Chapter 15 SDG 15. Protect, Restore, and Promote Sustainable Use of Terrestrial Ecosystems, Sustainably Manage Forests, Combat Desertification, Halt and Reverse Land Degradation, and Halt Biodiversity Loss 145

Chapter 16 SDG 16. Promote Peaceful and Inclusive Societies for Sustainable Development, Provide Access to Justice for All, and Build Effective, Accountable, and Inclusive Institutions at All Levels 157

Chapter 17 SDG 17. Strengthen the Means of Implementation and Revitalize the Global Partnership for Sustainable Development 167

Conclusions: Moving Forward with Territorial Identities – Concluding Perspectives 177

Index 189

Foreword

The separation of the environment from its social contexts may be seen at the root of the interlocking social, environmental, and climate crises we face today. With the adoption of Agenda 2030 in 2015, the international community finally acknowledged the need to address questions of the economy, society, and environment in one frame. This acknowledgment has entered international agreements through the 17 Sustainable Development Goals in Agenda 2030. But what might this mean in practice for different places and for the people living in these places in different parts of the world? As a recent issue on rural sustainability in Europe showed us (Arora-Jonsson et al., 2023), what sustainability means in one place may be quite different from another. This is where Salvatore Monaco's book on *Identity, Territories, and Sustainability* comes to our aid. The author takes on the arduous and much needed task of getting to the bottom of the relationship between territorial and collective identities, territorial policies, and what that might imply for sustainability.

Territories have been defined as bounded spaces – regulated, policed, and given meaning by the state and people. Territorial policies, including those seeking to promote sustainable development, may be seen as ways of influencing and controlling resources and people in a bounded space. The disregard of peoples, territories, and culture in policy-making in favor of the belief in science and economic development to solve our environmental and social problems are what I have come to see as the blind spots of policy-making. These blind spots lead us to overestimate our ability to do what is right and to act undemocratically without necessarily meaning to do so. Policymakers continue to treat as merely technical matters and decisions that are actually social and political ones and disregard the insight that culture too is politics (Arora-Jonsson, 2017).

Through the various chapters in his book, Salvatore Monaco brings culture, identity, and everyday relationships back into a discussion on sustainability. He stresses the importance of considering the complex interweaving of social, cultural, political, historical, and biophysical factors in shaping different sustainability trajectories in each place. Drawing on diverse case studies from around the world, the author demonstrates how environmental and social justice concerns have gained prominence in public debates and how territorial policies shape sustainability actions.

Sustainability in policy-making could be both positive and negative. As Stiernström (2023) shows us, defining a policy as sustainable can make it appear "just and good" regardless of what the policy infers and even if this entails the sacrifice of rural territories, such as by mining operations.

Salvatore Monaco's case studies examine diverse sustainability outcomes through the examination of grassroots movements and their role in shaping environmental and social justice discourses. He shows the pitfalls of territorial policies, such as those promoting the "green revolution" in countries in the global South, that disregarded traditional practices and local identities in favor of Western agricultural models. This resulted in the loss of biodiversity, environmental degradation, economic vulnerability, and lasting health problems.

Importantly, the book highlights the importance of taking the natural environment seriously and the differences that arise in different environments in relation to inland water bodies, land, forests, seas, or mountains. He brings attention to the work carried out by people, eco-social work, and championing social justice critical for sustainable territorial development.

As we navigate the many challenges with him, the book brings home to us all the importance of how collaboration and territorial identities can be catalysts for positive change, ushering in an equitable, inclusive, and prosperous future.

Seema Arora-Jonsson
Department of Urban and Rural Development
Swedish University of Agricultural Sciences
Uppsala, Sweden

References

Arora-Jonsson, S. (2017). Blind spots in environmental policy-making: How beliefs about science and development may jeopardize environmental solutions. *World Development Perspectives*, 5, 27–29.

Arora-Jonsson, S., McAreavey, R., Waldenström, C., Stiernström, A., Sandström, A., Asztalos Morell, I., Kuns, B., González-Hidalgo, M., Cras P., & Alarcon-Ferrari, C. (2023). Multiple dimensions of sustainability: Towards new rural futures in Europe. *Sociologia Ruralis*, 63(3), 377–378.

Stiernström, A. (2023). Sustainable development and sacrifice in the rural North. *Sociologia Ruralis*, 63(3), 661–682.

Introduction: Integrating Territorial Identity into SDGs

Abstract

The text introduces the theory of integrating territorial identity into the discourse on sustainability. It stresses the importance of considering for each place the complex interaction among social, cultural, political, historical, architectural, biophysical, geological, and hydrographic factors in shaping sustainable development trajectories. Sustainable development must certainly involve environmental, social, and economic aspects in an integrated manner, but it must be "territorially desirable" in the meantime. This vision represents a fundamental paradigm for a new way of approaching the Sustainable Development Goals (SDGs) and the path to sustainability. The proposed approach acknowledges that the way of achieving SDGs cannot be implemented without any differences worldwide. Instead, it must account for the specificities of each area and territory and the compatibility of actions with the identity of places.

Starting from '68 Movements around the world and growing out of the demands for social change, public awareness about the importance of sustainability has been increasing. Student protests, civil rights claims, and pacifism endorsed by 68ers contributed to creating a favorable context for discussing the interconnections between the struggle for social justice and environmental protection, which emphasized how social injustices often manifest as environmental injustices as well (Bryant & Bailey, 1997; Eckersley, 2004).

In the subsequent years, one of the regions where a strong commitment to the intersection of environmental and social issues was observed in the United States, where the civil rights movement, women's movement, and peace movement created a context for fruitful discussions on sustainability (Szasz, 2007). Opposition to the Vietnam War prompted many activists to reflect on the underlying causes of the conflict, including the impact of the military industry on the environment and human health (Young et al., 2004).

In Europe, during the '70s, the environmentalist movement gained strength and influence. Germany was one of the pioneering nations in promoting environmentally sustainable policies and practices. The German environmentalist movement addressed issues such as nature conservation, nuclear energy, and waste management (Dobson, 2007), setting the stage for claims that gradually spread to other regions.

The impact of the movements of the '60s and '70s extended well beyond the borders of the United States and Western Europe. In many other countries, both in the Global North and South, movements and organizations that embraced environmental issues as an integral part of the struggle for social justice emerged. In Latin America, for example, some indigenous movements and environmental organizations supported the defense of lands and natural resources against industrialization and the expansion of extractive activities (Martínez-Alier, 2003).

Attention to public participation and environmental justice has also been supported by new environmentalist movements, echoed by several scholars (Arora-Jonsson, 2013; O'Neill & Nicholson-Cole, 2009). In particular, the environmental justice movement has addressed the issue of environmental inequalities and highlighted the importance of including the voices of vulnerable communities in environmental decisions. The movement emerged in the United States in the '80s as a response to the environmental inequalities disproportionately affecting low-income and marginalized ethnic communities (Bullard & Johnson, 2000). The perspective of environmental justice highlighted how the most vulnerable communities are often exposed to greater environmental risks, since disadvantaged groups bear the negative effects of environmental decisions without real decision-making power. In this regard, Robert Bullard (1993) has introduced the concept of "environmental racism" to highlight how environmental inequalities are often linked to racial and socioeconomic factors. Anthony Giddens' work (2009) on the interconnection between social and power inequalities has further emphasized how inequalities are inherently linked to access to resources and opportunities which are necessary conditions for achieving sustainability. For instance, income inequalities can result in significant differences in individual ability to develop sustainable habits, such as purchasing eco-friendly products or accessing using low-impact technologies. Similarly, power inequalities can prevent certain social groups from political decisions and resource management.

The need to pursue environmental, economic, and social sustainability has led various actors to promote policies and practices aimed at fostering equitable economic growth, ensuring social inclusion, protecting the environment, and preserving natural resources. A key approach to achieving these goals has been the establishment of national sustainability councils or commissions which act as advisory bodies to the government, bringing together representatives from various sectors of society to formulate recommendations and strategies for sustainable development.

At the supranational level, bodies and institutions promoting sustainability have been established across different continents. In Europe, the European Union (EU) has a range of bodies and agencies working to promote sustainable policies and initiatives. The European Commission, the European Parliament, and the Council of the European Union play a key role in shaping and implementing environmental and climate policies at the community level. In Africa, the African Union (AU), founded in 2002 on the principles of equality and interdependence among member states, has established through its Agenda 2063 a series of goals for the continent, including peace, sustainable development, human rights, democracy, and promotion of local and regional economies. The first continental report on the implementation of Agenda 2063 was presented by President Alassane Ouattara of Ivory Coast on February 10, 2020, marking the beginning of a biennial reporting cycle through which progress toward the objectives in different areas of the Agenda and geographical regions are monitored. In the United States, the governmental body responsible for environmental protection and the promotion of sustainable development is the United States Environmental Protection Agency (EPA). The Agency was created on the proposal of President Nixon and became operational on December 2, 1970. The EPA is led by an administrator appointed by the President and confirmed by the Senate. It develops and implements environmental policies, regulations, and programs to reduce pollution, preserve natural resources, and promote sustainable practices.

To address global issues, the United Nations (UN) organization helps facilitate dialogue and collaboration among countries with the aim of fostering international cooperation. Through various specialized agencies, programs, and funds – such as the United Nations Environment Programme (UNEP) and the United Nations Industrial Development Organization (UNIDO) – the UN provides technical support, financial resources, and coordination efforts to promote sustainability on a global scale. The UN was founded on October 24, 1945, after World War II. Its mission is to promote peace, international security, and social and economic progress. It consists of several organs, including the General Assembly, the Security Council, the Economic and Social Council, the Secretariat, and the International Court of Justice. Each member state has a representative in the General Assembly, which is the principal organ responsible for decisions on global issues. The UN also organizes conferences and international summits that bring together world leaders, experts, and representatives of civil society to discuss global challenges and adopt concrete commitments.

The UN Conference on the Human Environment, held in Stockholm in 1972, represents a focal moment in the history of the environment and sustainable development. This global event marked the first attempt to bring together political leaders, experts, and representatives of civil society to discuss the environmental challenges the world was facing. The conference highlighted the importance of addressing environmental issues holistically, recognizing that economic and social development must go hand in hand with environmental conservation. It also sheds light on crucial topics such as pollution, deforestation, natural resource management, and biodiversity conservation. In addition, it recognized the interconnectedness between the environment and social development, emphasizing that sustainable natural resource management and greater social equity are both essential to ensure a sustainable society. The Stockholm Conference produced a declaration that presented guiding principles for international environmental action. Among these points is the principle of common but differentiated responsibility, underscoring the need for a shared global commitment to addressing environmental challenges while considering the differing responsibilities between developed and developing countries. The important role of governments in promoting sustainability through policies and concrete actions was pointed up too. The Conference also laid the groundwork for a growing commitment in the field of environment and sustainable development at the international level. It paved the way for the creation of organizations and initiatives addressing these issues. Moreover, it facilitated the adoption of international treaties aimed at protecting the environment, such as the Convention on International Trade in Endangered Species of Wild Fauna and Flora (CITES) and the United Nations Framework Convention on Climate Change. A series of initiatives and meetings that contributed to defining the concept of sustainable development followed, such as the establishment of the World Commission on Environment and Development, known as the Brundtland Commission. It was established in 1983 under the leadership of then-Norwegian Prime Minister Gro Harlem Brundtland, in order to address environmental and development issues. Emphasizing the need to strike a balance between socioeconomic needs and environmental conservation, the Brundtland Commission played a key role in defining and promoting the concept of sustainable development. In their seminal report "Our Common Future" (WCED, 1987), the Commission defined the concept of sustainable development as "development that meets the needs of the present without compromising the ability of future generations to meet their own needs." Recognizing that sustainable development cannot be compartmentalized into isolated concerns, the Brundtland Commission's assertion illuminated the need to view economic progress, social equity, and ecological resilience as interwoven threads within the fabric of progress. This interplay emphasized that promoting well-being for the present and safeguarding opportunities for future generations hinges upon a comprehensive understanding of how economic choices resonate through social dynamics and reverberate within the ecosystem.

Building on these developments, the UN Conference on Sustainable Development, commonly known as the Earth Summit, took place in Rio de Janeiro in 1992. This conference marked a turning point in the global promotion of sustainable development. World leaders, government representatives, and international organization officials gathered to discuss and put forward concrete, shared measures to address environmental challenges and promote balanced and equitable development. During the conference, a fundamental document known as Agenda 21 was adopted. This document was prepared as an action plan for the 21st century and provided guidelines for promoting sustainable development at the global, national, and local levels. Agenda 21 underscored the importance of active participation of civil society, local communities, and non-governmental organizations in the decision-making process, recognizing the fundamental role of collaboration and partnership among all stakeholders. One of the most significant aspects of the Rio Earth Summit was the commitment made by participating countries to adopt international instruments for the promotion of sustainable development. During the conference, three important non-legally binding instruments were adopted: the Rio Declaration on Environment and Development, the United Nations Framework Convention on Climate Change, and the Convention on Biological Diversity. These international agreements provided a regulatory framework to address issues regarding key environmental and climate change. The conference also paved the way for further international initiatives in the field of sustainable development, such as the subsequent UN Conferences on Climate Change (COP), which led to the adoption of the Kyoto Protocol in 1997 and the Paris Agreement in 2015, representing significant milestones in the fight against climate change. The Kyoto Protocol was an international treaty that established binding obligations for industrialized countries, historically major contributors to greenhouse gas emissions, to reduce the greenhouse effect. The protocol introduced the concept of "emission quotas" assigned to countries, which means that the countries were required to commit to reducing their emissions within a specified period. The document also introduced financial instruments such as the Clean Development Mechanism (CDM), which promoted collaboration between industrialized and developing countries to reduce emissions and promote sustainable development. The Paris Agreement, adopted in 2015 during COP21, marked a significant further step in the fight against climate change. Its main goal was to limit the increase in global average temperature well below 2 °C above pre-industrial levels and to pursue efforts to limit the increase to 1.5 °C. The agreement also established the objective of making global emission reduction efforts consistent with minimizing the negative impacts of climate change and adapting to its effects. The Paris Agreement garnered widespread support from countries, including major greenhouse gas emitters like China and the United States. This agreement also recognized the importance of climate adaptation and emphasized the need to provide financial and technological support to developing countries to address the challenges of climate change. The significance of this effort was further underscored during the COP28 in Dubai in 2023. In pursuit of climate justice, the 198 delegates formalized, within the framework of the "Global Stocktake," the establishment of a Fund dedicated to the group of 46 least developed nations, which, despite being among the least polluting, are among the most affected by global warming. This fund will be financed through voluntary contributions.

The relevance of the Brundtland Commission's definition of sustainable development also played a key role in shaping the Millennium Development Goals (MDGs), which were formulated in 2000. They represented a set of eight global objectives to be achieved by 2015. These goals included eradicating extreme poverty and hunger, promoting universal education, reducing child and maternal mortality, promoting gender equality, sustainable management of natural resources, and combating HIV/AIDS, malaria and other diseases. The adoption of the MDGs catalyzed global commitment to meet these challenges and led to better coordination of international efforts in achieving the established goals. Achieving the MDGs was a complex and challenging task that required concerted efforts from governments, international organizations, civil society, and the private sector. To check the progress toward the MDGs, a monitoring system at the global and national levels was established. The UN, along with other international organizations, played a key role in supervising and evaluating countries' efforts to achieve the MDGs. It is important to emphasize that not all MDG targets were achieved by 2015. However, substantial progress was made in many areas. For example, in the context of the MDGs, notable advancement was made in reducing extreme poverty in various countries. According to the "Millennium Development Goals Report" (UN, 2015), from 1990 to 2015, the percentage of people living in extreme poverty worldwide decreased from 37% to 13%. In particular, Brazil made significant strides in this aspect. Another example pertains the access to primary education. Albania was noted as the country that made the greatest progress in this area, with a substantial increase in enrollment rates. Another area of significant headway was the reduction of child mortality, with Cambodia being an example which made the main advances in this field. The adoption of the MDGs and the monitoring system contributed to raising awareness about the challenges of sustainable development and spurred concrete actions in many countries. During the UN Conference on Sustainable Development (Rio+20) held in Rio de Janeiro in 2012, recognition emerged that the MDGs had significant limitations. World leaders emphasized the importance of addressing the environmental, social, and economic dimensions of sustainable development in a more integrated manner. For instance, the conference highlighted the need for greater attention to equality and social justice in pursuing SDGs. Additionally, the conference recognized the need to strengthen the international institutional architecture for sustainability and proposed the idea of establishing new SDGs to guide the global post-2015 agenda (Andonova & Hoffmann, 2012).

Building on these reflections, an Open Working Group of the UN was established in 2013. Its major role was to discuss and negotiate SDGs. This group consisted of representatives from different countries, who spent two years trying consistently to define a set of new targets and objectives that would guide the sustainable development agenda. They consulted with civil society, the private sector, non-governmental organizations, and other stakeholders to unit diverse contributions and coordinate perspectives for the development of the new global sustainability strategy. In September 2014, the UN published the report "The Road to Dignity by 2030: Ending Poverty, Transforming All Lives and Protecting the Planet," which provided a basis for the discussion and formulation of new goals set to be achieved by 2030.

Just one year later, the UN General Assembly adopted unanimously the 2030 Agenda for Sustainable Development, which includes the new 17 SDGs and their related 169 specific targets. One of the distinctive features of the SDGs lies in their ambition and coverage. While the MDGs primarily focused on reducing extreme poverty and related social issues, the SDGs address the interconnectivity of contemporary societal challenges. Their definition was guided by principles of greater inclusiveness, and respecting human rights, within the limitations of the global arenas (Arora-Jonsson, 2023). The SDGs encompass themes ranging from poverty, health, education, gender equality, energy, environment, infrastructure, justice, and peace, to partnerships. This recognition reflects the understanding that achieving a specific SDG can influence the progress toward other social objectives. For example, improving access to education can have a positive impact on poverty reduction and gender equality. Another distinctive element of the SDGs is the universality. While the initial targets of MDGs were mainly developing countries, the SDGs were designed to involve all nations, recognizing that sustainability is a global challenge requiring the participation of all countries. This universal approach reflects the awareness that the challenges of sustainable development are interdependent and require a common commitment from all global actors. After the adoption of the SDGs, countries began working to integrate them into their national policies and define action plans for their achievement.

Despite the broad support for the SDGs as a tool to respond to sustainable development challenges, they are not without criticism. Some observers argue that the SDGs are overly ambitious and unrealistic given the complexity and magnitude of the challenges they address. Concerns have been raised that the SDGs may be too numerous and too extensive to be effectively implemented (Le Blanc, 2015; Sachs et al., 2019). Another criticism pertains to the lack of a clear financing strategy for the SDGs. Since achieving the goals requires substantial financial resources, a clear roadmap to ensure necessary funding would have been opportune (Biermann et al., 2017; Georgeson & Maslin, 2018; Mawdsley, 2018). Additionally, the ambiguous role of the private sector in achieving the SDGs has been highlighted, with some concerns about the possibility of economic interests prevailing over social and environmental benefits (Cavaliere, 2017; Spaiser et al., 2017). Other criticisms relate to the lack of effective reporting and monitoring mechanisms (Costanza et al., 2016). Even though a strengthened monitoring system has been developed to measure progress and make informed decisions to guide necessary policies and actions for achieving the SDGs, significant challenges in obtaining accurate and timely data on a global and national scale have been underscored (Ruggerio, 2021). The monitoring system relies on a set of indicators that measure progress toward each goal. Information is collected by querying various data sources, including national statistics, surveys, reports from international organizations, and independent assessments. Monitoring the SDGs poses a complex challenge due to the diversity of national contexts, limitations of available data, and difficulties in ensuring the coherence and accuracy of collected information (Klopp & Petretta, 2017; Mair et al., 2018; McArthur & Rasmussen, 2019). Furthermore, the concern that achieving the goals may promote a "tick-box" approach has been raised, with member states focusing solely on meeting the indicators without addressing the root causes of issues (Teichmann & Wittmann, 2022). Final, some observers have highlighted that certain goals may conflict with each other or require difficult choices (Hüsing et al., 2017; Pradhan et al., 2017). For example, the tension between promoting clean energy and protecting employment in the fossil fuel sector has been noted (Rosin et al., 2020). At the same time, historically the improvement of health and nutritional status globally also resulted in increasing greenhouse gas emissions and food waste (Hiç et al., 2016).

The aforementioned criticisms should not be perceived as a negation of the intrinsic value of the SDGs, but rather as crucial insights to initiate constructive debate on optimizing the feasibility and effectiveness of these goals in achieving concrete global sustainability. Addressing these criticisms with commitment and an open mind can contribute to enhancing the adaptability, realism, and efficacy of the SDGs in promoting real and lasting change toward tangible global sustainability. These critical reflections, proposed alternatives, and new ideas constitute the fundamental elements in shaping a clearer understanding of sustainability as an extremely complex and articulated social phenomenon.

This book aims to make a significant contribution to the ongoing and lively discourse surrounding sustainable development. It is rooted in the belief that the discussions on sustainable development, until now, have only scratched the surface of the intricate concept of territorial identity, only partially considering the true essence of territories and their specific needs. A territorial perspective of the world unfolds as a framework that values the cultural and natural specificities of places at the local, regional, or national scale. Despite the extensive debate on the need to adopt a territorial perspective (Jessop et al. 2008; Mitchell 1991; Storey, 2001), the concept of territory has not always received the attention it deserves (Agnew, 2020). According to Stuart Elden (2005) in most cases "territory tends to be assumed as unproblematic. Theorists have largely neglected to define the term, taking it as obvious and not worthy of further investigation" (p. 10). Often the term territory has been used interchangeably with "land" or "space," although it "connotes something more precise. Territory is land or space that has had something done to it, it has been acted upon. Territory land has been identified and claimed by a person or people..." (Cowen & Gilbert, 2008, p. 16). As suggested by Michel Lussault (2007), territory differs from other forms of space, being a "structured by principles of contiguity and continuity" that "depend less on the material aspects of space than on the systems of ideas (*systemès idéels*) that frame the space in question, as well as the related practices that take place there" (p. 113). There is also the "territorial trap," which is the mistaken assumption that the spatialities of state power and state territory are homomorphic (Agnew, 1994). Territory cannot be reduced to either national territory or state territory, as it possesses conceptual autonomy independent of the nation-state (Sassen, 2020). Instead, the territory must be interpreted as an intricate weaving of social, cultural, economic, political, historical, architectural, biophysical, geological, and hydrographic factors. Territorial identity gives rise to a rich tapestry, akin to a quilt, where each piece plays a fundamental role in completing the overall picture of a place.

The society that evolves within a territory serves as the needle that weaves the diverse patches of this identity quilt. Shared stories, cultural traditions, social dynamics, and interpersonal relationships are the invisible threads that bind every individual to the environment around them. In this context, a form of "territorial imagination" emerges, uniting people and making them feel like integral parts of a broader whole. This intricacy is made up of various societal groups, with

Introduction: Integrating Territorial Identity into SDGs   9

diverse backgrounds, beliefs, cultures, and histories. These groups contribute to the richness and depth of the overall fabric. Each group brings a unique perspective that adds to the collective narrative, enhancing the multifaceted nature of the whole. In each context, minorities play a vital role in the formation of territorial identity, since they are active contributors to the ongoing narrative of the place. Their presence often carries with them stories of resilience, adaptation, and cultural preservation.

The economic activities that unfold within a territory not only sustain livelihoods but also shape the distinctive contours of the identity, extending beyond mere commercial transactions. Thus, the economic asset encompasses the intricate networks of trade, commerce, and industry that contribute to a place's distinctiveness. Whether activities revolve around agriculture, industry, services, or innovation, the economic landscape echoes the aspirations, skills, values, and innovative spirit of the local population. Economic practices are reflective of local wisdom, resource endowments, and historical trajectories, revealing the way people live, work, and interact with their environment.

The interplay of political and historical dimensions within the tapestry of territorial identity weaves a complex narrative that bridges the past with the present. Just as the stitches in a quilt hold together the layers of fabric, political and historical threads constitute the layers of time, forming an integral part of the overall design. Political choices, often shaped by ideologies, and the pursuit of power, imprint their mark on the identity of a territory. These choices stand the test of time, leaving behind a legacy that can be both inspiring and cautionary. Whether through the establishment of institutions, the formulation of policies, or the negotiation of alliances, politics influences not only the governance of a place but also the perception of its identity, orienting the societal norms, values, and aspirations (Harvey, 1996).

A further exploration of the intricate metaphor of the tapestry would relate to architecture and urban planning which emerge as additional esthetic components, akin to the material patches that contribute to the quilt of territorial identity. Within this multifaceted fabric, monuments, buildings, infrastructures, and public spaces stand as potent symbols, each possessing the power to define the narrative of the territory. Monuments stand as a testament to the ingenuity and craftsmanship of their creators, echoing stories of bygone eras, influential figures, and cult events. As spectators traverse through these architectural marvels, they are endowed with the power to travel through time, experiencing the layered history and the cultural evolution of the territory. In the same vein, buildings rise as contemporary witnesses of the aspirations of the present community. These structures embody the architectural language of their era and represent the technological advancements and societal ideals of their time. Infrastructures interlace the territory with the threads of connectivity and mobility (Urry, 2012). Roads, bridges, tunnels, and utilities create the arteries and veins that allow the lifeblood of a community to flow seamlessly. These infrastructural elements shape how people move, interact, and access resources, thereby influencing the way each society functions and thrives. Public spaces, perhaps the most democratic of architectural interventions, are the common threads that bind people together within a territory. Parks, plazas, squares, and markets serve as meeting points and communal arenas, providing space for social interaction, celebration, and exchange. These spaces become canvases for cultural expression, where festivals, performances, or parades enrich the identity of a place.

Territorial identity is not solely molded by human experiences. Biotic elements, encompassing the diverse array of living organisms, and abiotic factors, encompassing the non-living components such as soil, water, and climate, combine to create ecosystems that shape the character of a territory in profound ways. Just as different fabric patches offer unique colors and textures to a quilt, the biodiversity within ecosystems adds variety to the identity of a territory. From the smallest microbes to the towering trees, each organism plays a distinct role in the narrative of life, contributing to the intricate story of each place. Mountains, valleys, and plains shape the physical character of a territory, influencing factors such as temperature, rainfall, and soil. These abiotic elements set the stage for the thriving ecosystems that develop, defining the natural rhythm of society and influencing the basic needs of human communities. Water flows as a vital thread through the fabric of ecosystems. Rivers, lakes, and oceans nourish life and serve as lifebloods for movement and interaction. The water shapes not only the natural landscape but also the way of human activities, illustrating the interconnectedness between nature and culture. Climate, another crucial abiotic factor, exerts its influence throughout the quilt of territorial identity. Temperature, precipitation, and prevailing winds create distinct climatic zones, influencing the types of ecosystems that can flourish and the species that can thrive within a territory. Just as the tones of a quilt can evoke different moods, the climate of a region can shape the character of its identity, influencing everything from agricultural activities to social practices.

The central theme of this book revolves around the notion that a just sustainable development must inevitably take into account all the aforementioned pieces that contribute to the identity of a territory, in addition to the economic, social, and environmental implications. In fact, for the pursuit of the SDGs, some policies and initiatives gravitate toward specific aspects of nurturing and amplifying territorial identity, occasionally without taking into consideration its full complexity. This partial approach can be attributed to the need to address issues in a targeted manner, for yielding tangible short-term results. Within the enthusiasm for pursuing specific goals lies the risk that key elements of territorial identity are perceived by both public and private initiatives in a fragmented manner, detached from the broader context that envelops them. It is worth noting that pursing a specific goal while focusing solely on immediate objectives can at times neglect the multifaceted nature of territorial identity, potentially resulting in unintended consequences. For instance, sustainable development policies exclusively oriented toward economic aspects might disregard the rich cultural nuances that contribute to the intricate tapestry of territorial identity. Similarly, initiatives aimed at improving environmental conditions could inadvertently overlook the economic or socio-cultural context that shapes the overall well-being of a community.

This scenario of compromise highlights a greater dilemma: How can the pursuit of a SDG lead to conflict with the broader realm of territorial identity? Reflection on the intricacies of balancing goals with the broader desideratum of territorial identity is necessary, in order to acknowledge the potential conflicts and synergies that might emerge. The pursuit of sustainable development necessitates a comprehensive consideration of environmental, social, and economic dimensions, seamlessly integrated in a manner that is concurrently "territorially desirable." This perspective underscores the importance of laying equal importance on specific concerns and the distinctiveness of individual territories as well as their identities. The concept of "territorial desirability" recognizes that the meaning of sustainability can vary across different geographic contexts. Solutions must be grounded in the specific context of a place, interweaving the aspirations, and defining characteristics that shape its identity. The recognition and appreciation of territorial identity assume paramount importance as a central step toward forging a more harmonious, equitable, and sustainable future for present and future generations. As the world grapples with the intricacies of the 21st century, the bedrock of resilience and progress lies in understanding and recognizing the multifaceted assets that constitute a territory's identity. It is through this lens that complexities can be truly comprehended, historical narratives can be acknowledged, and connections can be forged between the land and its inhabitants. Consequently, an imperative arises to integrate identity preservation with strategies for sustainable development.

Contrary to the misconception that safeguarding identity implies resisting transformation, the concept of preserving territorial identity acknowledges the dynamic nature of societies and environments. The very essence of identity is rooted in the relentless interplay among tradition and progress, history, and innovation. The assertion that preserving territorial identity entails stasis would give rise to overlooking that the territory itself is not static. As suggested by Joe Painter (2010) "territory is never complete, but always becoming" (p. 1094). Regarding the dynamic nature of territorial identity, Doreen Massey developed the concept of "places in relation" (2005) to illustrate that territories are continually evolving entities shaped by the relationships that develop among people, communities, and the environment in which they inhabit. This flexibility is an inherent aspect nature of territories, reflecting the resilience and adaptability of communities as they navigate among the currents of change. In this sense, the notion of preserving identity emphasizes the integration of progress, technological advancements, and social changes within the framework of a territory's cultural, historical, and natural context. Just as new patches might be added to a quilt, the introduction of novel elements can enhance and enrich the territorial identity, offering fresh narratives that complement the existing fabric, as long as they co-exist in a consistent and appropriate manner. History is replete with examples of societies that have successfully merged tradition and innovation, thereby enriching their identity. The challenge lies in the delicate art of integrating change without compromising the core values and essence that define a territory. While the path toward sustainable development can bring new opportunities, it also poses the risk of homogenization or harm to the unique cultural, social, and environmental identities. Striking a proper balance between embracing change and safeguarding identity requires a nuanced approach that considers the multifaceted aspects that define a territory. It is an essential challenge that, if overcome, can lead to the formulation of truly sustainable practices, policies, initiatives, and actions.

On the basis of these considerations, the structure of the book unfolds with a deliberate progression, dedicating each chapter to a specific SDG. This structured arrangement facilitates an evolving narrative that adheres to a coherent pace. Each chapter begins with a general introduction to the designated goal, an endeavor that situates it within the intricate web of global sustainability. This contextual grounding becomes even more enhanced by the development of a comprehensive theoretical framework which encapsulates essential definitions and nuanced concepts orbiting the focal goal, strengthening its comprehension. This conceptual underpinning is designed to intricately bolster the forthcoming exploration of an array of case studies that fall within its extensive scope. The resulting picture of case studies ranges across a spectrum, spanning from references to public policies, law, regulations, and private initiatives. These case studies systematically illustrate the dynamic interplay between sustainability and territorial identity in concrete and detailed manners. Diverse in nature, these cases encompass local communities, regions, or urban contexts, and they were carefully selected for their relevance and heterogeneity. The depth of each case study analysis delves into a myriad of experiences and situations. This spectrum extends from triumphant exemplars of best practices that have achieved a harmonious coexistence between sustainability and territorial identity, to the cautionary narratives that emerged where the pursuit of sustainability may have inadvertently veered from the tenets of territorial identity, thus precipitating discord, tension, or practical implementation quandaries. Each case study is not only strengthened by empirical data but also accompanied by contextual analysis. This approach ensures that the readers would feel themselves in the specific scenario as if they were truly present at every junction.

The book concludes with a synthesis of the principal findings that have emerged from the analysis of these diverse case studies, followed by a series of final reflections. These suggestions form a guiding light, illuminating the path toward more contextually sensitive and all-encompassing policies and strategies for sustainable development. With an expanded perspective, these recommendations lay the groundwork for fostering an era of inclusive progress resonating with the essence of each territory, capturing the very core of its identity.

References

Agnew, J. (1994). The territorial trap: The geographical assumptions of international relations theory. *Review of International Political Economy*, *1*, 53–80.

Agnew, J. (2020) (Ed.). *The confines of territory*. Routledge.

Andonova, L. B., & Hoffmann, M. J. (2012). From Rio to Rio and beyond: Innovation in global environmental governance. *The Journal of Environment & Development*, *21*(1), 57–61.

Arora-Jonsson, S. (2013). *Gender, development and environmental governance: Theorizing connections*. Routledge.
Arora-Jonsson, S. (2023). The sustainable development goals: A universalist promise for the future. *Futures, 146*, 103087.
Biermann, F., Kanie, N., & Kim, R. E. (2017). Global governance by goal-setting: The novel approach of the UN sustainable development goals. *Current Opinion in Environmental Sustainability, 26*, 26–31.
Bryant, B., & Bailey, S. (1997). *Third world political ecology*. Routledge.
Bullard, R. D. (1993). The threat of environmental racism. *Natural Resources & Environment, 7*(3), 23–56.
Bullard, R. D., & Johnson, G. S. (2000). Environmentalism and public policy: Environmental justice: Grassroots activism and its impact on public policy decision making. *Journal of Social Issues, 56*(3), 555–578.
Cavaliere, C. T. (2017). Foodscapes as alternate ways of knowing: Advancing sustainability and climate consciousness through tactile space. In S. Slocum & C. Kline (Eds.), *Linking Urban and Rural Tourism: Strategies for Sustainability*. CABI International.
Costanza, R., Daly, L., Fioramonti, L., Giovannini, E., Kubiszewski, I., Mortensen, L. F., Pickett, K. E., Vala Ragnarsdottir, K., De Vogli, R., & Wilkinson, R. (2016). Modelling and measuring sustainable well-being in connection with the UN sustainable development goals. *Ecological Economics, 130*, 350–355.
Cowen, D., & Gilbert, E. (2008) (Eds.). *War, citizenship, territory*. Routledge.
Dobson, A. (2007). *Green political thought*. Routledge.
Eckersley, R. (2004). *The green state: Rethinking democracy and sovereignty*. MIT Press.
Elden, S. (2005). Missing the point: Globalization, deterritorialization and the space of the world. *Transactions of the Institute of British Geographers, 30*, 8–19.
Georgeson, L., & Maslin, M. (2018). Putting the United Nations sustainable development goals into practice: A review of implementation, monitoring, and finance. *Geo: Geography and Environment, 5*(1), e00049.
Giddens, A. (2009). *The politics of climate change*. John Wiley & Sons.
Harvey, D. (1996). *Justice, nature and the geography of difference*. Wiley-Blackwell.
Hiç, C., Pradhan, P., Rybski, D., & Kropp, J. P. (2016). Food surplus and its climate burdens. *Environmental Science & Technology, 50*(8), 4269–4277.
Hüsing, B., Kulicke, M., Wydra, S., Stahlecker, T., Aichinger, H., & Meyer, N. (2017). *Evaluation der "Nationalen Forschungsstrategie BioÖkonomie 2030"*. BMBF.
Jessop, B., Brenner, N., & Jones, M. (2008). Theorizing sociospatial relations. *Environment and Planning D: Society and Space, 26*, 389–401.
Klopp, J. M., & Petretta, D. L. (2017). The urban sustainable development goal: Indicators, complexity and the politics of measuring cities. *Cities, 63*, 92–97.
Le Blanc, D. (2015). Towards integration at last? The sustainable development goals as a network of targets. *Sustainable Development, 23*(3), 176–187.
Lussault, M. (2007). *L'homme spatial: La construction sociale de l'espace humain*. Seuil.
Mair, S., Jones, A., Ward, J., Christie, I., Druckman, A., & Lyon, F. (2018). A critical review of the role of indicators in implementing the sustainable development goals. In W. Leal Filho (Ed.), *Handbook of sustainability science and research* (pp. 41–56). Springer.
Martínez-Alier, J. (2003). *The environmentalism of the poor: A study of ecological conflicts and valuation*. Edward Elgar Publishing.
Massey, D. (2005). *For space*. Sage.
Mawdsley, E. (2018). From billions to trillions. *DHG, 8*, 191–195.
McArthur, J. W., & Rasmussen, K. (2019). Classifying sustainable development goal trajectories: A country-level methodology for identifying which issues and people are getting left behind. *World Development, 123*, 104608.

Mitchell, T. (1991). The limits of the state: Beyond statist approaches and their critics. *American Political Science Review*, *85*, 77–96.

O'Neill, S., & Nicholson-Cole, S. (2009). "Fear won't do it" promoting positive engagement with climate change through visual and iconic representations. *Science Communication*, *30*(3), 355–379.

Painter, J. (2010). Rethinking territory. *Antipode*, *42*(5), 1090–1118.

Pradhan, P., Costa, L., Rybski, D., Lucht, W., & Kropp, J. P. (2017). A systematic study of sustainable development goal (SDG) interactions. *Earth's Future*, *5*(11), 1169–1179.

Rosin, Z. M., Hiron, M., Żmihorski, M., Szymański, P., Tobolka, M., & Pärt, T. (2020). Reduced biodiversity in modernized villages: A conflict between sustainable development goals. *Journal of Applied Ecology*, *57*(3), 467–475.

Ruggerio, C. A. (2021). Sustainability and sustainable development: A review of principles and definitions. *Science of the Total Environment*, *786*, 147481.

Sachs, J. D., Schmidt-Traub, G., Mazzucato, M., Messner, D., Nakicenovic, N., & Rockström, J. (2019). Six transformations to achieve the sustainable development goals. *Nature Sustainability*, *2*(9), 805–814.

Sassen, S. (2020). When territory deborders territoriality. In J. Agnew (Ed.), *The confines of territory* (pp. 83–106). Routledge.

Spaiser, V., Ranganathan, S., Swain, R. B., & Sumpter, D. J. (2017). The sustainable development oxymoron: Quantifying and modelling the incompatibility of sustainable development goals. *International Journal of Sustainable Development & World Ecology*, *24*(6), 457–470.

Storey, D. (2001). *Territory*. Prentice Hall.

Szasz, A. (2007). *Shopping our way to safety: How we changed from protecting the environment to protecting ourselves*. University of Minnesota Press.

Teichmann, F. M. J., & Wittmann, C. (2022). How can sustainability be effectively regulated? *Journal of Financial Crime*.

UN (United Nations). (2015). *The millennium development goals report*. https://www.un.org/millenniumgoals/2015_MDG_Report/pdf/MDG%202015%20rev%20(July%201).pdf

Urry, J. (2012). *Sociology beyond societies: Mobilities for the twenty-first century*. Routledge.

WCED (World Commission on Environment and Development). (1987). *Our common future*. Oxford University Press.

Young, A. L., Giesy, J. P., Jones, P. D., & Newton, M. (2004). Environmental fate and bioavailability of Agent Orange and its associated dioxin during the Vietnam War. *Environmental Science and Pollution Research*, *11*, 359–370.

Chapter 1

SDG 1. End Poverty in All Its Forms Everywhere

Abstract

The chapter delves into the intricate relationship among poverty alleviation policies, cultural identities, and community-specific development in the context of sustainable development. Through various case studies, the chapter underscores the need for policies that empower communities and encourage active participation in decision-making processes. It argues that inclusive development should consider local knowledge, traditions, aspirations, and advocates for partnerships between stakeholders to ensure effective and culturally appropriate strategies. The chapter presents the view that recognizing and preserving cultural identities can not only help fight against poverty but also enhance social unity and well-being. In conclusion, the chapter advocates for a paradigm shift in poverty alleviation strategies: Appreciating and leveraging cultural diversity, empowering communities, and embracing a multifaceted approach to development. Through this approach, a holistic and community-specific stance can yield more effective, sustainable, and equitable outcomes in poverty reduction.

From a classical perspective, income and wealth are the primary indicators in assessing the economic condition of individuals. This viewpoint holds that poverty is evident when people lack sufficient financial resources, giving them limited access to the production and consumption of goods.

Adam Smith (1776) emphasized the importance of labor and income as sources of wealth and well-being. He placed particular emphasis on the fundamental role of labor as a productive factor and a generator of wealth. In his opinion, income derived from labor is the primary means through which individuals can access the goods and services necessary to satisfy their needs and pursue well-being. He argued that labor not only generates income for workers but also contributes to economic growth and the development of society as a whole. The cornerstone of Smith's theory is based on identifying a nation's wealth, which is correlated to the proportion of productive workers within its population. Productivity develops hand in hand with the division of labor, which, in turn, is connected with market expansion. Smith's perspective was based on the idea that a prosperous society is characterized by sustained economic growth, which can only be achieved through free competition and a price system guided by the invisible hand of the market. In other words, he believed that, in a context of free trade and adherence to the natural laws of economics, it is possible to achieve an equitable distribution of resources and greater prosperity for all members of society, thereby reducing the risk of poverty.

Smith's theory regarding the creation of wealth through labor and the free market significantly influenced the thinking of the economist David Ricardo, who developed the concept of wages as determinants of poverty. Ricardo (1817), however, defined poverty as the outcome of low income primarily caused by unemployment or insufficient wages. He argued that in a market economy, a worker's wage is determined by the balance between labor supply and demand. If the supply of labor exceeds demand, wages tend to decrease as workers compete for a limited number of jobs. In such cases, workers may be compelled to accept wages below the subsistence level, resulting in poverty. Conversely, if labor demand surpasses supply, wages tend to increase, and thus enhancing the economic well-being of workers. Ricardo discussed that the equilibrium between labor supply and demand is influenced by various factors, such as population growth, birth and mortality rates, as well as changes in productivity and efficiency. He recognized that technology and innovation can contribute to increase productivity and, consequently, higher wages. At the same time, technological progress has also been described as a potential factor contributing to the substitution of human labor with mechanized work, thereby posing a risk of unemployment, consequently, and poverty.

Subsequent studies have expanded the understanding of the intricate nature and various facets of poverty. Notably, sociology has played a critical role in delving deeper into the poverty debate, moving beyond the classical economic approach and offering a broader, multidimensional perspective. In this respect, the work of Karl Marx (1867) stands as a landmark in providing a materialistic interpretation of history, which serves to integrate the economic, social, and political dimensions. Marxist theory suggests that poverty cannot be solely attributed to a lack of financial resources since it is characterized as a complex social phenomenon stemming from a social organization that fosters capital accumulation and inequality. In his theory of historical materialism, Marx highlighted how social structures and production relations lie at the core of the marginalization of the poorer classes. According to Marx, the capitalist system inherently rests on the exploitation of the working class by the dominant class of capitalists. This exploitation arises from the inequality in the possession of the means of production, with workers selling their labor for a wage lower than the value created by their activity. The consequence is a concentration of wealth and power in the hands of a small group of individuals who own the means of production while workers remain trapped in a state of poverty and oppression. The working class not only lacks decision-making power in economic matters but also suffers from exploitation due to the lack of control over the means of production. This leads to an inequitable distribution of wealth and a condition of poverty for the working masses. Marxist analysis of poverty significantly influenced subsequent sociological thoughts on the social and economic dynamics that determine poverty.

Pierre Bourdieu introduced the concept of "cultural capital" (1979). This term refers to the cultural resources that an individual possesses, such as education, skills, and knowledge. At the core of the Bourdieusian perspective is the idea that cultural capital plays a key role in structuring social opportunities, influencing access to employment, social mobility, and economic success. The theory of cultural capital has provided a valuable analytical lens for understanding the complexity of poverty and its social facets. One of the main aspects of Bourdieu's theory pertains to the importance of education as a means of acquiring cultural capital. Access to quality education is essential for expanding knowledge, skills, and career prospects. However, educational inequalities are widespread, with wealthier families having greater resources to ensure quality education for their children, while impoverished ones may be disadvantaged due to limited economic and social resources. This can perpetuate poverty across generations, with intergenerational transmission of inequalities and advantages associated with cultural capital. In addition to education, Bourdieu highlighted the role of social networks in determining access to cultural capital. Influential social networks can provide job opportunities, support, and valuable information that can facilitate social advancement and the accumulation of cultural capital. Individuals living in poverty may have limited access to influential social networks, compromising their ability to secure quality employment or access resources and opportunities that could improve their social and economic status. The lack of cultural capital can also influence how individuals interpret and navigate the social and economic context. Bourdieu argued that the dominant culture and its cultural practices are often deemed "legitimate" by society, while other cultural forms may be marginalized or devalued. This can create disparities in values, norms, and behaviors that can make individuals whose cultural capital is different from the dominant one feel uncomfortable. For instance, unfamiliarity with widely accepted social conventions, linguistic practices, or forms of behavior considered appropriate can limit opportunities for social integration and professional success.

Within the reflections on the multidimensional nature of poverty, Erik Olin Wright elaborated his theory of "triple oppression" (1985). According to Wright, poverty cannot be comprehended solely through the lens of social class, since it must also be considered in relation to other identity factors, such as ethnicity and gender. Wright argued that these three dimensions of oppression are interconnected and intersect, resulting in complex forms of inequality and marginalization. Social class membership determines access to resources, economic opportunities, and individual autonomy in decision-making. Individuals belonging to lower or less privileged classes are more inclined to live in poverty, with limited work and income opportunities. Gender represents a second important dimension in the analysis of poverty, as women in many social and territorial contexts face gender-based discrimination that limits their work, income, and resource access opportunities. Finally, racial discrimination can influence job opportunities, income, and resource access for many individuals, impacting entire communities as well. Thus, individuals at the intersection of these forms of oppression can experience multiple oppressions and may be more vulnerable to poverty compared to those facing only one form of oppression.

Peter Townsend (1979) contributed to the understanding of poverty, identifying four interconnected and interdependent dimensions that mutually influence each other. Material poverty is considered the most evident and visible aspect of poverty. It refers to the lack of financial and material resources necessary to meet basic needs such as food, housing, clothing, and access to essential services. In addition to material poverty, social poverty represents another critical dimension. It can be defined as the lack of social resources, often accompanied by a sense of isolation and social exclusion. Social poverty can manifest through a lack of support networks, social participation, and opportunities for integration. This condition can lead to a range of negative consequences, including social isolation, discrimination, and marginalization. Educational poverty is another relevant dimension of poverty. It pertains to limited access to quality education and educational opportunities. People in poverty may face financial, social, and cultural obstacles that restrict their participation in the education system and their prospects for academic success. Educational poverty can significantly impact individuals' future opportunities and their ability to acquire skills necessary for entering the job market and overcoming life's challenges. Finally, health poverty represents a significant dimension of poverty concerning limited access to healthcare services and medical treatment. The lack of financial resources and adequate healthcare can lead to chronic health issues, reduced life expectancy, and greater vulnerability to diseases. Health poverty can also be exacerbated by social factors such as a lack of health information, unfavorable living conditions, and a lack of social support.

SDG 1 underscores the importance of addressing poverty as a global and integrated issue, recognizing it as a multidimensional phenomenon still affecting millions of people worldwide. It aims to end poverty in all its forms by 2030. This goal entails an approach that goes beyond the economic dimension and considers the various facets of the phenomenon, including lack of access to education, healthcare, clean water, clean energy, decent employment, other essential resources, and services. The UN has emphasized that to sustainably tackle poverty, particular attention to social inclusion must be paid. This involves ensuring that all individuals, regardless of their ethnic origin, gender, age, disability, or socio-economic status, enjoy equal opportunities for economic, political, and social participation. Furthermore, it is important to address the economic inequalities that contribute to the perpetuation of poverty. This requires policies that promote resource redistribution and create opportunities for income increase for all people. Particularly, fiscal and income redistribution policies can play a crucial role in reducing inequalities and ensuring a more equitable distribution of resources.

Integrating the discourse on territorial identity into the SDGs would ensure sustainability-based anti-poverty policies which consider the specific cultures and needs of different local communities. A case of good practice that has achieved significant results in promoting integrated and culturally respectful sustainability is the "Whānau Ora" community development program, implemented in New Zealand. It was introduced in 2010 by the New Zealand government led by the Labor Party, under the leadership of Prime Minister John Key. The program has received praise and recognition from various key stakeholders, including the New Zealand government itself, academic institutions, civil society organizations, and Māori communities. This program was established with the aim of reducing poverty and promoting the well-being of Māori families, who represent the indigenous population of the country. In fact, the term "Whānau Ora" means "family well-being" and highlights the program's approach, which focuses not only on the individual as a sole beneficiary but also as a member of a broader family network (Boulton & Gifford, 2014). "Whānau Ora" was implemented by recognizing the importance of family relationships, cultural traditions, and support networks within the Māori community, valuing them as essential resources for well-being and fighting against poverty. The initiative was based on the principle that the well-being of a Māori family is closely linked with a balance between physical, social, emotional, and cultural aspects. Therefore, the program aimed to ensure that Māori families could live in adequate socio-economic conditions. A key aspect of the program has been its empowerment approach: Māori families were given the power to make decisions about their own lives and well-being. Families were actively involved in defining their development goals and personalized their approach to achieve them. "Whānau Ora" promoted participation and self-determination of families, aiming to remove the dependence on welfare services and foster autonomy and self-efficacy. Another key element of this program has been the integration of services. The program has involved collaborations among different government agencies, local communities, and non-profit organizations, in order to provide all-round and coordinated support to beneficiaries. This approach has helped overcome bureaucratic barriers and has ensured that families receive a range of support services specially tailored to meet their needs. Noticeably, "Whānau Ora" deserves credit for its recognition of the importance of cultures and traditions while effectively promoting family well-being. The program encouraged active participation in Māori culture, supporting language learning, involvement in traditional dance and music, and access to cultural knowledge and practices. This approach not only succeeded in reducing the risk of vulnerability and marginalization of indigenous families but also contributed to the preserving and giving full play to the role of Māori identity, strengthening the sense of belonging to their territory.

In Canada as well, various similar programs have been established to support indigenous addressing the structural and multidimensional problems of poverty. These policies and strategies served contextually to reduce poverty and promote their socio-economic well-being while respecting their cultural identity. They have been mainly implemented by the Canadian federal government in collaboration with various indigenous communities and associated organizations. Remarkable headways have been made with increased attention and commitment in recent decades. A great stride was made in 2021 when the "United Nations Declaration on the Rights of Indigenous Peoples Act" received Royal Assent and immediately came into force (Borrows et al., 2019; Wood, 2020). This legislation strengthened the Canadian Government's relationship with indigenous people and established a legal basis for implementing specific policies and programs aimed at reducing poverty in indigenous communities. The results of these policies have been varied, depending on the specific initiatives and programs implemented in different regions of Canada. However, there have been positive signs of progress and significant impacts across the board. For example, important outcomes have been achieved in the field of education, with increased access to higher education by young indigenous individuals and greater support for bilingual and intercultural education. Successes have also been observed in promoting indigenous entrepreneurship and tradition-based economic development, with the creation of cooperatives and enterprises that value the products and craftsmanship of indigenous communities. These latter initiatives have been pursued to provide economic opportunities for indigenous communities within the country, fully respecting their traditional practices, and thus preserving their identity and autonomy.

In order to ensure the right to decent housing for people living in makeshift shelters due to their poverty in Africa, socially and environmentally sustainable experimental projects have been implemented in recent years. These projects have been developed to construct strong, durable, and affordable houses made of recycled waste, which served to address the housing shortage while protecting the local environment. The construction process involved shredding plastic waste and mixing it with other elements. Over the coming years, multi-story buildings will be built, and will be constructed in close collaboration with local communities. The local government plans to adopt the same methodology for the construction of refugee centers, schools, and hospitals. All building modules are produced locally, creating jobs, and earning opportunities for the local population (Quaye et al., 2022), so as to actively address the plague of poverty.

The overarching goal of welfare policies is to lift individuals out of poverty, offering them a chance to meet their basic needs, and enhancing their quality of life. Nevertheless, some initiatives can inadvertently contribute to perpetuating the marginalization of disadvantaged individuals, especially when they are designed without a comprehensive understanding of the unique characteristics of each territory. Indeed, welfare policies characterized by stringent impositions, or rigorous controls can paradoxically exacerbate the life struggles of people. As territories possess distinct identities, the realization of sustainable welfare policies entails the integration of territorial desirability, considering the unique characteristics and aspirations of a place and its inhabitants. For this reason, solutions must be grounded in the specific context of a region, acknowledging the multifaceted elements that shape its identity, including its economic opportunities, cultural heritage, and social fabric.

A study conducted to assess the effectiveness of initiatives undertaken in accordance with the MDGs in Papua New Guinea – an emerging Pacific Island nation characterized by over 600 islands and more than 850 linguistic groups – revealed that the "one-size-fits-all" development models implemented until 2015 only led to apparent improvements. While there was a recorded increase in per capita income, citizens continued to experience widespread discomfort due to the lack of meaningful engagement of local communities in development policies (Paton & Valiente-Riedl, 2016). The "one-size-fits-all" approach involves applying the same standardized policies to different communities without considering the cultural, social, and economic specificities of each of them. This kind of approach may disregard the needs and perspectives of local communities, thus reducing the effectiveness of poverty alleviation policies. The case of Papua New Guinea prompts important reflections on the need to adopt a more culturally sensitive and community-specific approach when developing poverty alleviation policies, avoiding the possible gap between development policies and territorial identity. It underlines the need for a holistic approach that recognizes the fact that the success of welfare policies is not solely determined by their short-term impacts on poverty rates, but also by their long-term implications for the overall well-being and identity of the region.

An additional concrete illustration of how the implementation of standardized development policies can have adverse effects on local communities is also evident in the context of housing and public construction initiatives. As highlighted earlier, these endeavors hold a key role in ensuring equitable access to decent housing for marginalized individuals, thereby contributing to the reduction of socioeconomic disparities and the enhancement of overall living conditions. However, the achievement of such objectives hinges on the careful calibration of these policies to suit the unique requirements of each distinct territory and its population. In certain instances, housing policies might suffer from undue standardization or an overemphasis on abstract models, leading to solutions that might be ill-suited to the actual needs, and contexts of the regions they serve. This mismatch between policy design and territorial desirability can yield outcomes that may be less appropriate, which in turn leads to ineffective implementation, aggravation of problems or new conflicts and social tensions. For instance, even though the well-intentioned construction of sizable residential complexes was designed to address housing shortages or improve living conditions, they turned out to disrupt the already existing equilibrium and harmony of the community. The altered urban dynamics can strain the social ties that have been built over generations. This shift in the community's makeup and character can result in a sense of estrangement among its members, eroding the shared values, traditions, and relationships that once defined the territory's identity. Moreover, a notable array of public housing or urban renewal initiatives have been undertaken with a singular focus on immediate quantitative outcomes. The emphasis on numerical targets or economic metrics, though important, can sometimes overshadow the need to embed these interventions within the nuanced context of territorial identity. Consequently, these initiatives might not only overlook the significance of historical heritage, cultural preservation, and community cohesion but also miss the opportunity to harness the unique strengths and assets that each territory possesses. This kind of situation occurred with urban revitalization efforts in the city of Rio de Janeiro, Brazil. Preparing for the 2016 Olympic Games, authorities initiated a large-scale campaign to renovate and modernize urban areas. This initiative entailed the demolition of numerous informal settlements and low-income neighborhoods without adequate resettlement of local communities and consideration of their requirements and cultural identities. One of the most well-known examples was the case of Vila Autódromo, a community situated near the Olympic Park. Inhabited by a low-income population, this area was subjected to an urban renewal plan that involved demolishing a significant portion of the housing to make room for new Olympic infrastructure. Despite strong resistance and community protests, many houses were demolished, and most residents were forced to leave their dwellings to relocate to other parts of the city. This case generated social tensions and conflicts because, despite the promise of improved housing, the Vila Autódromo community had a deep attachment to their territory and cultural roots. Residents took pride in their communal identity and local traditions, and they would have preferred to continue residing in their favela instead of being displaced to modern accommodations far from their neighborhood. In this case, the implemented policy resulted not only in the destruction of traditional housing but also in a blow to territorial identity and community cohesion, threatening the social fabric, historical continuity, and cultural authenticity that constituted the Brazilian territorial identity. In light of these considerations, it becomes clear that the successful implementation of housing and public construction policies hinges on more than just providing physical infrastructure. They require a deeper understanding of the interplay between policy objectives and the distinct intricacies of territorial identity. The mere delivery of solutions might overcome immediate challenges but risks sidelining the long-term desirability and authenticity of the places being transformed.

More in general, the lens of territorial identity compels policymakers to approach development initiatives with attention to the several elements shaping a territory's identity. By embracing the unique qualities, historical narratives, and cultural expressions that define each place, policies can be shaped to not only improve the standard of living but also enrich the intangible aspects that form the essence of a community. Policy frameworks must vigilantly avoid paternalistic approaches that erode community autonomy. Instead of top-down imposition, an inclusive and participatory line seeks to build a bottom-up consensus. Beyond standardized solutions, this path resonates with immediate necessities and enduring community aspirations (Bryer & Prysmakova-Rivera, 2018; Canduela et al., 2014). In the pursuit of such endeavors, it is imperative to ensure that the adoption of inclusive and community-specific policies does not inadvertently perpetuate other form of exclusion or marginalization. Rather, the thrust should be to put forward policies that give importance to active participation, self-determination, and equal opportunities for all community members. Diverse stakeholders represent different interests, perspectives, and aspirations. Embracing a variety of viewpoints cultivates a comprehensive understanding of community challenges and opportunities, identifying synergies and trade-offs among different groups. While some solutions might appear favorable from one perspective, they could hinder progress from another angle (Boon & Farnsworth, 2011; Ravi & Engler, 2015). By fostering a territorially desirable participatory approach in the fight against poverty, communities are empowered as active stakeholders, nurturing ownership over processes that shape their destinies. This transformative engagement contributes to the sustainable enhancement of territories, safeguarding and enriching their distinct identities.

References

Boon, B., & Farnsworth, J. (2011). Social exclusion and poverty: Translating social capital into accessible resources. *Social Policy & Administration, 45*(5), 507–524.

Borrows, J., Chartrand, L., Fitzgerald, O. E., & Schwartz, R. (Eds.). (2019). *Braiding legal orders: Implementing the United Nations declaration on the rights of Indigenous peoples*. CIGI.

Boulton, A. F., & Gifford, H. H. (2014). Whānau Ora; he whakaaro ā whānau: Māori family views of family wellbeing. *The International Indigenous Policy Journal, 5*(1), 1–16.

Bourdieu, P. (1979). *La Distinction. Critique sociale du jugement*. Les Éditions de Minuit.

Bryer, T. A., & Prysmakova-Rivera, S. (2018). *Poor participation: Fighting the wars on poverty and impoverished citizenship*. Lexington Books.

Canduela, J., Lindsay, C., Raeside, R., & Graham, H. (2014). Employability, poverty and the spheres of sociability – Evidence from the British Household Panel Survey. *Social Policy & Administration, 49*(5), 571–592.

Marx, K. (1867). *Das Kapital: Kritik der politischen Oekonomie. Vol. 1: Der Produktionsprozess des Kapitals* (1st ed.). Verlag von Otto Meissner.

Paton, J., & Valiente-Riedl, E. (2016). Is globalizing 'development' ethical? A view from the Pacific. In H. Gaisbauer, G. Schweiger, & C. Sedmak (Eds.), *Ethical issues in poverty alleviation*. Studies in Global Justice (Vol. 14). Springer.

Quaye, I., Amponsah, O., Azunre, G. A., Takyi, S. A., & Braimah, I. (2022). A review of experimental informal urbanism initiatives and their implications for sub-Saharan Africa's sustainable cities' agenda. *Sustainable Cities and Society, 83*, 103938.

Ravi, S., & Engler, M. (2015). Workfare as an effective way to fight poverty: The case of India's NREGS. *World Development, 67*, 57–71.

Ricardo, D. (1817). *On the principles of political economy and taxation* (1st ed.). John Murray.

Smith, A. (1776). *An inquiry into the nature and causes of the wealth of nations* (Vol. 1, 1st ed.). W. Strahan.

Townsend, P. (1979). *Poverty in the United Kingdom: A survey of household resources and standards of living*. University of California Press.

Wood, C. (2020). Protecting Indigenous rights at home: A comparative analysis of the way forward for domestic implementation of the United Nations Declaration on the Rights of Indigenous Peoples. *Australian International Law Journal, 27*, 77–101.

Wright, E. O. (1985). *Classes*. Verso.

Chapter 2

SDG 2. End Hunger, Achieve Food Security and Improved Nutrition and Promote Sustainable Agriculture

Abstract

Drawing on initiatives held in various countries, the chapter advocates for a multi-stakeholder approach in making decisions related to food systems. By prioritizing local perspectives, diverse stakeholder participation, and equitable decision-making, this approach ensures policies that are responsive to unique contexts, thus contributing to sustainable and culturally sensitive development. Within these forums, local communities share traditional knowledge and expertise, influencing policy formulation that respects social specifics. Importantly, direct engagement of communities in land use, resource management, and agricultural practices helps preserve territorial identities. The chapter also discusses historical examples where development policies, such as the "green revolution," disregarded traditional practices and local identity in favor of Western agricultural models. This resulted in negative consequences, including the loss of biodiversity, environmental degradation, and economic vulnerability among small farmers.

The annual report produced by the Global Network Against Food Crises (GNAFC, 2023) has revealed a negative situation of acute food insecurity in 2022, with approximately 258 million people in 58 countries and territories facing this severe issue. The severity of acute food insecurity has increased to 22.7% from 21.3% in 2021, indicating a global trend of deteriorating food security. This represents the highest number of people affected by acute food insecurity in the seven-year history of the report.

Conditions of acute hunger and destitution were observed in seven countries during 2022. More than half of these dire circumstances were concentrated in

Somalia, where 57% of the population faced acute hunger. Similar extreme conditions were also observed in Afghanistan, Burkina Faso, Haiti (for the first time in the country's history), Nigeria, South Sudan, and Yemen. These countries have experienced severe humanitarian crises and conflicts that worsened the food and nutritional shortage of the people (Resnick, 2021).

Among those most affected by the effects of acute food insecurity are children under the age of 5. As reported in the study, in 30 of the 42 main countries affected by the food crisis, over 35 million children suffered from wasting or acute malnutrition, with 9.2 million of them facing the most dangerous form of malnutrition, severe wasting. This physical condition poses a serious threat to their lives and contributes to the increase in child mortality.

The causes of food insecurity and malnutrition are multiple and complex. Catastrophes such as droughts, floods, cyclones, and heatwaves are becoming more frequent and intense due to climate change. They can severely damage crops and natural resources, reducing food availability and exacerbating food shortages (Connolly-Boutin & Smit, 2016; Yadav et al., 2019).

The COVID-19 pandemic has even worsened the situation, with worldwide economic impacts. Lockdown measures and restrictions on commercial activities have disrupted global food systems, leading to supply and chain problems. Additionally, people have lost their means of livelihood and income due to job losses and changes in economic conditions, leading to increased food insecurity in many regions (Arndt et al., 2020; Béné et al., 2021; von Grebmer et al., 2021).

The conflict in Ukraine has also had a particularly significant impact on global food security, as both Ukraine and Russia have traditionally played a crucial role in the production and trade of essential agricultural commodities (Abay et al., 2023; Behnassi & El Haiba, 2022). About 50 countries that depended on Russia and Ukraine for most of their wheat imports found themselves struggling in order to find alternative suppliers (Galanakis, 2023; Jagtap et al., 2022). This situation added oil to the persistent food inflation since the second half of 2020. By March 2022, global food prices had reached the highest levels ever recorded. Compared to the previous year, cereal prices increased by 37%, cooking oil prices by 56%, and meat prices by 20%. In 2023, they decreased slightly compared to those of the previous year but still remained higher than those in 2021 (FAO, 2023).

The scenario described above highlights the ongoing challenge of food insecurity and malnutrition worldwide. Against this backdrop, SDG 2 recognizes that hunger and malnutrition are problems that must be overcome by implementing holistic and interconnected solutions. Therefore, it is necessary not only to ensure access to safe and nutritious food but also to end all forms of malnutrition. By 2025, the internationally agreed goal is to achieve nutrition targets for children under the age of 5, adolescents, pregnant and lactating women, and the elderly. This implies a greater focus on the specific nutritional needs of these population groups and the implementation of targeted policies and strategies to improve their nutrition.

Another crucial aspect of SDG 2 concerns improving agricultural productivity and income for small-scale food producers, including indigenous people, farming families, pastoralists, and fishermen. Women, in particular, must have secure and equal access to productive resources, knowledge, financial services, markets, and employment opportunities. Doubling the agricultural productivity and income of these producers is essential to ensure food security and the well-being of rural communities.

Another goal of SDG 2 is the promotion of sustainable food production systems. The UN is pushing for the implementation of agricultural practices that increase productivity and production while protecting ecosystems and improving the adaptability to climate change and natural disasters. Furthermore, land and soil improvement are crucial to the sustainability of agricultural resources and the resilience of rural communities.

To achieve this goal, the UN considers it necessary to increase investments in rural infrastructure, agricultural research and extension services, technological development, and plant and animal genetic banks. International cooperation is described as essential to enhance agricultural productive capacity, especially in less developed countries. At the same time, it is crucial to remove trade restrictions and distortions in global agricultural markets. Proper regulation of food commodity markets and their derivatives is necessary to avoid excessive food price volatility and ensure timely access to food resources (Calvin, 2017; Goncharova & Merzlyakova, 2021; Timmer, 2016).

An exemplary local intervention aimed at achieving SDG 2 is embodied by the Shimodu3 project (GHI, 2022). This initiative has been implemented in the post-COVID period in the Diffa region of Niger, where populations face various crises threatening their food and nutritional security at the same time. In this region, land degradation, health epidemics, floods, and displacements caused by insecurity generated by armed groups have reduced agricultural production and strained vulnerable communities. Only 11% of the people living in the communities were able to make a living through their own production. The project has been designed to improve the living conditions and resilience of vulnerable groups, including displaced people, refugees, and host populations. Shimodu3 not only endeavors to address hunger but also seeks to make full use of the inherent resources within the territory in terms of knowledge and competencies. This territorially sensitive approach is underpinned by the recognition that each community is unique, harboring specific resources, traditions, and social dynamics. The project has involved community members, local authorities, volunteers, and a consortium of international organizations. One output has been the creation of food and fodder banks, managed by the communities themselves, where stocks accumulated during periods of abundance are offered at fixed prices during general assemblies. These stocks are then resold to communities during lean seasons or challenging situations to guard against the premium prices of staple foods and fodder. The management of the banks is entrusted to local committees that maintain regular contact with government authorities and receive technical support and training for financial and stock management. The project works closely with regional and departmental authorities to ensure a coordinated and aligned response to the needs of vulnerable communities. In addition, plans for humanitarian response and support to local communities have been developed in collaboration with the UN Office for the Coordination of Humanitarian Affairs and government authorities. The multifaceted nature of the intervention embraces the ethos that combating hunger is not just about the issue of nutrition but involves a comprehensive understanding of the intricate web of social, economic, and cultural factors influencing food security, recognizing and respecting the unique identity of the territory. Despite the objective difficulties, the initiative has led to significant results in the Diffa region. Approximately 28,000 people from 4,000 crisis-affected families have found lasting integration into the local economy, through sustainable access to basic social services. Social cohesion has been strengthened, promoting more inclusive local governance, and significantly improving food and nutritional security. In addition to these successes, the project has promoted the creation of networks between communities and district institutions, facilitating coordination and peer learning. These collaborations not only address immediate needs related to hunger but also play a key role in fortifying territorial identity by preserving and giving advantages to local resources within the context of long-term sustainable development. Through experience sharing, vulnerable families and communities have been able to improve their living conditions, reducing negative response strategies. Additionally, various collective entities have emerged to provide financial and agricultural services, such as savings and loan associations in villages, agricultural shops, and food processing and marketing services. Among these activities, food fodder banks and producers of dense malnutritional blocks for animals stand out, facilitating a connection between local development initiatives and private sector actors in the area, thus contributing to strengthening social cohesion.

In some contexts, monitoring policies have been implemented to quickly identify critical areas where improvement policies for food and agricultural resource management are needed (Iruhiriye et al., 2022; Smith & Haddad, 2015). For example, in the course of 2022 in the Mangochi district of Malawi, the Community Initiative for Self Reliance (CISER) was established. It involved the collaboration between the local government and several civil society organizations to develop community assessments in the 2020–2021 agricultural season. These assessments collected locals' experiences with the Affordable Inputs Program (AIP), one of the flagship initiatives of the national government that provides subsidized fertilizers and seeds to farmers in economic difficulty. Through the evaluation of locals and officials from the District Agriculture Office, several weaknesses of the program were identified, including issues in the procedures to redeem purchased vouchers, delays in refunds, difficulties in accessing voucher distribution sites due to poor roads, issues for those who had lost their national identity cards, and a lack of procedures to file complaints or report problems. The District Agriculture Office communicated these issues to the central government, which took action to address them in the subsequent agricultural season. Some changes were introduced, such as the possibility to receive vouchers at a different location and in advance. The assessments also considered gender-based discrimination in receiving subsidized fertilizers and seeds, and they are included as a new indicator, in order to better monitor gender equality and women's involvement in the agricultural sector.

Multistakeholder platforms, as exemplified in the scenario described, constitute a valid tool for fostering dialogue and collaboration within the realm of agricultural and food governance (Hermans et al., 2017; Thorpe et al., 2022). These platforms, renowned for their efficacy, offer a dynamic arena where diverse perspectives and needs can converge and be comprehensively addressed (Delaney et al., 2018), serving as inclusive spaces surpassing traditional boundaries and hierarchies. The collaborative nature of these platforms creates synergies that lead to innovative solutions and informed decision-making. The diversity of participants, each bringing their unique expertise and experiences to the table, enriches the discourse and propels the development of effective strategies in line with the territorial identity. Built on this collaborative approach, multistakeholder platforms emerge not merely as facilitators of dialogue but as catalysts for positive change in agricultural and food governance. Among the multiple benefits offered by multistakeholder platforms, their role in promoting the right to food among citizens is particularly appreciated (HLPE, 2022). The participation of representatives from civil society, non-governmental organizations, the private sector, and the government makes possible the improved access to safe and nutritious food for all, especially for the most vulnerable groups, such as children, the elderly, and rural populations.

However, it is important to recognize that the establishment of these platforms can also raise some concerns, for example, creating unrealistic expectations about the outcomes of policy actions by participants. Thus, it is necessary to ensure that expectations are managed realistically and that participants are aware of the limits of decisions made through the platform (Resnick & Birner, 2010). Another critical aspect could concern the risk of reinforcing the asymmetries of existing power in the food system (Gleckman, 2018). As some stakeholders may enjoy access to greater resources, knowledge, or exert greater influence over the decision-making process, it is essential to ensure that participation is inclusive and that all voices are heard and considered (Herens et al., 2022). Such is the only way to avoid situations where some groups are at a greater disadvantage than others. These issues are particularly significant in local contexts where forms of patriarchy and other asymmetric power relations are entrenched. In these contexts, decision-making processes can be influenced by gender dynamics and social inequalities, which could limit the participation of certain groups of people (Fuchs et al., 2009; Park & White, 2018).

Discussion forums or roundtables finalized to ensure that decision-making processes are inclusive of the population's diversity – adopting a gender- and power-sensitive approach – have been established in various countries, including Bolivia, Brazil, Ethiopia, Indonesia, and Peru (Barletti, 2022). These initiatives aim to promote the participation of all stakeholders, encouraging open and inclusive dialogue and seeking to ensure the fairness and transparency of decision-making. Through these discussion forums, participants from different interest groups have the equal opportunity to voice their opinions and collaborate in defining policies and strategies for the agricultural and food sectors. The goal is to reach shared decisions through continuous feedback, so that the adopted policies truly address the actual needs and respond to challenges of the local context. In order to be truly effective, all interest groups have the equal opportunity to participate and express their opinions, including disadvantaged and marginalized ones. Furthermore, several measures are implemented in order to ensure that the voices of vulnerable groups are heard and considered in final decisions.

The described initiatives also represent an important signal of the safeguarding of territorial identities, as they encourage active and inclusive participation of local communities in decision-making processes related to agriculture and food. Within the context of these platforms, local communities have the opportunity to share their knowledge and expertise about traditional agricultural and food systems, as well as their specific needs and challenges. This information becomes an integral part of the decision-making process, helping to shape policies and strategies that take into account the cultural and social specificities of diverse communities. The direct involvement of local communities in decisions regarding land use, natural resource management, and agricultural practices helps protect territorial identities and preserve the diversity and richness of local traditions.

However, to achieve these outcomes is not always an easy task. Development policies promoted by international organizations in some countries have sometimes overlooked the importance of the identity of the involved communities, leading to negative consequences for people and the environment. For example, a typical case is the so-called "green revolution," which intensified in the second half of the 20th century, aimed to improve agricultural productivity, and reduce poverty in rural areas and the Global South (Evenson & Gollin, 2003; Glaeser, 2010). This approach often disregarded traditional practices and local knowledge of farming communities, preferring to promote the application of Western agricultural technologies and models. One of the most problematic aspects of these policies was the promotion of intensive monocultures, the extensive use of chemical pesticides and fertilizers, and the introduction of new high-yielding crop varieties. These practices led to the destruction of traditional agriculture, which was closely tied with the identity of communities, and the loss of agricultural biodiversity. The excessive use of pesticides also had negative impacts on the environment and people's health, undermining food security and long-term sustainability (Frankema, 2014; Shiva, 1991). Development policies without considering territorial identity also had bad effects on the economy and sustainability of small farmers. Abandoning traditional crops made rural communities dependent on hybrid or genetically modified seeds, which often require high external inputs and can be costly for small farmers. This contributed to the vulnerability of some rural communities to economic shocks and fluctuations in seed and fertilizer prices. In pursuit of the commendable goals of enhancing agricultural productivity and alleviating poverty, the policies enforced by international organizations, often contingent upon accessing funding or technical assistance, have, regrettably, tended to overlook the unique needs and priorities of local communities.

References

Abay, K. A., Breisinger, C., Glauber, J., Kurdi, S., Laborde, D., & Siddig, K. (2023). The Russia-Ukraine war: Implications for global and regional food security and potential policy responses. *Global Food Security*, *36*, 100675.

Arndt, C., Davies, R., Gabriel, S., Harris, L., Makrelov, K., Robinson, S., Levy, S., Simbanegavi, W., van Seventer, D., & Anderson, L. (2020). Covid-19 lockdowns, income distribution, and food security: An analysis for South Africa. *Global Food Security*, *26*, 100410.

Barletti, J. P. (2022). Learning from adaptive collaborative management: A participatory tool to support adaptive and reflective learning in multi-stakeholder forums. In C. Colfer, P. Ravi, & A. Larson (Eds.), *Adaptive collaborative management in forest landscapes: Villagers, bureaucrats, and civil society* (pp. 159–184). Routledge.

Behnassi, M., & El Haiba, M. (2022). Implications of the Russia–Ukraine war for global food security. *Nature Human Behaviour*, *6*(6), 754–755.

Béné, C., Bakker, D., Chavarro, M. J., Even, B., Melo, J., & Sonneveld, A. (2021). Global assessment of the impacts of COVID-19 on food security. *Global Food Security*, *31*, 100575.

Calvin, M. (2017). *No hunger in paradise: The players. The journey. The dream.* Random House.

Connolly-Boutin, L., & Smit, B. (2016). Climate change, food security, and livelihoods in sub-Saharan Africa. *Regional Environmental Change*, *16*, 385–399.

Delaney, A., Evans, T., McGreevy, J., Blekking, J., Schlachter, T., Korhonen-Kurki, K., Tamás, P. A., & Rist, S. (2018). Governance of food systems across scales in times of social-ecological change: A review of indicators. *Food Security*, *10*(2), 287–310.

Evenson, R. E., & Gollin, D. (2003). Assessing the impact of the Green Revolution, 1960 to 2000. *Science*, *300*(5620), 758–762.

FAO (Food and Agriculture Organization of the United Nations). (2023). *FAO food price index*. https://www.fao.org/worldfoodsituation/foodpricesindex/en/

Frankema, E. (2014). Africa and the green revolution a global historical perspective. *NJAS: Wageningen Journal of Life Sciences*, *70*(1), 17–24.

Fuchs, D., Kalfagianni, A., & Arentsen, M. (2009). Retail power, private standards, and sustainability in the global food system. In J. Clapp, & D. Fuchs (Eds.), *Corporate power in global agrifood governance* (pp. 29–59). MIT Press.

Galanakis, C. M. (2023). The "vertigo" of the food sector within the triangle of climate change, the post-pandemic world, and the Russian-Ukrainian war. *Foods*, *12*(4), 721.

GHI (Global Hunger Index). (2022). *Global Hunger Index. 2022 Report*. https://www.global-hungerindex.org/

Glaeser, B. (Ed.) (2010). *The Green Revolution revisited: critique and alternatives* (Vol. 2). Taylor & Francis.

Gleckman, H. (2018). *Multistakeholder governance and democracy: A global challenge*. Routledge.

GNAFC (Global Network Against Food Crises). (2023). *Global report on food crises*. Brussels.

Goncharova, N. A., & Merzlyakova, N. V. (2021). Food shortages and hunger as a global problem. *Food Science and Technology*, *42*, e70621.

Herens, M. C., Pittore, K. H., & Oosterveer, P. J. (2022). Transforming food systems: Multi-stakeholder platforms driven by consumer concerns and public demands. *Global Food Security*, *32*, 100592.

Hermans, F., Sartas, M., Van Schagen, B., van Asten, P., & Schut, M. (2017). Social network analysis of multi-stakeholder platforms in agricultural research for development: Opportunities and constraints for innovation and scaling. *PloS One*, *12*(2), e0169634.

HLPE (High Level Panel of Experts). (2022). *Report on sustainable forestry for food security and nutrition*. High Level Panel of Experts.

Iruhiriye, E., Olney, D. K., Frongillo, E. A., Niyongira, E., Nanama, S., Rwibasira, E., Mbonyi, P., & Blake, C. E. (2022). Translation of policy for reducing undernutrition from national to sub-national levels in Rwanda. *Food Security*, *14*(4), 977–993.

Jagtap, S., Trollman, H., Trollman, F., Garcia-Garcia, G., Parra-López, C., Duong, L., Martindale, W., Munekata, P. E. S., Lorenzo, J. M., Hdaifeh, A., Hassoun, A., Salonitis, K. & Afy-Shararah, M. (2022). The Russia-Ukraine conflict: Its implications for the global food supply chains. *Foods*, *11*(14), 2098.

Park, C. M. Y., & White, B. (2018). We are not all the same: Taking gender seriously in food sovereignty discourse. In E. Holt-Giménez, A. Alonso-Fradejas, T. Holmes, & M. J. Robbins (Eds.), *Food sovereignty: Convergence and contradictions, condition and challenges* (pp. 154–169). Routledge.

Resnick, D. (2021). *Political economy of wheat value chains in post-revolution Sudan*. [Sudan Strategy Support Program Working Paper 1. International Food Policy Research Institute].

Resnick, D., & Birner, R. (2010). Agricultural strategy development in West Africa: The false promise of participation? *Development Policy Review*, *28*(1), 97–115.

Shiva, V. (1991). *The violence of the green revolution: Third world agriculture, ecology and politics*. Zed Books.

Smith, L. C., & Haddad, L. (2015). Reducing child undernutrition: Past drivers and priorities for the post-MDG era. *World Development*, *68*, 180–204.

Thorpe, J., Sprenger, T., Guijt, J., & Stibbe, D. (2022). Are multi-stakeholder platforms effective approaches to agri-food sustainability? Towards better assessment. *International Journal of Agricultural Sustainability*, *20*(2), 168–183.

Timmer, C. P. (2016). The world food economy: A 40 year perspective on the past, and a look forward. *World Food Policy*, *2*(2–1), 121–134.

von Grebmer, K., Bernstein, J., Delgado, C., Smith, D., Wiemers, M., Schiffer, T., Hanano, A., Towey, O., Ní Chéilleachair, C., Foley, C., Gitter, S., Ekstrom, K., & Fritschel, H. (2021). *Global hunger index: Hunger and food systems in conflict settings*. Welthungerhilfe and Concern Worldwide.

Yadav, S. S., Redden, R. J., Hatfield, J. L., Ebert, A. W., & Hunter, D. (Eds.). (2019). *Food security and climate change*. John Wiley & Sons.

Chapter 3

SDG 3. Ensure Healthy Lives and Promote Well-Being for All at All Ages

Abstract

The chapter is focused on the multifaceted challenges and concerted efforts aimed at improving health, within the context of SDG 3, which aims at ensuring healthy lives and promoting well-being for all. It explores the intricate interconnections among physical, mental, and social well-being, acknowledging their reciprocal influence on overall health. Focusing on Africa, a particularly vulnerable region, the chapter sheds light on the complex landscape of healthcare, where governments, non-governmental organizations, professionals, institutions, and communities play pivotal roles. The African continent, though marked by progress, still lags behind in terms of healthcare performance. Several barriers, including limited financial resources, high treatment costs, fragile healthcare systems, and cultural resistance exist. Starting from the analysis, the chapter concludes with a comprehensive picture of the healthcare landscape in Africa, navigating challenges through collaborative efforts, innovative strategies, and tailored interventions. It underscores the imperative of culturally sensitive approaches, community involvement, and international partnerships in realizing the SDG 3 and ultimately achieving improved health and well-being for all African populations.

Health is a fundamental human right, and access to adequate and quality medical care is essential for the progress and prosperity of societies. As a central aspect of human existence, health has been a subject of discussion across various disciplines for centuries. Traditionally, health was narrowly defined within the biomedical framework as the absence of disease or infirmity, emphasizing a reductionist perspective that centered on physiological dysfunction (Anderson, 1998; Lyng, 1990). The biomedical model, with its focus on diagnosing and treating diseases, has long been dominant in the medical field. While this approach has undoubtedly advanced medical knowledge and contributed to life-saving interventions, it largely disregarded the complex interplay of social determinants that shape health performance.

The World Health Organization's (WHO) seminal definition of health in 1948, defining health as "a state of complete physical, mental, and social well-being, and not merely the absence of disease or infirmity," marked a pivotal transformation from the traditional biomedical perspective. This holistic definition has been driven by the recognition that health is a multifaceted and dynamic state, intricately influenced by a myriad of social, economic, and cultural factors.

Social sciences have been instrumental in driving this paradigm shift by acknowledging the interconnectedness between individual well-being and the broader socio-environmental contexts in which people live (Shakespeare, 2012). Several scholars have unveiled the significant impact of socioeconomic status, education, employment, housing conditions, access to healthcare services, and cultural norms on health outcomes (Galabuzi, 2004; Richardson & Norris, 2010; Williams, 1999). They have highlighted that health disparities, far from being solely determined by genetic or biological factors, are heavily influenced by systemic inequities, discrimination, and structural determinants present in societies. For instance, Michael Marmot (2005, 2015) conducted groundbreaking research on exploring the social determinants of health, revealing a strong correlation between social status and health outcomes. He found that individuals who work in junior positions had a significantly higher risk of developing chronic diseases and experiencing premature mortality compared to their senior counterparts, even when factors such as diet and smoking were under control.

Another influential figure in this field is Achille Ardigò (1997), who argued that the medical profession should not limit itself to curing diseases but should actively consider other crucial elements in the overall health equation. Ardigò proposed a holistic perspective that encompassed the bio-psychological dimension of the individual together with the external environment and the wider social system. The external nature, for instance, constitutes the environment where pathogens emerge, and the paths of prevention, treatment, and rehabilitation must be taken into account. Meanwhile, the social system represents the theater where individuals interact through interpersonal relationships, forming simple social groups like families, as well as complex ones such as the State. Ardigò recognized the individuals as entities immersed in their vital worlds, encompassing both the ego and the self, with their bio-psychological dimensions deeply intertwined. This comprehensive approach underscores the need for a broader understanding of health and well-being, comprising not only the medical domain but also the social, psychological, and environmental aspects influencing human health.

Among many others, Paul Farmer (2004) also played crucial roles in extending and enriching the understanding of the social determinants of health and highlighting the importance of interdisciplinary research to address health disparities and promote equitable health outcomes. He was an American medical anthropologist and physician who focused on addressing the root causes of health inequities, examining the social and economic factors influencing disease distribution and access to healthcare. Farmer (2001) delved into the structural determinants of health disparities and emphasized the need to deal with these issues for meaningful improvements in public health. Exploring the links among poverty, human rights, and health, he also highlighted how systemic inequalities perpetuated suffering and illness among the poor and marginalized communities, calling for a comprehensive approach that addresses social and economic injustices as essential components of achieving human well-being, reinforcing the necessity for collective efforts in achieving health equity worldwide. Farmer's work has also extended to his co-founding of the nonprofit organization "Partners in Health" (PIH), which has been instrumental in providing medical services and advocating for health equity in some of the most impoverished regions of the world. Through PIH, Farmer has demonstrated the importance of community-based care and the integration of social and economic support systems to effectively address health disparities and promote sustainable improvements in health outcomes.

Starting from this awareness, SDG 3 focuses on the health of populations worldwide. Its goal is to ensure healthy lives and promote physical, mental, and social well-being, recognizing that these domains are closely interconnected, and they mutually influence an individual's overall health status (WHO, 2021). Physical well-being pertains to the health of the body, its ability to function properly, and to support daily activities without significant limitations, in the absence of illnesses or disorders. Good physical health is fundamental to enabling individuals to lead an active and fulfilling life, allowing them to participate in daily activities, work, and leisure without hindrances. Mental well-being encompasses psychological health and emotional stability, including the ability to cope with stress, emotions, and life challenges in a balanced manner. Mental well-being also involves the effective management of emotions and interpersonal relationships, the ability to adapt to changes, and to confront difficulties with resilience. Good mental health is crucial in fostering greater self-awareness, recognition of others, enhancing self-esteem, and boosting confidence in one's abilities. Finally, social well-being refers to the health of human relationships, social cohesion, and the ability to actively participate in the community. Social well-being includes elements such as mutual support, a sense of belonging, and active engagement in community life. A robust network of social relationships and a sense of community can significantly impact an individual's well-being, providing a support system during challenging times.

To achieve SDG 3, several sub-priorities have been identified, including reducing maternal and child mortality, combating infectious diseases, strengthening healthcare systems, and improving access to basic healthcare services.

Rural and remote areas in many underdeveloped countries, mainly those in various regions of Africa, represent particularly vulnerable territories from a health perspective. These communities often face significant challenges due to the lack of adequate healthcare infrastructure, geographical isolation, and limited access to medical care. In many African countries, qualified healthcare personnel are scarce or even absent, making it even more difficult for people to receive the medical assistance they need, especially for pregnant women and children (Grimett, 2023; Mugo et al., 2015). The healthcare situation in these areas can be further exacerbated by issues such as poverty, poor environmental conditions, and a lack of adequate resources to address diseases and health emergencies. Such was evident during the COVID-19 health crisis. At the beginning of 2020, within three months, the pandemic had affected all African countries. In addition to the health impact, the pandemic has also had a series of harsh indirect effects on the economic, social, and political aspects of the sub-Saharan region. The pandemic has hit African economies hard, which was manifested by a sharp decline in international demand for commodities and agricultural products, the halt suspension of foreign investments, and capital flight. Lockdown measures adopted by African governments have led to job losses and income reductions for the economies of the region, which remains the poorest on the planet, despite the progress that has been made in the last two decades (Lone & Ahmad, 2020; Maeda & Nkengasong, 2021).

The health, social, and economic sufferings that COVID-19 has inflicted on African populations have significantly increased interest and awareness regarding the topic of health, driven in part by the African Union (AU). It is an intergovernmental continental organization composed of 55 African member states. Established on May 26, 2001, in Durban, South Africa, the AU succeeded the Organization of African Unity (OAU), which was created in 1963 with the aim of promoting unity and solidarity among African countries during the decolonization period. The AU is led by various organs, including the Assembly of Heads of State and Government, the Executive Council, and the African Union Commission. Among the AU's objectives are the promotion of peace, security, and stability of the continent, the protection of human rights, and the promotion of democracy and sustainable development. To this day, its actions are fundamental to ensuring a shared vision that can lay the foundations for a coherent and coordinated regulation of health policies of African states, while recognizing and promoting the rights associated with Universal Health Care (UHC).

The current strategic policy direction on the African continent is the Africa Health Strategy 2016–2030, which was developed by WHO and the AU through a participatory process involving African countries, regional organizations, civil society, and international partners. It is a programmatic document that collects and renews the commitment to pursue all health-related goals, in line with the SDGs framework, recognizing the unique health challenges of Africa, including issues of access to health services, limited resources, and the presence and impact of endemic diseases.

Although there is shared consensus in recognizing the progress made over the past decades, it is equally true that the African continent continues to have the worst health performance among the various regional areas of the globe (WHO, 2023a). According to the World Health Statistics 2022 (WHO, 2023b), in 2019 deaths related to communicable diseases, maternal, and nutritional conditions in Africa accounted for over 50% of the total, the highest percentage among various regions of the world. The document also reports critical data concerning healthcare infrastructure. As of 2022, much of sub-Saharan Africa recorded a hospital bed density below the minimum threshold of 18 per 10,000 inhabitants.

Furthermore, public health spending in Africa is still inadequate, failing to respond to the actual needs of the region and to ensure potential access to essential services to less than half of the population.

Despite the challenging realities, effective solutions must be developed to improve access to healthcare services and ensure quality care for all individuals. In this regard, the Africa Health Strategy 2016–2030 embodies a joint commitment to achieve sustainable development goals in health in Africa, considering also territorial identities as essential tools for promoting positive and sustainable change in the health of African populations. The preparation of the document duly took into account the vastness and cultural diversity of the continent, characterized by a multiplicity of territories with their own specificities. Africa cannot be considered a homogeneous area. It is a large continent composed of many independent countries, each with its own culture, and traditions. Thus, the adoption of a single health strategy would be unsuitable for addressing the health needs of all the diverse communities present on this vast continent. On the contrary, an effective strategy to promote health in Africa must consider the cultural and social specificities of each region and adapt to local peculiarities to yield lasting and significant results.

This approach toward desirable territorial development has been translated into a series of interventions and healthcare policies based on the specific identity of each community, all united by the overarching goal of improving the living conditions and well-being of all citizens.

Taking these aspects into account, the Health Strategy for Africa revolves around the following four fundamental pillars: Firstly, the emphasis is placed on strengthening healthcare systems, aiming to improve people's access to healthcare, the quality of services offered, and universal health coverage. The document advocates for the resilience of healthcare systems to cope with emergencies and epidemics, recognizing the importance of a timely and coordinated response in times of crisis. Secondly, a crucial pillar is the prevention and control of diseases, with a specific focus on the major afflictions affecting Africa, such as HIV/AIDS, malaria, tuberculosis, and non-communicable diseases like heart diseases and diabetes. Moreover, the strategy considers the threat of emerging infectious diseases, such as Ebola, urging policymakers to commit to implementing effective prevention and control measures to safeguard the health of citizens in individual African countries. The third pillar promotes the health and well-being of populations through targeted programs, including nutrition interventions, maternal and child health, reproductive health, mental health, and non-communicable disease prevention. These initiatives aim to improve the quality of life for individuals, ensuring access to adequate care and promoting well-being and a satisfactory state of health throughout all stages of life. Finally, the strategy underscores the importance of research and innovation as essential tools to address Africa's health challenges. Research is seen as a driver to develop innovative solutions tailored to the specific community's profile, contributing to improving production capacity and access to affordable drugs and health technologies. This pillar is essential to support Africa's autonomy in the healthcare sector and promote equity in access to care and healthcare services.

The guidance of the AU plays a crucial role in defining and implementing the health policies of the continent. However, it is important to emphasize that this guidance does not have binding regulatory power. This means that individual African states are the only ones that can effectively make decisions and formulate health policies at the national level, even though the AU and other continental institutions provide guidelines and recommendations to promote public health. Thus, each individual African state has decision-making power over its own health policies, considering the specificities and needs of its populations, choosing what other actors to involve in health governance.

In Nepal, significant progress in community health was achieved in 2021 through the action of the civil society organization Aasaman. This initiative actively engaged residents, municipal representatives, and service providers from two municipalities in the Madhesh province, creating a participatory process of health performance assessment and action plan development to improve them (Crawley et al., 2023; Khatri et al., 2023). Initially, community members gathered to discuss expectations regarding healthcare facilities and the quality of medical services, identifying a series of indicators necessary to assess performance. These indicators were then assessed separately for each healthcare facility and service. Subsequently, participants reconvened to collaborate and develop an action plan in case the performance of a healthcare facility fell below an agreed-upon threshold. In this action plan, specific roles and responsibilities were identified to improve individual performance. A key element of the approach was transparency, as each action plan was made public and regularly monitored to ensure effective implementation. Annually, performance is subject to reassessment, which is conducted to monitor progress and make any additional corrective actions. This interactive and participatory process is an effective tool to engage local communities and enhance healthcare facilities and services in the involved areas. Aasaman's initiative can be considered as a best practice that can be implemented in other geographical areas interested in promoting the health and well-being of local populations, with full respect for the territorial identity.

International organizations, governments of other countries, and development agencies also play a critical role in supporting health goals in marginalized countries through financial, technical, and logistical assistance. Among the major funding agencies operating in this field, the Global Fund to Fight AIDS, Tuberculosis, and Malaria stands out. Founded in 2002, the Global Fund is a public-private partnership aimed at mobilizing and investing resources in the fight against these three deadly diseases worldwide. The Global Fund has provided funds for HIV antiretroviral treatment, tuberculosis diagnosis and management, and the distribution of insecticide-treated bed nets for malaria prevention. These programs have had a significant impact on the health of African populations, contributing to reducing the spread of these diseases and improving access to intervention. The Global Fund works closely with governments of developing countries to ensure effective use of funds and proper program implementation. African governments are responsible for managing and implementing projects funded by the Fund, while the Fund commits to providing the necessary technical and logistical support. This partnership between the Global Fund and local governments is essential to ensure that health programs are tailored to the specific identities of countries and communities.

In addition to the Global Fund, other international organizations such as UNICEF and UNITAID have played a significant role in supporting efforts to improve health in Africa. UNICEF focuses on maternal and child health, working to reduce neonatal and child mortality through promoting breastfeeding, access to vaccinations, and prevention of mother-to-child HIV transmission. UNITAID is dedicated to combating communicable diseases, with a focus on providing affordable drugs and diagnostics for vulnerable populations.

Some governments of other countries, such as the United States, the United Kingdom, and France, have also made significant contributions to financing health programs in Africa through foreign aid and bilateral partnerships. These contributions have been crucial in supporting the prevention, diagnosis, and treatment of diseases, as well as improving access to basic healthcare services in rural and remote areas.

Despite the efforts of these organizations and governments, there are still significant challenges in improving health in Africa. Financial resources are often limited, and the cost of treatments and drugs can be a barrier to accessing care for many people. Furthermore, healthcare systems in many African countries are still fragile or lack adequate materials and equipment.

Challenges related to cultural resistance also exist. For instance, when the National Tuberculosis Control Program (PNCT) was first implemented in Angola, integrating PNCT activities into the basic healthcare service network was not easy. The project was perceived, especially at the provincial level, as an external intervention that could not be integrated into basic healthcare services because it was too different from other health services (Santini, 2007). Various cultural resistances were mainly advanced by the Angolan medical class. This resistance led to the persistence of a clear separation between tuberculosis treatment and other basic healthcare services. Inertia in collaboration and integration among different healthcare sectors posed a challenge to the project and limited the effectiveness and efficiency of care. The effort to seek dialogue and participation from provincial health authorities often clashed with this dominant mindset. This is just one of many cases where the work of an external humanitarian organization required a contextualized and culturally sensitive approach to ensure the effectiveness of interventions. Cultural views, traditional practices, and local belief systems still influence the perception and acceptance of health initiatives by African communities in some cases.

Such an example is useful to emphasize once again how taking into consideration the identity of a place appears essential to pursue sustainable initiatives that are territorially desirable.

In order to foster a climate of collaborative trust in pursuit of SDG 3, solutions should involve a wide range of stakeholders, including governments, non-governmental organizations, healthcare professionals, institutions, and the community itself. In cases of misunderstanding or resistance, it may be helpful to have cultural mediators and local health workers work closely together, to ensure understanding and safe implementation, especially in the case of imported programs and interventions. The most effective interventions are those carried out involving community members actively in decisions regarding their health and well-being. This approach is able to create a sense of belonging and responsibility in the involved communities, leading to greater acceptance and adherence to health initiatives.

References

Anderson, N. B. (1998). Levels of analysis in health science: A framework for integrating sociobehavioral and biomedical research. *Annals of the New York Academy of Sciences, 840*(1), 563–576.

Ardigò, A. (1997). *Società e salute. Lineamenti di sociologia sanitaria*. Franco Angeli.

Crawley, L., Singh, J., Sah, V., Yadav, N., Mcquaige, F., Nash, L., & Mishra, B. (2023). 562 Development of an online Case Based Discussion (CBD) group for health professionals in Nepal as part of the NNEPCP programme. *Archive of Disease in Childhood, 108*(2), 310–311.

Farmer, P. (2001). *Infections and inequalities: The modern plagues*. University of California Press.

Farmer, P. (2004). *Pathologies of power: Health, human rights, and the new war on the poor* (Vol. 4). University of California Press.

Galabuzi, G. E. (2004). Social exclusion. In D. Raphael (Ed.), *Social determinants of health: Canadian perspectives*. Canadian Scholars' Press.

Grimett, L. (2023). Understanding the plight and challenges facing South African. *American Journal of Industrial and Business Management, 13*(6), 532–567.

Khatri, R. B., Assefa, Y., & Durham, J. (2023). Multidomain and multilevel strategies to improve equity in maternal and newborn health services in Nepal: Perspectives of health managers and policymakers. *International Journal for Equity in Health, 22*(1), 1–16.

Lone, S. A., & Ahmad, A. (2020). COVID-19 pandemic – An African perspective. *Emerging Microbes & Infections, 9*(1), 1300–1308.

Lyng, S. (1990). *Holistic health and biomedical medicine: A countersystem analysis*. SUNY Press.

Maeda, J. M., & Nkengasong, J. N. (2021). The puzzle of the COVID-19 pandemic in Africa. *Science, 371*(6524), 27–28.

Marmot, M. (2005). Social determinants of health inequalities. *The Lancet, 365*(9464), 1099–1104.

Marmot, M. (2015). The health gap: The challenge of an unequal world. *The Lancet, 386*(10011), 2442–2444.

Mugo, N., Zwi, A. B., Botfield, J. R., & Steiner, C. (2015). Maternal and child health in South Sudan: Priorities for the post-2015 agenda. *Sage Open, 5*(2), 2158244015581190.

Richardson, L. D., & Norris, M. (2010). Access to health and health care: How race and ethnicity matter. *Mount Sinai Journal of Medicine: A Journal of Translational and Personalized Medicine, 77*(2), 166–177.

Santini, S. (2007). Tubercolosi, Angola, Fondo globale. *Cooperazione Sanitaria, 3*(7), 29–40.

Shakespeare, T. (2012). Still a health issue. *Disability and Health Journal, 5*(3), 129–131.

WHO (World Health Organization). (1948). *Preamble to the constitution of the World Health Organization*. https://www.who.int/about/governance/constitution

WHO (World Health Organization). (2021). *Social determinants of health.* https://www.who.int/health-topics/social-determinants-of-health

WHO (World Health Organization). (2023a). *Technical efficiency of health systems in the WHO African Region.* World Health Organization. Regional Office for Africa.

WHO (World Health Organization). (2023b). *World health statistics 2023: Monitoring health for the SDGs, sustainable development goals.* World Health Organization. Regional Office for Africa.

Williams, D. R. (1999). Race, socioeconomic status, and health the added effects of racism and discrimination. *Annals of the New York Academy of Sciences, 896*(1), 173–188.

Chapter 4

SDG 4. Ensure Inclusive and Equitable Quality Education and Promote Lifelong Learning Opportunities for All

Abstract

After discussing the fundamental importance of education, touching upon its role in cognitive and social development, the chapter highlights the urgency of ensuring equitable access to quality education for all children, regardless of their social backgrounds, and tackling the barriers that hinder educational access for marginalized groups. Subsequently, the chapter examines the historical challenges that indigenous communities have faced, particularly in relation to oppressive educational policies imposed by colonial powers and dominant governments. Drawing from the context of SDG 4 and the broader 2030 Agenda, the chapter concludes by emphasazing the critical role of education in safeguarding cultural diversity and promoting social inclusion, while showcasing the innovative efforts in helping indigenous communities reclaim and revitalize their linguistic and cultural heritage on a global scale.

Education is a crucial aspect of the social and economic development of a society, and it is considered one of the primary drivers of human progress.

It enables individuals to acquire knowledge, skills, and abilities for them to understand the world around them, interpret information, and make informed decisions. In his functional analysis, Émile Durkheim (1922) emphasized that education is not only a means of providing technical knowledge but also a device for developing a sense of belonging and social identity. He highlighted that education could contribute to social cohesion by providing moral and civic respect for rules and social institutions. Through the main agencies of socialization, education plays a fundamental role in shaping the culture, identity, and values of a society, as well as in fostering an active socially conscious citizenship. It empowers individuals to learn the tangible and intangible elements that characterize their territory, thus contributing to safeguarding and sharing their cultural heritage.

Education exposes individuals to other cultures and perspectives too, fostering mutual understanding and tolerance. Furthermore, education is essential for the economic development of a society. Quality education equips individuals with the skills and knowledge needed to engage in productive work activities and participate in the labor market. Educated and skilled workers are more productive and capable of contributing to innovation and the development of new technologies, thus promoting economic growth (Mannheim & Stewart, 1997).

Education also contributes to reducing social and economic inequalities. People with quality education gain better opportunities to secure well-paid job opportunities and access resources and services that enhance their quality of life. Conversely, those without access to education can find themselves trapped in situations of poverty and marginalization (Friedman, 2016).

For these reasons, it is safe to argue that education promotes social mobility (Collins, 1974). Education enables individuals to improve their own social status and that of their families, thereby breaking the cycle of poverty and inequalities. Education offers opportunities for personal growth and self-realization, allowing individuals to pursue their goals and aspirations.

Several Marxist and neo-Marxist authors have proposed a critical reading of education, noting that the educational system can be a means of reproducing social inequalities. This perspective contrasts with the functionalist view. Conflict theorists have not only postulated the existence of conflicts over education among various social groups but have also argued that education itself, in its agencies and dynamics, is actually a manifestation of the broader social conflict that exists among groups of people. Considering these premises, conflict theorists have provided a general view of education as a tool of exploitation and oppression wielded by powerful groups against subordinate ones. Regarding the American school system, for example, Samuel Bowles and Hebert Gintis (2002) emphasized a direct relationship between education and class structure, suggesting that these cannot be analyzed independently of each other. The underlying idea of their thought is that school education primarily serves to maintain and reproduce class inequalities. As a result, basic schooling instructs individuals on how to obey those in possession of greater power. The autonomy of thought and decision-making skills required for leadership roles are only taught at the university level, accessible only to the limited circles of elites who already possess the economic and social resources to access this type of education.

According to Louis Althusser (2014), in the capitalist society, the reproduction of production relations is ensured by the exercise of state power in state apparatuses, such as the public school system. From his perspective, the educational system represents the most important ideological apparatus, as it acts as a socialization agent capable of perpetuating dominant ideologies, ensuring their internalization from generation to generation.

In the scientific field, there are several views that criticize the perception of students as passive recipients of knowledge, proposing a more participatory and emancipatory conception of individuals within the school environment. On this topic, Paulo Freire (1970) argued that education can stimulate dialogue and interaction between teachers and students, in which students become active participants in their learning. This approach enables them to gain greater awareness of their social reality and become agents of change within their communities.

The significance of education as a key factor in addressing complex social challenges, such as gender discrimination, racism, and intolerance, has been widely supported by a vast body of academic research. One relevant study in this context is the one conducted by James Banks (1993), which examined the impact of multicultural education on society. The multicultural approach to education aims to incorporate culturally diverse perspectives into the curriculum, thereby promoting a deeper and more respectful understanding of different cultures and identities. Banks' research revealed that multicultural education can play a crucial role in promoting acceptance and empathy among diverse communities. In addition, students exposed to multicultural education are more likely to challenge stereotypes and develop more tolerant attitudes toward cultural differences, thus contributing to the fight against racism and discrimination (Grant & Tate, 1995).

Other studies have confirmed the importance of education in promoting diversity and tolerance. For example, research by Thomas Pettigrew and Linda Tropp (2008) examined the effects of education on individuals' attitudes toward ethnic minorities. The results showed that a higher level of education is correlated with greater open-mindedness and a reduced tendency toward racial prejudice. This indicates that quality education can help eradicate discriminatory attitudes and promote greater tolerance among society members.

Another relevant research area concerns gender education and its role in combating discrimination. Studies have demonstrated that equitable and inclusive education can challenge traditional gender expectations and promote equality between men and women. Such programs can support students in developing a greater awareness of gender inequalities, thus promoting equality (Kane, 1995; Kollmayer et al., 2018; Pekkarinen, 2012).

Furthermore, studies have shown that quality education can help combat intolerance and hatred by fostering critical thinking and mutual understanding. A study by Haider-Donald Markel and Mark Joslyn (2008) examined the impact of higher education on individuals' perception of the rights of minority groups in the United States. The results revealed that individuals with higher levels of education were more supportive of minority rights and had a greater understanding of social issues related to discrimination and intolerance.

Although education alone cannot completely overcome the social challenges associated with discrimination and intolerance, research unequivocally demonstrates that quality education can provide a solid foundation for building a more inclusive and harmonious society.

Having recognized the power of education as a fundamental tool for addressing global challenges, promoting sustainable development, and building a better future for all, SDG 4 was articulated.

It is further divided into 10 sub-goals, each of which targets specific aspects of education. It aims to increase access to pre-school education, providing young minds with a solid foundation for future learning. Early childhood education has been shown to have a significant impact on cognitive and social development. Furthermore, the goal aims to ensure that all children, regardless of their social or cultural background, have access to free, equitable, and quality primary education. This can be achieved by removing the financial and geographical obstacles that prevent children from accessing basic education. In line with this purpose, the UN calls on governments worldwide to increase sources of funding and scholarship opportunities, with a particular emphasis on developing countries where enrollment rates are still too low. SDG 4 also aims to eliminate social and cultural barriers that sometimes hinder opportunities for quality education for individuals from sexual minorities, ethnic minorities, disadvantaged groups, or people with disabilities. In this context, the training of teaching staff also plays a central role. In order to provide quality education to all students, it is essential to increase the number of qualified, well-trained, and motivated teachers who can provide the necessary skills and knowledge. The importance of education is not limited to the school age. SDG 4 also promotes the improvement of technical and professional skills in the post-school period. This growth can be achieved through technical education and continuous vocational training throughout one's lifetime. This purpose has become essential to prepare individuals to meet the demands of the ever-evolving job market and daily life within a rapidly changing social context. Transversally, the UN hopes that themes related to environmental protection and sustainable development are integrated into all educational programs. This means educating global citizens capable of addressing challenges such as climate change, poverty, and inequality.

In order to make education respectful of local identities and thus promote desirable territorial development, it appears appropriate to promote educational and training programs capable of preserving the territorial identities and traditional practices of communities, in contrast to what has been observed throughout history. To better understand this point, it is important to explore the intricate interplay among education and language revitalization, with a particular focus on indigenous communities and cultural minorities. This operation is necessary since they have often seen their cultures and traditions threatened or even denied due to oppressive and discriminatory educational policies.

In the past, educational policies imposed by colonial powers and dominant governments often sought to homogenize different cultures and traditions under a single monocultural and uniform vision. This process of cultural homogenization has often led to the loss of local languages, traditional practices, and knowledge, with serious consequences for the identity and autonomy of the communities involved (Nwanosike et al., 2011; Ocheni & Nwankwo, 2012; Simpson, 2007). Such policies have also contributed to marginalizing the voices and perspectives of some, preventing them from fully participating in society and shaping their own educational initiatives.

Throughout history, various forms of assimilation often disregarded the cultural needs and traditional practices of local communities.

At times, throughout history, assimilation by individuals was seemingly voluntary, appearing as a response to the pressure of a more dominant culture. As a result, conformity was adopted as a solution to stay safe even if it went against the will. This phenomenon can be found, for example, during the Spanish Inquisition, when Jews and Muslims formally accepted the Roman Catholic Church as their religion out of fear of retaliation, while still privately practicing their traditional religions (Ward, 2004).

In America as well, various forms of assimilation, including forced cultural assimilation, were particularly relevant for indigenous groups during colonialism in the 18th, 19th, and 20th centuries. This type of assimilation included religious conversion, separation of families, changes in gender roles, division of property among foreign powers, elimination of local economies, and lack of sustainable food supply (Ellinghaus, 2006). Many welfare policies aimed to integrate indigenous populations into Western culture and society, attempting to end their traditions and cultural practices. To this end, indigenous language schools were closed and replaced with educational institutions that promoted Western values and language. Such assimilation had devastating consequences for indigenous languages and cultural identities, leading to the loss of valuable knowledge and the fragmentation of traditions passed down orally through generations. Over time, many indigenous communities have struggled to resist these assimilation policies and tried to preserve their cultures. However, the challenges have been immense, and the damage caused by past policies has had a lasting impact on indigenous communities. Even today, many of these communities continue to fight to preserve and revitalize indigenous languages and traditional cultural practices. Significant efforts have been made to recognize and value the cultural diversity of indigenous populations, but the road to fully valuing their cultural identities is still long.

The adoption of the United Nations Declaration on the Rights of Indigenous Peoples in 2007 represented a momentous first step toward recognizing the rights and cultures of indigenous communities at the international level. This declaration emphasized the importance of preserving the languages, traditions, and cultural practices of indigenous populations, as well as their right to self-determination and participation in decisions that affect their communities.

Furthermore, significant efforts have been made by indigenous organizations and activists to promote cultural and linguistic education within communities. Programs for language revitalization and cultural preservation have been implemented in various regions, aiming to counteract the loss of indigenous languages and promote greater recognition of their importance. These efforts have proven essential in strengthening the cultural identity of indigenous communities and promoting a sense of pride and belonging.

The 2030 Agenda has spurred the implementation of various educational programs aimed at linguistic revitalization and cultural preservation, with initiatives being carried out in different regions of the world. These efforts have been guided by an awareness of the importance of preserving and valuing indigenous languages and cultures, considered as an integral part of the cultural heritage of humanity.

One of the most significant initiatives has been promoted by the United Nations Educational, Scientific and Cultural Organization (UNESCO) through its Endangered Languages Safeguarding Initiative (LSI). This program aims to preserve endangered languages and promote their revitalization. UNESCO has collaborated with indigenous communities and local organizations to develop concrete action plans for the safeguarding of at-risk languages, promoting the teaching and use of these languages in schools and cultural institutions.

Another successful example is the establishment of cultural centers and institutions dedicated to promoting indigenous languages and traditions. In Canada, for example, the federal government established the "National Centre for Truth and Reconciliation" at the University of Manitoba in November 2015, following the recognition of the serious abuses suffered by indigenous children in the so-called "residential schools." This center is tasked with documenting and preserving the culture and history of indigenous peoples in Canada, including their traditional languages, in order to promote greater awareness and understanding of past injustices and support the reconciliation process.

In Australia, the government initiated a program to teach indigenous languages in schools, with the aim of supporting and promoting the teaching of Aboriginal languages. Nowadays, there are 82 schools offering 96 Aboriginal language programs. This includes 11 South Australian Aboriginal languages and 1 Queensland Aboriginal language. This initiative aims to preserve and promote the rich linguistic and cultural diversity of Aboriginal communities, recognizing the central role of traditional languages in their identity and well-being. The initiatives for linguistic revitalization and cultural preservation have also involved indigenous communities themselves, with the support of non-governmental organizations and civil society actors.

In addition to national and regional initiatives, the UN has also played an important role in promoting the recognition and appreciation of indigenous languages and traditions on a global level. In 2019, the UN General Assembly declared 2019 the International Year of Indigenous Languages, in order to raise public awareness about the challenges that indigenous languages face and promote their preservation and appreciation. In this context, numerous events and initiatives were organized worldwide to celebrate and promote indigenous languages and cultures. Subsequently, the UN General Assembly, with Resolution A/RES/74/135, proclaimed the years 2022 to 2032 as the "International Decade of Indigenous Languages," to draw the international community's attention to the loss of these languages and to adopt urgent measures to preserve them through specific training programs.

References

Althusser, L. (2014). *On the reproduction of capitalism: Ideology and ideological state apparatuses*. Verso Books.
Banks, J. A. (1993). *Multicultural education: Historical development, dimensions, and practice*. Teachers College Press.
Bowles, S., & Gintis, H. (2002). Schooling in capitalist America revisited. *Sociology of Education, 1*, 1–18.
Collins, R. (1974). Where are educational requirements for employment highest? *Sociology of Education, 1*, 419–442.
Durkheim, E. (1922). *Éducation et Sociologie*. Félix Alcan.
Ellinghaus, K. (2006). Indigenous assimilation and absorption in the United States and Australia. *Pacific Historical Review, 75*(4), 563–585.
Freire, P. (1970). *Pedagogy of the oppressed*. Herder and Herder.
Friedman, S. (2016). Habitus clivé and the emotional imprint of social mobility. *The Sociological Review, 64*(1), 129–147.
Grant, C. A., & Tate, W. F. (1995). Multicultural education through the lens of the multicultural education research literature. In J. A. Banks (Ed.), *Handbook of research on multicultural education* (pp. 89–105). Jossey-Bass.
Haider-Markel, D. P., & Joslyn, M. R. (2008). Beliefs about the origins of homosexuality and support for gay rights: An empirical test of attribution theory. *Public Opinion Quarterly, 72*(2), 291–310.
Kane, E. W. (1995). Education and beliefs about gender inequality. *Social Problems, 42*(1), 74–90.
Kollmayer, M., Schober, B., & Spiel, C. (2018). Gender stereotypes in education: Development, consequences, and interventions. *European Journal of Developmental Psychology, 15*(4), 361–377.
Mannheim, K., & Stewart, W. A. C. (1997). *An introduction to the sociology of education* (Vol. 9). Taylor & Francis.
Nwanosike, O. F., Onyije, L. E., & Eboh, L. (2011). Colonialism and education. *Mediterranean Journal of Social Sciences, 2*(4), 41–47.
Ocheni, S., & Nwankwo, B. C. (2012). Analysis of colonialism and its impact in Africa. *Cross-Cultural Communication, 8*(3), 46–54.
Pekkarinen, T. (2012). Gender differences in education. *Nordic Economic Policy Review, 1*(1), 165–194.
Pettigrew, T. F., & Tropp, L. R. (2008). How does intergroup contact reduce prejudice? Meta-analytic tests of three mediators. *European Journal of Social Psychology, 38*(6), 922–934.
Simpson, M. K. (2007). From savage to citizen: Education, colonialism and idiocy. *British Journal of Sociology of Education, 28*(5), 561–574.
Ward, S. (2004). Crypto-Judaism and the Spanish Inquisition. *Shofar: An Interdisciplinary Journal of Jewish Studies, 22*(4), 167–169.

Chapter 5

SDG 5. Achieve Gender Equality and Empower All Women and Girls

Abstract

This chapter emphasizes the interconnectedness of legal frameworks, socio-cultural norms, and policy interventions in forging a more inclusive and just society for girls and women. Despite substantial strides, gender disparities still persist across the Western world, highlighting the need for targeted actions. The chapter explores the "glass ceiling" phenomenon, the wage gap, gender-based violence, emphasizing their persistence, and the imperative of transformative policies. Shifting focus to the East, the narrative navigates through distinct trajectories of women's rights advocacy. Religious beliefs have historically reinforced gender inequality in some Eastern societies, shaping cultural norms and limiting women's public participation. In the context of Islam, varying interpretations have led to differing perspectives on gender roles. The chapter showcases instances of progress, such as Saudi Arabian women gaining voting rights, while acknowledging enduring challenges like female genital mutilation and forced marriages. In the conclusion part, the chapter highlights the need for sustained efforts to dismantle barriers and elevate women's voices, fostering a global landscape marked by gender equality and women's empowerment.

The roots of gender disparity are embedded in the history of human societies, where many cultures established patriarchal systems that limited the rights and opportunities of women. A historical example of such a patriarchal system is evident in ancient Greece, where the role of women was tightly confined to the domestic sphere. Greek women had little or even no participation in the political and social life of the polis (city-state), and their main duty was to manage the household and raise children. The philosophical thinking of the time, expressed by figures like Plato and Aristotle, justified the subordination of women and considered them inferior to men (Fant & Lefkowitz, 2016; Schidel, 1995).

In ancient Rome, the role of women was heavily influenced by culture and prevailing laws. Historical evidence, such as the writings of historians and philosophers like Tacitus, Seneca, and Cicero, reflected the patriarchal conception and traditional ideas about the position of women in Roman society. These authors often described women as emotional and fragile beings, portraying women as submissive and inferior to men (MacLachlan, 2013). The Roman patriarchal system granted the head of the family, known as the "pater familias," absolute authority over his family, including wife, children, and domestic slaves (Johnson, 2007; Saller, 1999). Married women were under the guardianship of their husbands, who had the power to make legal and financial decisions on their behalf. Married Roman women could not own personal property and needed legal representation from their husbands in legal proceedings. Furthermore, Roman women were excluded from political participation and public institutions (Gardner, 2008; Saller, 1994).

It is important to note that the role of Roman women varied depending on their social class (Gerkens & Vigneron, 2000). Women from higher social classes, such as matrons of patrician families, had greater access to education and could be involved in cultural and religious activities. They also held a certain degree of social and political influence within their social circles. Women from lower social classes, such as slaves and lower-class free women, had fewer opportunities and rights. Slave women were completely subject to the will of their masters and often subjected to violence and abuse. Lower-class free women, although having more autonomy than slaves, still had to contend with legal and social limitations (Harris, 1999).

Gender disparity was also evident in the feudal system of medieval Europe. In this system, power and property were concentrated in the hands of male feudal lords, while women were generally excluded from participating in public affairs and decision-making processes. Women in the Middle Ages were often subject to male guardianship and the law of their father or husband, so they were deprived of freedom and autonomy (Erler & Kowaleski, 1988; Morewedge, 1975; Stewart & Ostrove, 1998).

The modern age witnessed a growing recognition of human and civil rights, but gender disparity persisted. In the 17th and 18th centuries, for instance, women's emancipation in Europe was limited and often contentious. Marie Gouze, known as Olympe de Gouges, was one of the first feminists to raise the issue of women's rights during the French Revolution (Siess, 2005). In 1791, she wrote the "Declaration of the Rights of Woman and of the Female Citizen", emphasizing gender equality and calling for the extension of political rights to women. Her ideas were widely rejected, and the French Revolution did not lead to significant improvements in the condition of women (Groult, 2013).

The 19th century marked a period of significant change for women's rights in some parts of the world. Among the most significant and influential movements of this period was the suffragette movement in the United Kingdom. Suffragettes were women activists who fought for the right to vote, which was considered an exclusive right of men at the time. The movement began to take shape in the late 19th century, with activists like Emmeline Pankhurst and her daughter Christabel leading the fight for women's suffrage (Crawford, 2003; Gilman, 2023). The suffragette movement employed various tactics to draw public attention to the cause and intensify pressure on governments, such as mass demonstrations, marches, hunger strikes, acts of civil disobedience, and public protests. Suffragettes faced resistance from authorities and were often arrested and imprisoned for their actions. The movement achieved a major victory in 1918 when the British Parliament granted the right to vote to women over the age of 30 who owned property. In 1928, the right to vote was extended to all women over the age of 21, based on gender equality in electoral rights. This marked a turning point in the history of women's rights in the United Kingdom (Holton, 2003).

Outside of the United Kingdom, other countries granted women the right to vote during the 19th and 20th centuries. In 1893, New Zealand became the first country in the world to grant women's suffrage, followed by South Australia in 1894 (Franceschet et al., 2019; Grimshaw, 1987; Millar, 2018). Other nations that granted women the right to vote in the decades that followed include Finland (1906), Norway (1913), Russia (1917), Sweden (1919), Ireland (1922), and many others (Daley & Nolan, 1994). In the United States, the 19th Amendment to the United States Constitution, ratified in 1920, granted women the right to vote (DuBois, 1999).

These significant advancements in the 19th and 20th centuries paved the way for further struggles for women's rights in the subsequent years, contributing in part to deconstructing the expectations and gender roles that often define what was considered appropriate or inappropriate for men and women. For example, in many societies, women have traditionally been assigned the primary role of taking care of the home and family, while men were seen as the primary breadwinners and responsible for external work. These long-standing cultural norms have limited people's life choices and opportunities based on their gender, generating systemic discrimination characterized by legal and institutional barriers, as well as cultural expectations and attitudes toward women (Butler, 2002; De Lauretis, 1989). During the 20th century, the feminist movement marked a turning point in the fight for women's rights in many parts of the Western world. This movement, which gained momentum in the 1960s and 1970s, had a significant impact on promoting gender equality and challenging social norms that discriminated against women. Throughout the 20th century, women gained increasing access to education and work opportunities. Many laws discriminating against women in the workplace were repealed, paving the way for greater female participation in the workforce and allowing highly educated women to take leadership and responsibility positions. This led to greater economic independence for women and contributed to reducing dependence on male figures. Another significant outcome of the feminist movement has been the increase in women's political representation. In many countries, there has been a growing participation of women in politics and their presence in governmental institutions. Women have started to attain positions of power and leadership in political institutions, thereby contributing to a more equitable gender perspective in the formulation of public policies

(Conway, 2001; Dolan et al., 2021). The feminist movement has also highlighted the issue of reproductive rights. In 1973, in the United States, the Roe vs Wade case was a turning point for women's right to make autonomous decisions about their bodies and reproductive health. This decision granted women the right to abortion, supporting the concept of autonomy and self-determination for women regarding maternity (Levine et al., 1999), which was subsequently adopted in many other legal systems.

It is important to underline that gender disparities persist in many parts of the Western world. Even though women have made significant strides toward achieving equality, there are sectors where they remain underrepresented or face discrimination. In leadership positions and senior-level corporate roles, women are often outnumbered by men. Gender pay gap disparities continue to exist, with women frequently earning less than their male counterparts for performing the same work. Moreover, the phenomenon of the "glass ceiling" often hinders women from reaching the highest positions within organizations, thereby limiting opportunities for professional advancement (Cotter et al., 2001). The term "glass ceiling" was coined in 1978 by Marilyn Loden in an interview and was later used in March 1984 by Gay Bryant, the founder and former editor of *Working Woman* magazine. As emphasized by Joan Acker (1988), even when the job market seems open to all regardless of gender, implicit organizational patterns allocate different responsibilities, roles, and wages to men and women, confirming that gender-based disparities persist even in seemingly democratic contexts.

Several authors argue that gender inequalities persist within the domestic sphere too, with many women still bearing the brunt of household and family care responsibilities (Collins, 2019).

Another critical issue to address is gender-based violence. Women continue to be victims of physical, sexual, and psychological violence, and the phenomenon of femicide is widespread in many parts of the world. Domestic violence and stalking also pose threats to many women, underscoring the need to address the issue of gender-based violence and promote a culture of respect and equality. According to the Every Woman Treaty Association, approximately one in three women globally has experienced physical or sexual violence from a partner or others in their lifetime (EWT, 2023).

In the Eastern world, the struggle for women's rights and gender equality has taken a different trajectory. Historically, many Eastern societies adopted patriarchal systems similar to those in the Western world. In these contexts, religious beliefs have contributed to justifying and legitimizing gender inequality, imposing social and cultural norms that still confine women to the domestic sphere and limit their opportunities for public and political participation.

One of the significant examples of how religion has influenced traditional gender roles can be found in some Middle Eastern countries where Islam is the predominant religion. It is important to note that interpretations of Islam can vary widely from one region to another. Furthermore, within Islamic communities, alternative interpretations of sacred texts promoting gender equality and women's rights also exist (Ahmed, 2021; Engineer, 2008). In more conservative interpretations of sacred texts, women are often regarded as "guardians of virtue" and they are required to adhere to strict rules regarding their behavior and attire. These interpretations have often led to gender segregation and limited opportunities for women to actively participate in society. For instance, until 2015, Saudi women were not allowed to vote, and it was only in that year that they were permitted to participate in municipal elections, marking a significant step forward for women's political participation (Quamar, 2016). Nonetheless, some discriminatory laws and social norms concerning marriage, inheritance, and child custody continue to restrict women's autonomy in Saudi Arabia and other Middle Eastern societies. Female genital mutilation (FGM) is still prevalent in some African countries like Somalia and Guinea. According to UNICEF estimates (2023), at least 200 million girls and women alive today in 31 countries have undergone FGM. Forced marriage is also a persistent issue in some regions, with many girls compelled to marry against their will, suffering devastating consequences for their freedom and well-being (Atim, 2017).

In some parts of sub-Saharan Africa, women also face persistent challenges to their rights and gender equality. In Niger, for example, discriminatory laws and cultural practices limit women's opportunities for participation in political and public life. Women encounter difficulties accessing education and economic opportunities, and the practice of early marriage is still prevalent, with many girls forced into marriage at a young age, disrupting their education and jeopardizing their health.

In Somalia, armed conflict and political instability have exacerbated gender-based violence and discrimination against women. Somali women are at risk of sexual and gender-based violence, both within their communities and during armed conflicts.

Even in other non-Islamic Eastern communities, gender roles are often defined within a patriarchal framework. For instance, in Thailand, a nation with a significant Buddhist population, Buddhist nuns (bhikkhuni) have faced discrimination and restrictions throughout history. The presence of bhikkhuni has long been hindered and is a subject of debate even within traditional Buddhist communities (Barua, 2023).

Similarly, in India, which is home to a substantial population of practitioners of Hinduism and Buddhism, women have encountered gender inequalities deeply rooted in culture and religious traditions. In many Indian communities, women are excluded from important religious rituals and leadership positions, despite formal guarantees of gender equality and women's rights in its Constitution (Rodrigues, 2023).

The above cited cases underscore the vastly diverse situation of women in different territorial contexts, varying from country to country and community to community. While some nations and cultures have made some progress in promoting gender equality and challenging patriarchal norms, others still grapple with deep-seated gender inequalities and discrimination.

This makes it evident why targeted actions and transformational policies are necessary to create a more inclusive and just society where women can fully participate and contribute to all aspects of life. SDG 5 endeavors to attain gender equality and empower all women and girls. It acknowledges that gender equality is not just a fundamental human right but also an essential prerequisite for fostering a peaceful, prosperous, and sustainable world. This goal is a dedicated effort to confront and rectify the enduring gender disparities and discrimination that persist in societies across the globe (Walby, 2009). A critical focus of this goal revolves around recognizing and addressing the often undervalued and overlooked aspect of women's reproductive work. It emphasizes the need to acknowledge and appreciate the significant contribution of women in this often marginalized and underappreciated sphere. SDG 5 also places great emphasis on eradicating all forms of violence and harmful practices that women and girls face. This includes domestic violence, sexual harassment, trafficking, and harmful cultural practices like child marriage and FGM.

A critical milestone in this direction is the passing of legislation and the implementation of policies aimed at addressing these issues. For example, Morocco took a significant step toward combatting violence against women by enacting a new law that criminalized various forms of violence, including domestic violence, sexual harassment, and forced marriage. The law, which came into effect in 2018, obligates public authorities to adopt prevention measures, including awareness programs on violence against women. It also provides for the establishment of specialized units to address the needs of women and children in courts, government agencies, security forces, and local, regional, and national committees dealing with women and children's issues. However, this law, while representing a significant step forward for a country with a high rate of violence against women, also has serious gaps and shortcomings, including a lack of funding sources for reforms. In the country, there are fewer than 10 shelters to accommodate domestic violence victims, and in addition, they have limited capacity. Non-governmental groups manage them all, but only a few of them receive government funding. Many victims of domestic violence are compelled to return to violent partners because they lack the means to support themselves or have a home. Additionally, standardized monitoring mechanisms have not been planned (HRW, 2018).

In addition to legislative actions, awareness-raising campaigns, and educational initiatives have played a crucial role in advancing gender equality and promoting women's rights. Various organizations and advocacy groups have been working tirelessly to raise awareness about gender-based violence, challenge harmful gender norms, and empower women and girls. For instance, the "HeForShe" campaign, launched by the UN, has been engaging men and boys as advocates for gender equality, encouraging them to take action to end violence against women and promote women's rights (Harvey, 2020; Stache, 2015).

In recent years, protests and resistance movements led by women in various contexts have sought to challenge social norms and laws that discriminate against and restrict their freedom of choice. A significant example comes from Iran, where in 2019, thousands of women participated in the "White Wednesdays" protests, a movement of civil disobedience aimed at supporting the demand for greater clothing choice freedom. During these protests, women wore white veils as a symbol of opposition to the government-imposed veil requirement (Nashat, 2021). The Iranian authorities responded firmly and repressively, using coercion, public humiliation, and violence to suppress women participating in the protests.

Activists and protesters were arrested, intimidated, and persecuted, while women who resisted the veil requirement faced severe and often violent consequences. This authoritative stance epitomizes a rigidly uniform vision of society that neither recognizes nor respects the plurality of identities within the country although Iran has formally taken some steps towards achieving SDG 5 (HRW, 2023). In 2016, the Iranian government released a national document named the "Charter of Citizenship's Rights" to promote a range of social issues based on local and national considerations, including the improvement of women's rights, judicial justice, and access to information (Biglari et al., 2017). However, the events described illustrate that significant challenges still persist regarding the attainment of gender equality (Sachs et al., 2021).

The resistance by Iranian women illustrates how laws and social norms inadequately reflect the diversity and complexity of identities in a country. The veil requirement is a contentious issue in Iran, with divergent opinions regarding its application. While some women choose to wear the hijab for religious or cultural reasons, many others view it as a symbol of oppression and desire the right to decide how to dress as they wish. This exemplifies the intricate and multifaceted landscape surrounding the pursuit of gender equality and women's rights. These complexities highlight the ongoing struggle to reconcile traditional values with modern principles of human rights and individual autonomy, fully respecting the various voices that make up the territorial identity. Thus, initiatives like the "Charter of Citizenship's Rights" signal a commitment to advancing women's rights, but substantive change requires a comprehensive reevaluation of cultural norms and social structures to create a more inclusive and equitable society. While the eradication of discriminatory laws and policies is undoubtedly paramount, it is imperative to recognize that a comprehensive approach to this struggle extends beyond legal frameworks. The imposition of norms by institutions and expectations upon the behaviors and lifestyles of women can profoundly misalign with the authentic territorial identity. The impositions perpetuate cultural hegemony, stifling the expressions of women who challenge or deviate from prescribed behaviors. As a result, such interventions can be perceived as external impositions that fail to resonate with the authentic essence of the community, ultimately impeding the organic evolution of territorial identity.

On the opposite side, various initiatives have been implemented worldwide to address the issue of girls' education and promote women's empowerment while respecting their cultural identity and background. One such initiative is the "Let Girls Learn" program, launched in 2015 by the United States Agency for International Development (USAID) in collaboration with the Peace Corps and led by Michelle Obama (Biressi, 2018). The "Let Girls Learn" program aimed to dismantle barriers preventing girls from accessing quality education and to empower them to reach their full potential. It acknowledged that girls encounter unique challenges in pursuing education, including cultural norms, early marriage, gender-based violence, poverty, and limited school access. Thus, the program laid significant emphasis on providing culturally relevant education and training to empower girls. It acknowledged that curricula and teaching methodologies should be in line with the experiences of the girls, in order to make education more engaging and meaningful. Furthermore, the "Let Girls Learn" program recognized the importance of engaging communities and transforming social norms to support girls' education. It involved collaboration with parents, religious leaders, and community members to challenge stereotyped harmful practices and beliefs that hindered girls' access to education. By involving these stakeholders, the program aimed to create an enabling environment for girls' education and promote long-term sustainability. The impact of the program was substantial in numerous communities, leading to increased enrollment and retention of girls in schools. It helped challenge traditional gender roles and stereotypes, empowering girls to pursue their aspirations. The program raised global awareness about the significance of girls' education and women's empowerment, mobilizing support and resources to address this critical issue. While primarily led by the United States, the "Let Girls Learn" program inspired similar initiatives subsequently taken by other international organizations, governments, and non-profit entities to promote girls' education and women's empowerment in diverse contexts.

This type of initiative not only fully addressed the social expectations that characterize SDG 5 but also took into account the intrinsic value of territorial identity. The program ensured that school facilities were designed in accordance with cultural norms and practices, providing spaces for girls to comfortably observe religious practices or rituals. But "Let Girls Learn" went beyond mere infrastructure development and renovation, ensuring that schools were inclusive and accommodating to the distinct needs of girls from different cultural backgrounds. Recognizing that girls hail from varied ethnicities, religions, and social contexts, the initiative aimed to create an educational environment that valued and celebrated their diversity, adopting a culturally sensitive approach to enhancing school quality and safety.

When initiatives aimed at gender equality are designed and implemented with a keen understanding of territorial identity, they take on a deeper resonance. Rather than imposing uniform solutions, these initiatives engage with the experiences and aspirations of local communities. They recognize that the challenges and opportunities presented by gender equality are refracted through the unique prism of territorial identity. By anchoring gender equality efforts within this broader context, initiatives harness the power of local agency and cultural significance.

Such initiatives act as catalysts for transformative change that resonates across societal dimensions, paving the way for more inclusive economic systems, participatory political structures, and resilient communities. Moreover, initiatives that honor territorial identity would amplify the voices of all groups. They provide a platform for women with different identity backgrounds to articulate their unique needs and aspirations. These initiatives ensure that solutions are contextually relevant and culturally sensitive. This approach also empowers women to challenge and transform discriminatory norms from within, driving a more sustainable and organic process of change. However, it is crucial to acknowledge that this approach is not without challenges. The interplay between gender equality and territorial identity can be complex, and tensions may arise between traditional practices and modern aspirations. Balancing the preservation of cultural heritage with the advancement of gender equality requires delicate navigation. Also, in this case, open and inclusive dialogues within communities are essential to ensure that the transformative goals of gender equality are not misconstrued or misaligned with the values held dear.

SDG 5 also aims to reduce gender disparities in the workplace overcoming the obstacles that women encounter. Through the European Gender Equality Strategy 2020–2025, proposed under NextGenerationEU, Europe has established a substantial body of laws and guidelines regarding employment and training. Gender dimensions have been integrated into all European policies and actions, with the goal of accelerating the progress in women's empowerment and safeguarding the achievements made in gender equality over the 25 years following the adoption of the Beijing Declaration. The uniqueness of this strategy lies in the willingness to recognize and respect the socio-cultural characteristics of everyone (Corbisiero & Nocenzi, 2023), moving beyond the tendency to devise standardized and universally applicable solutions.

Ensuring women's reproductive health and rights is another fundamental aspect of SDG 5. This encompasses access to family planning, maternal healthcare, and comprehensive sexual and reproductive health services.

To advance this goal, in 2015 the United Nations Population Fund (UNFPA) launched the "Safeguard Young People" program, focusing on promoting adolescent sexual and reproductive health and rights. This initiative addresses the specific needs and challenges that young people face in accessing information and services related to sexual and reproductive health. By offering age-appropriate and comprehensive education, the program aims to empower young women and girls to make informed choices regarding their sexual and reproductive health.

Furthermore, governments and organizations have taken steps to enhance maternal healthcare services to ensure safer pregnancies and childbirths. The World Health Organization (WHO) has been at the forefront of promoting maternal health through initiatives like the "Safe Childbirth Checklist," introduced in 2015 to reduce maternal mortality rates by enhancing the quality of care during childbirth (Perry et al., 2017).

In the context of comprehensive sexual and reproductive health services, the International Planned Parenthood Federation (IPPF) has played a crucial role in advocating for women's reproductive rights and providing access to a wide range of reproductive health services. Over time, the IPPF has increased its commitment to ensuring that all women have access to quality reproductive healthcare services through its network of member associations (Weydner, 2018).

Women's reproductive rights have been underscored through international agreements too. The Nairobi Summit on ICPD25, held in Kenya in 2019, marked a 25th anniversary since the International Conference on Population and Development (ICPD) held in Cairo in 1994. This summit brought together government representatives and stakeholders to renew commitments toward advancing women's reproductive rights and health, with a focus on achieving the ICPD Programme of Action by 2030 (Mahmood & Bitzer, 2020).

Lastly, SDG 5 acknowledges the pivotal role women play in decision-making processes and calls for increased women's voices across all levels of governance and leadership. This encompasses political participation, corporate boardrooms, and community decision-making bodies. The United Nations Entity for Gender Equality and the Empowerment of Women (UN Women) actively promotes women's leadership through initiatives like the "Leadership and Political Participation Program." Nonetheless, the underrepresentation of women in leadership positions and politics persists, necessitating ongoing efforts to address barriers and promote gender balance in decision-making spheres.

In this regard, a virtuous example comes from a developing country. In Rwanda, women's activism and inclusive policies have contributed to enhancing women's political participation and promoting gender equality. The preamble of the new Constitution, enacted in 2003, enshrined equal rights between men and women, setting a 30% representation target for women at all levels of government. The Constitution also established the position of "gender monitor" to ensure the alignment of public programs with the country's equality and equal opportunity goals. The turning point came in 2008. Rwanda became the first country in the world to have a female-majority parliament, with a 56% representation. This record was furthered to 64% in 2013. The female-majority parliament worked extensively to improve the status of women in the country, implementing various policies and initiatives to reduce the gender gap in the workforce and combat gender-based violence (Inter-Parliamentary Union, 2023).

These initiatives facilitated a cultural shift, which initially began as a survival mechanism after the genocide but, through targeted policies, allowed the country to come closer to narrowing the gender gap.

References

Acker, J. (1988). Class, gender, and the relations of distribution. *Signs: Journal of Women in Culture and Society*, *13*(3), 473–497.

Ahmed, L. (2021). *Women and gender in Islam: Historical roots of a modern debate*. Veritas.

Atim, G. (2017). Girls not brides: Ending child marriage in Nigeria. *Journal of Gender, Information and Development in Africa (JGIDA)*, *6*(1–2), 73–94.

Barua, S. (2023). The status of women in Vedic and Buddha's periods. *Journal of International Buddhist Studies*, *13*(2), 61–74.

Biglari, S., Beiglary, S., & Arthanari, T. (2022). Achieving sustainable development goals: fact or Fiction?. *Journal of Cleaner Production*, *332*, 130032.

Biressi, A. R. (2018). From the girl to the world: Good girls as political endorsers and agents of change. *Communication Culture & Critique*, *11*(3), 399–417.

Butler, J. (2002). *Gender trouble*. Routledge.

Collins, C. (2019). *Making motherhood work: How women manage careers and caregiving*. Princeton University Press.

Conway, M. M. (2001). Women and political participation. *Political Science and Politics*, *34*(2), 231–233.

Corbisiero, F., & Nocenzi, M. (2023). Intersezionalità e divario di genere: un paradigma alternativo per il policy-making europeo. In A. Scialdone (Ed.), *PNRR. Promesse da mantenere e miglia da percorrere* (pp. 93–121). Editoriale Scientifica.

Cotter, D. A., Hermsen, J. M., Ovadia, S., & Vanneman, R. (2001). The glass ceiling effect. *Social Forces*, *80*(2), 655–681.

Crawford, E. (2003). *The women's suffrage movement: A reference guide 1866–1928*. Routledge.
Daley, C., & Nolan, M. (Eds.). (1994). *Suffrage and beyond: International feminist perspectives*. NYU Press.
De Lauretis, T. (1989). *The violence of representation*. Routledge.
Dolan, J., Deckman, M. M., & Swers, M. L. (2021). *Women and politics: Paths to power and political influence*. Rowman & Littlefield.
DuBois, E. C. (1999). *Feminism and suffrage: The emergence of an independent women's movement in America, 1848–1869*. Cornell University Press.
Engineer, A. (2008). *The rights of women in Islam*. Sterling Publishers.
Erler, M., & Kowaleski, M. (Eds.). (1988). *Women and power in the Middle Ages*. University of Georgia Press.
EWT (Every Woman Treaty). (2023). *Safer Now*. Full Report. https://everywoman.org/safer-now-report/
Fant, M. B., & Lefkowitz, M. R. (2016). *Women's life in Greece and Rome: A source book in translation*. Bloomsbury Publishing.
Franceschet, S., Krook, M. L., & Tan, N. (Eds.) (2019). *The Palgrave handbook of women's political rights. Gender and politics*. Palgrave Macmillan.
Gardner, J. F. (2008). *Women in Roman law and society*. Routledge.
Gerkens, J. F., & Vigneron, R. (2000). The emancipation of women in ancient Rome. *Revue internationale des droits de l'Antiquité*, *47*, 108–121.
Gilman, C. P. (2023). *Women's economic writing in the nineteenth century*. Routledge.
Grimshaw, P. (1987). *Women's suffrage in New Zealand*. Auckland University Press.
Groult, B. (2013). *Ainsi soit Olympe de Gouges: La déclaration des droits de la femme et autres textes politiques*. Grasset.
Harris, W. V. (1999). Demography, geography and the sources of Roman slaves. *The Journal of Roman Studies*, *89*, 62–75.
Harvey, R. (2020). Twitter reactions to the UN's# HeForShe campaign for gender equality: A corpus-based discourse analysis. *Journal of Corpora and Discourse Studies*, *3*, 31–50.
Holton, S. S. (2003). *Feminism and democracy: Women's suffrage and reform politics in Britain, 1900-1918*. Cambridge University Press.
HRW (Human Rights Watch). (2018). *Morocco: New violence against women law*. https://www.hrw.org/news/2018/02/26/morocco-new-violence-against-women-law
HRW (Human Rights Watch). (2023). *Unveiling resistance: The struggle for women's rights in Iran*. https://www.hrw.org/news/2023/06/26/unveiling-resistance-struggle-womens-rights-iran
Inter-Parliamentary Union. (2023). *Women in national parliaments*. https://data.ipu.org/women-ranking?month=10&year=2023
Johnson, E. (2007). Patriarchal power in the Roman republic: Ideologies and realities of the paterfamilias. *Hirundo*, *5*, 99–117.
Levine, P. B., Staiger, D., Kane, T. J., & Zimmerman, D. J. (1999). Roe v Wade and American fertility. *American Journal of Public Health*, *89*(2), 199–203.
MacLachlan, B. (2013). *Women in ancient Rome: A sourcebook* (Vol. 19). A&C Black.
Mahmood, T., & Bitzer, J. (2020). Accelerating progress in sexual and reproductive health and rights in Eastern Europe and central Asia – Reflecting on ICPD 25 Nairobi Summit. *European Journal of Obstetrics & Gynecology and Reproductive Biology*, *247*, 254–256.
Millar, G. (2018). Women's lives, feminism and the New Zealand journal of history. *New Zealand Journal of History*, *52*(2), 134–152.
Morewedge, R. T. (Ed.). (1975). *The role of woman in middle ages* (Vol. 6). SUNY Press.
Nashat, G. (2021). *Women and revolution in Iran*. Routledge.

Perry, W. R. G., Nejad, S. B., Tuomisto, K., Kara, N., Roos, N., Dilip, T. R., & Dhingra-Kumar, N. (2017). Implementing the WHO safe childbirth checklist: Lessons from a global collaboration. *BMJ Global Health*, *2*(3), e000241.
Quamar, M. M. (2016). Municipal elections in Saudi Arabia, 2015. *Contemporary Review of the Middle East*, *3*(4), 433–444.
Rodrigues, H. P. (2023). *Introducing Hinduism*. Taylor & Francis.
Sachs, J., Schmidt-Traub, G., Kroll, C., Lafortune, G., Fuller, G., & Woelm, F. (2021). Sustainable Development Report 2020: The Sustainable Development Goals and Covid-19 Includes the SDG Index and Dashboards. Cambridge: Cambridge University Press.
Saller, R. P. (1994). *Patriarchy, property and death in the Roman family*. Cambridge University Press.
Saller, R. P. (1999). Pater familias, mater familias, and the gendered semantics of the Roman household. *Classical Philology*, *94*(2), 182–197.
Schidel, W. (1995). The most silent women of Greece and Rome: Rural labour and women's life in the ancient world (I) 1. *Greece & Rome*, *42*(2), 202–217.
Siess, J. (2005). Un discours politique au féminin. Le projet d'Olympe de Gouges. *Mots. Les langages du politique*, *1*(78), 9–21.
Stache, L. C. (2015). Advocacy and political potential at the convergence of hashtag activism and commerce. *Feminist Media Studies*, *15*(1), 162–164.
Stewart, A. J., & Ostrove, J. M. (1998). Women's personality in middle age: Gender, history, and midcourse corrections. *American Psychologist*, *53*(11), 1185.
U.S. Agency for International Development (USAID). (2015). *Let girls learn*. https://www.usaid.gov/what-we-do/gender-equality-and-womens-empowerment/let-girls-learn
UNICEF (UN Children's Fund). (2023). *Female genital mutilation (FGM)*. https://data.unicef.org/topic/child-protection/female-genital-mutilation/
Walby, S. (2009). *Globalization and inequalities: Complexity and contested modernities*. Sage.
Weydner, S. (2018). Reproductive rights and reproductive control: Family planning, internationalism, and population control in the international planned parenthood federation. *Geschichte und Gesellschaft*, *44*(1), 135–161.

Chapter 6

SDG 6. Ensure Availability and Sustainable Management of Water and Sanitation for All

Abstract

The chapter focuses on universal access to clean water, examining diverse strategies to address the escalating global water crisis. Through case studies, it exemplifies how innovation and sustainable design can harmonize with local culture and traditions. By aligning projects and initiatives with territorial identity, societies can alleviate the water crisis while safeguarding their heritage and ecosystems for future generations. These kinds of solutions contrast with other initiatives that are not respectful of territorial identities, such as the intensive groundwater extraction practices prevalent in various countries, which endanger local ecosystems. In this aspect, the chapter highlights borehole drilling's limitations, specifically in arid regions, where complex geological conditions often lead to suboptimal outcomes.

Water is an essential element for human life and ecosystem. According to WHO, UNICEF, and the World Bank, between 2000 and 2020, the global population with access to safely managed drinking water at home increased by over 2 billion, rising from 3.8 billion to 5.8 billion people (WHO, 2022). Despite these advancements, nearly 2 billion people still do not have access to safely managed drinking water. National, regional, and global averages often conceal significant inequalities in service levels between countries and within them. While in 2020, three out of four people globally used safely managed drinking water services, regional coverage varied from 96% in Europe and North America to just 30% in sub-Saharan Africa. Unsafe drinking water is a major cause of over 1.5 million deaths each year due to diarrhea, with the majority being infants and young children. Diarrheal diseases range from mild and self-limiting to severe illnesses such as typhoid fever and cholera, which are endemic in 69 countries and are estimated to cause 2.9 million cases annually, leading to rapid death if untreated. Estimates suggest that between 94 and 220 million people are at risk of exposure to high concentrations of arsenic in groundwater, with the majority (94%) located in Asia. Millions of children attend schools without basic access to clean water. In 2021, 546 million children lacked basic water services in their schools, with 288 million having no access to drinking water services.

Water resources are becoming increasingly scarce due to various factors.

First, many low-income countries lack the capacity to access and distribute water. This challenge is particularly pronounced in areas that lack the financial or technological resources to make the necessary investments to accommodate urban population growth and the resulting increased demand for both human consumption and food production, agriculture, and farming. An example of this is the Dead Sea, which is experiencing a significant reduction in water levels due to growing irrigation and domestic water demands along its watershed. This has even led to a higher concentration of salts in the remaining water, with severe impacts on the local ecosystem and the availability of drinking water for surrounding communities (Yakushev et al., 2022).

Water availability is also threatened by climate change, which contributes to a widening global gap between wet and arid regions. The effects of climate change, such as global warming and precipitation variability, are already impacting the quantity and quality of water resources, with devastating consequences for communities and ecosystems dependent on them. One of the primary consequences of climate change is the increased frequency and intensity of extreme weather events, such as droughts, floods, and storms. These events strain the water resource management capacity of communities and governments, leading to greater uncertainty and vulnerability in water supply (Allan et al., 2020; Pokhrel et al., 2021; Stewart et al., 2020). For instance, prolonged droughts can drastically reduce water availability, negatively affecting agricultural production, food security, and public health. Conversely, floods can lead to water source contamination, jeopardizing public health and community safety. The consequences of climate change vary across different regions of the world. In some regions of Northern Europe, such as Scandinavia, an increase in precipitation, and water availability is projected, while other regions, like Sub-Saharan Africa, are expected to face higher temperatures and reduced rainfall, leading to more frequent drought events (Adaawen, 2021; Martel et al., 2021). The impact of climate change on water is particularly severe in already vulnerable regions with water-related issues, such as arid and semi-arid areas. These regions, where water is scarce, and surface water resources are limited, are highly sensitive to climate change, with devastating effects on the water and food security of local communities (Costa et al., 2023; Tabari et al., 2021; Vicente-Serrano et al., 2020). Under these circumstances, certain regions in East Africa, like the Horn of Africa, have experienced prolonged droughts and irregular rainfall patterns in recent years, leading to severe food crises and mass migrations to other areas.

Another significant contributing factor to the water crisis is the pollution of lakes, rivers, and seas. Often, industrial or urban wastewater is discharged into these water bodies without proper treatment, compromising water quality and rendering it unsuitable for agricultural use and human consumption. Among the most polluted rivers in the world are the Ganges, the Motagua River, and the Citarum River. The Ganges, considered the holiest river in India and believed by Hindus to cleanse sins, suffers from massive water pollution due to the discharge of untreated sewage and chemicals. Today, its surface is covered by a carpet of plastic and other debris (Batabyal & Beladi, 2020; Nelms et al., 2021). Similar circumstances characterize the Motagua River, flowing through Guatemala and into the Atlantic Ocean. It has become known as one of the most polluted rivers globally due to improper waste disposal practices in the region. Pollution in the Motagua River is primarily caused by untreated industrial and domestic discharges. Near cities and industrial zones, factory and human settlement wastewater is directly released into the river without proper treatment. This situation stems from weak environmental regulations and inadequate control systems. As a result, the river is contaminated with toxic chemicals from industries and residues of pesticides and fertilizers from agricultural activities (Berger et al., 2022; Mazariegos-Ortíz et al., 2020). The situation of Indonesia's Citarum River has become so dire that it has been labeled a "river of trash" due to immense amounts of waste floating on its now blackened waters. Stretching around 300 kilometers, it traverses a densely populated and industrialized area (Ferdinand et al., 2023; Fridayani, 2020).

Communities' livelihoods, whether through fishing, agriculture, or trade, are intrinsically linked to the health of the water systems they depend on. Water scarcity and pollution undermine the sustainability of marine and freshwater ecosystems, thus forcing natural habitats to change and threatening biodiversity. In addition, from a socio-anthropological perspective, it is safe to argue that water has played a fundamental role in shaping the course of human history and the development of countless civilizations. It is not an overstatement to say that water is often at the heart of societies, influencing their culture, identity, and way of life. For centuries, communities around the world have thrived by the side of rivers, lakes, and oceans, not only relying on water for basic survival, but also forging deep cultural and spiritual connections to their aquatic environments. Many of these places are regarded as sacred sites or locations for ritual ceremonies, further underlining the profound significance of water in their lives (Groenfeldt, 2019; Willems & Van Schaik, 2015). This interdependence fosters a profound connection between these communities and their natural surroundings. As a consequence, when effective river management policies are lacking or poorly implemented, and pollution threatens the water sources that have been the lifeblood of these societies for generations, their identities and social cohesion are placed in jeopardy (Posey, 1999). Similarly, changes in the quantity and quality of water resources can have a negative impact on tourism and the local economy. Coastal and lakeside areas that were once attractive tourist destinations due to their clear and uncontaminated waters may lose their appeal. This, in turn, can influence the features of places closely tied to tourism and the sustainable use of natural resources (Thushari & Senevirathna, 2020). The erosion of traditions, the decline of economies, and the degradation of environment all pose a significant threat to the territorial identity that has been woven over centuries (Hommes et al., 2019).

In light of this, SDG 6 focuses on universal and sustainable access to clean drinking water, as well as the sustainable management of water resources by 2030. To achieve this goal, it is necessary to invest in water and sanitation infrastructure, improve water treatment technologies, and promote hygienic practices at the community level. This also requires the implementation of targeted government policies and programs, as well as partnerships amongst governments, international organizations, civil society, and the private sector.

An innovative solution to address the growing water crisis in some of the world's most vulnerable regions is represented by emerging "air-to-water" (WFA) devices. These devices provide a low-cost and environmentally friendly solution for supplying drinking water to the population by harnessing the condensation process of moisture from the air. Technologies used vary depending on the device, but in general, they are equipped with hydrophilic materials that capture and collect humidity from the air, such as spiderweb-like nets or specially treated layers of materials. The condensed water is then filtered and treated for safe consumption before being stored in tanks or containers (Qadir et al., 2018; Siddiqui et al., 2023).

A concrete example of using WFA devices is the "Warka Tower" project, which was implemented in Ethiopia in 2015 (Aslan et al., 2022). This project not only caters to environmental, social, and economic sustainability needs, but it is also evidently in line with territorially desirable development, as implied by its name. The tower is named after Warka, a tree of great significance in Ethiopia. It is equipped with a spiderweb-like network made of hydrophilic materials to withstand the adverse climatic conditions of the region. It does not require the use of electricity or other energy resources. The condensed water flows along the network to a tank located at the bottom of the tower, where it is stored. From here, the water can be easily accessed and used by the local community for domestic, agricultural, and personal purposes. The Warka Tower represents an innovative solution that respects the identity of the territory, as the tower's shape, with its slender and articulated structure, recalls the distinctive features of Warka trees, which are symbolic and culturally relevant elements for local communities in Ethiopia. In the architecture and design of the Warka Tower, special attention has been given to the use of local and traditional materials, such as bamboo and rattan. This choice not only reduces the project's environmental impact but also contributes to preserving and strengthening the cultural and historical identity of the territory. The use of local materials allows the tower to align with the surrounding environment, creating a harmonious connection between the structure and the natural landscape. Another aspect that makes the Warka Tower a solution respectful of territorial identity is its ability to be managed and maintained by the local community itself. The active involvement of people in the construction, maintenance, and use of the tower creates a sense of belonging and responsibility. This process contributes to consolidating the identity and autonomy of the local community. The Warka Tower is an example of how technological innovation and sustainable design can be integrated with culture, traditions, and local needs, contrasting with other initiatives that, while driven by the need to respond to the growing demand for water for agricultural, industrial, and domestic purposes, appear less capable of respecting territorial identity. Nowadays, such a practice is widespread in many parts of the world, especially in arid and semi-arid regions characterized by water scarcity and limited surface water resources (He et al., 2018; Mancuso et al., 2020; Olea-Olea et al., 2020).

On the opposite side, it is possible to place some solutions that, over time, have led to a rapid decline in groundwater levels and aquifer depletion, such as intensive groundwater exploitation for agricultural irrigation. In India, China, the United States, Pakistan, and many other regions, water is extracted from underground aquifers using pumps to irrigate vast stretches of land, enabling the cultivation of intensive crops such as rice, wheat, and cotton. It has caused a loss of groundwater resources and habitat for natural wetlands, thus threatening the territorial identity of some local communities that depend on land and water for their sustenance (Custodio et al., 2016; Hoogesteger & Wester, 2015).

The industrial sector is also involved in intensive groundwater exploitation practices since it requires large amounts of water for production and cooling purposes. Mining, electricity generation, and manufacturing industries are some sectors that particularly require intensive use of groundwater resources. This exploitation can have serious consequences for human health and the surrounding environment, putting at risk not only safety but also the identity of local communities that depend on these water resources for their livelihoods.

Another long-standing solution for accessing clean water has been borehole drilling, especially in countries of southern and eastern Africa where freshwater availability is often limited and lands are predominantly arid. This practice has been plagued by numerous challenges and limitations which render borehole drilling success unreliable, with success rates of less than 50% in many areas (Aghazadeh & Mogaddam, 2010; Al-Khashman & Jaradat, 2014). This means that more than half of the dug wells ultimately yielded no water, resulting in a waste of resources and effort. The complex geological terrain in these regions is one of the main reasons for the high failure rate of borehole drilling. Rocks and sediments in the subsurface can impede the flow of water, making it difficult to find consistent sources of freshwater sufficient to support the needs of the population and agriculture (Kim & Jackson, 2012). Additionally, the presence of shallow or poor-quality aquifers can make it even more difficult to reliably locate water sources through borehole drilling.

Borehole drilling also has negative effects on the natural environment and landscape. The creation of deep wells alters the structure of the soil and subsurface, affecting local ecosystems and biodiversity. The lowering of the water table can also lead to soil subsidence, resulting in damage to structures and surrounding vegetation. These landscape changes are not territorially desirable, as they can also significantly impact the territorial identity of local communities, influencing their traditions, land uses, and relationships with the surrounding environment. A concrete example of the challenges and limitations of borehole drilling can be found in some regions of East Africa, such as Somalia and Kenya, where freshwater availability is particularly scarce. Here, access to clean water is a daily challenge for many rural communities, and well-digging has often been seen as a potential solution. However, due to the complexity of the subsurface and geological conditions, many drilling efforts have proven unsuccessful, leaving communities still without a reliable water source (Comte et al., 2016).

To overcome the challenges of drilling and ensure sustainable access to clean water that respects territorial identity, the "More Water More Life" initiative was launched in 2021 as a pilot project in Madagascar (UNICEF, 2021). The project, carried out by UNICEF in collaboration with the European Union Joint Research Centre (EU-JRC), aims to increase the likelihood of success in borehole drilling by mapping aquifers using satellites, geospatial images, and data. The data-driven approach helps identify aquifers before drilling even begins, leading to more effective outcomes. Water extraction occurs sustainably for the environment, as there are no long-term negative socio-economic or environmental impacts, such as aquifer depletion. With the success rate of water extraction doubling, providing hundreds of families with access to clean water, "More Water More Life" will be expanded to many other African countries and vulnerable territories.

Final, regarding the protection of aquatic ecosystems, in line with the guidelines of SDG 6, the World Bank has been collaborating with several countries for years through investments, technical assistance, knowledge, and innovative solutions. One of the most fruitful collaborations has been with Brazil. In Amazonian regions, underground water resources are of vital importance to local communities, providing drinking water, agricultural support, and assistance for industrial activities. However, these water reservoirs are threatened by various factors, including deforestation, surface water pollution, and rapid urbanization. Increasing temperatures and climate variations are also heavily influencing precipitation patterns and the hydrological balance of the region, making the conservation of groundwater resources even more difficult (Barbosa et al., 2016, 2017; Carvalho & Spataru, 2018). The World Bank has placed a significant focus on providing analytical products and consultancy services, as well as leveraging the latest and most comprehensive international knowledge and know-how to drive changes in the local water sector.

This kind of initiative can be deemed territorially desirable as it takes into account the preservation of the Brazilian identity, in addition to the well-established economic, social, and environmental dimensions of sustainability. The World Bank's water team has worked closely not only with stakeholders from agriculture, urban development, rural development, disaster management, energy, health, and other sectors, but also with local people to safeguard and monitor aquifers. The direct involvement of local communities is essential to ensure that initiatives align with the needs, traditions, and values of people who directly live on the region's water resources.

References

Adaawen, S. (2021). Understanding climate change and drought perceptions, impact and responses in the rural Savannah, West Africa. *Atmosphere*, *12*(5), 594.

Aghazadeh, N., & Mogaddam, A. A. (2010). Assessment of groundwater quality and its suitability for drinking and agricultural uses in the Oshnavieh area, Northwest of Iran. *Journal of Environmental Protection*, *1*(1), 30–40.

Al-Khashman, O. A., & Jaradat, A. Q. (2014). Assessment of groundwater quality and its suitability for drinking and agricultural uses in arid environment. *Stochastic Environmental Research and Risk Assessment, 28*, 743–753.

Allan, R. P., Barlow, M., Byrne, M. P., Cherchi, A., Douville, H., Fowler, H. J., Gan, T., Pendergrass, G., Rosenfeld, D., Swann, A., Wilcox, L., & Zolina, O. (2020). Advances in understanding large-scale responses of the water cycle to climate change. *Annals of the New York Academy of Sciences, 1472*(1), 49–75.

Aslan, D., Selçuk, S. A., & Avinç, G. M. (2022). A biomimetic approach to water harvesting strategies: An architectural point of view. *International Journal of Built Environment and Sustainability, 9*(3), 47–60.

Barbosa, M. C., Alam, K., & Mushtaq, S. (2016). Water policy implementation in the state of São Paulo, Brazil: Key challenges and opportunities. *Environmental Science & Policy, 60*, 11–18.

Barbosa, M. C., Mushtaq, S., & Alam, K. (2017). Integrated water resources management: Are river basin committees in Brazil enabling effective stakeholder interaction? *Environmental Science & Policy, 76*, 1–11.

Batabyal, A. A., & Beladi, H. (2020). A political economy model of the Ganges pollution cleanup problem. *Natural Resource Modeling, 33*(4), e12285.

Berger, M., Canty, S. W., Tuholske, C., & Halpern, B. S. (2022). Sources and discharge of nitrogen pollution from agriculture and wastewater in the Mesoamerican Reef region. *Ocean & Coastal Management, 227*, 106269.

Carvalho, P., & Spataru, C. (2018). Advancing the implementation of SDGs in Brazil by integrating water-energy nexus and legal principles for better governance. *Sustainability in Environment, 3*(3), 277–304.

Comte, J. C., Cassidy, R., Obando, J., Robins, N., Ibrahim, K., Melchioly, S., Mjemah, I., Shauri, H., Bourhane, A., Mohamed, I., Noe, C., Mwega, B., Makokha, M., Join, J., Banton, O., & Davies, J. (2016). Challenges in groundwater resource management in coastal aquifers of East Africa: Investigations and lessons learnt in the Comoros Islands, Kenya and Tanzania. *Journal of Hydrology: Regional Studies, 5*, 179–199.

Costa, F. R., Schietti, J., Stark, S. C., & Smith, M. N. (2023). The other side of tropical forest drought: Do shallow water table regions of Amazonia act as large-scale hydrological refugia from drought? *New Phytologist, 237*(3), 714–733.

Custodio, E., Andreu-Rodes, J. M., Aragón, R., Estrela, T., Ferrer, J., García-Aróstegui, J. L., Manzano, M., Rodríguez-Hernández, L., Sahuquillo, A., & Del Villar, A. (2016). Groundwater intensive use and mining in south-eastern peninsular Spain: Hydrogeological, economic and social aspects. *Science of the Total Environment, 559*, 302–316.

Ferdinand, F., Darma, A., & Savitri, A. (2023). Analysis of water pollution due to development activities and its impact on the Citarum River in Indonesia. *Leader: Civil Engineering and Architecture Journal, 1*(3), 318–323.

Fridayani, H. D. (2020). The government's role in facing SDGs 2030 Citarum River clean-up program, Indonesia: An analysis. *Journal of Governance and Public Policy, 7*(1), 41–50.

Groenfeldt, D. (2019). *Water ethics: A values approach to solving the water crisis.* Routledge.

He, Y., Lin, K., Zhang, F., Wang, Y., & Chen, X. (2018). Coordination degree of the exploitation of water resources and its spatial differences in China. *Science of the Total Environment, 644*, 1117–1127.

Hommes, L., Boelens, R., Harris, L. M., & Veldwisch, G. J. (2019). Rural–urban water struggles: Urbanizing hydrosocial territories and evolving connections, discourses and identities. *Water International, 44*(2), 81–94.

Hoogesteger, J., & Wester, P. (2015). Intensive groundwater use and (in)equity: Processes and governance challenges. *Environmental Science & Policy, 51*, 117–124.

Kim, J. H., & Jackson, R. B. (2012). A global analysis of groundwater recharge for vegetation, climate, and soils. *Vadose Zone Journal, 11*(1), vzj2011-0021RA.

Mancuso, M., Santucci, L., & Carol, E. (2020). Effects of intensive aquifers exploitation on groundwater salinity in coastal wetlands. *Hydrological Processes, 34*(11), 2313–2323.

Martel, J. L., Brissette, F. P., Lucas-Picher, P., Troin, M., & Arsenault, R. (2021). Climate change and rainfall intensity–duration–frequency curves: Overview of science and guidelines for adaptation. *Journal of Hydrologic Engineering, 26*(10), 03121001.

Mazariegos-Ortíz, C., de los Ángeles Rosales, M., Carrillo-Ovalle, L., Cardoso, R. P., Muniz, M. C., & Dos Anjos, R. M. (2020). First evidence of microplastic pollution in the El Quetzalito sand beach of the Guatemalan Caribbean. *Marine Pollution Bulletin, 156*, 111220.

Nelms, S. E., Duncan, E. M., Patel, S., Badola, R., Bhola, S., Chakma, S., Chowdhury, G. W., Godley, B. J., Haque, A. B., Johnson, J. A., Khatoon, H., Kumar, S., Napper, I. E., Niloy, M. N. H., Akter, T., Badola S., Dev, A., Rawat, S., Santillo, D., Sarker, S., Sharma, E., & Koldewey, H. (2021). Riverine plastic pollution from fisheries: Insights from the Ganges River system. *Science of the Total Environment, 756*, 143305.

Olea-Olea, S., Escolero, O., Mahlknecht, J., Ortega, L., Silva-Aguilera, R., Florez-Peñaloza, J. R., & Zamora-Martinez, O. (2020). Identification of the components of a complex groundwater flow system subjected to intensive exploitation. *Journal of South American Earth Sciences, 98*, 102434.

Pokhrel, Y., Felfelani, F., Satoh, Y., Boulange, J., Burek, P., Gädeke, A., et al. (2021). Global terrestrial water storage and drought severity under climate change. *Nature Climate Change, 11*(3), 226–233.

Posey, D. A. (Ed.) (1999). *Cultural and spiritual values of biodiversity*. UNEP and Intermediate Technology Publications.

Qadir, M., Jiménez, G. C., Farnum, R. L., Dodson, L. L., & Smakhtin, V. (2018). Fog water collection: Challenges beyond technology. *Water, 10*(4), 372.

Siddiqui, M. A., Azam, M. A., Khan, M. M., Iqbal, S., Khan, M. U., & Raffat, Y. (2023). Current trends on extraction of water from air: An alternative solution to water supply. *International Journal of Environmental Science and Technology, 20*(1), 1053–1080.

Stewart, I. T., Rogers, J., & Graham, A. (2020). Water security under severe drought and climate change: Disparate impacts of the recent severe drought on environmental flows and water supplies in Central California. *Journal of Hydrology X, 7*, 100054.

Tabari, H., Hosseinzadehtalaei, P., Thiery, W., & Willems, P. (2021). Amplified drought and flood risk under future socioeconomic and climatic change. *Earth's Future, 9*(10), e2021EF002295.

Thushari, G. G. N., & Senevirathna, J. D. M. (2020). Plastic pollution in the marine environment. *Heliyon, 6*(8), e04709.

UNICEF. (2021). *Finding water in the driest places*. https://www.unicef.org/innovation/stories/finding-water-driest-places

Vicente-Serrano, S. M., McVicar, T. R., Miralles, D. G., Yang, Y., & Tomas-Burguera, M. (2020). Unraveling the influence of atmospheric evaporative demand on drought and its response to climate change. *Wiley Interdisciplinary Reviews: Climate Change, 11*(2), e632.

WHO (World Health Organization). (2022). *State of the world's drinking water: An urgent call to action to accelerate progress on ensuring safe drinking water for all*. https://www.who.int/publications/i/item/9789240060807

Willems, W. J., & Van Schaik, H. (2015). *Water and heritage: Material, conceptual and spiritual connections*. Sidestone Press.

Yakushev, E. V., Andrulionis, N. Y., Jafari, M., Lahijani, H. A., & Ghaffari, P. (2022). How climate change and human interaction alter chemical regime in Salt Lakes, case study: Lake Urmia, Aral Sea, the Dead Sea, and Lake Issyk-Kul. In P. Ghaffari & E. V. Yakushev (Eds.), *Lake Urmia. The handbook of environmental chemistry* (Vol. 123, pp. 275–296). Springer.

Chapter 7

SDG 7. Ensure Access to Affordable, Reliable, Sustainable, and Modern Energy for All

Abstract

As the global push for renewable energy intensifies, it becomes imperative to critically assess the socio-territorial repercussions of some of these initiatives in local communities and their environments. The emergence of certain "eco-blind projects" serves as a reminder of situations where innovative modern solutions, although environmentally friendly, fail to acknowledge and safeguard territorial identity and the surrounding landscape. Within this comprehensive framework, the chapter emphasizes the pressing need to strike a delicate equilibrium between the pursuit of energy transition goals and the preservation of local traditions, and ecosystems. By considering the socio-territorial ramifications and fostering community engagement, policymakers, researchers, and stakeholders can collectively chart a path that leads toward a more sustainable and inclusive renewable energy landscape. This approach encapsulates not only the imperative of curbing climate change and alleviating energy poverty but also the crucial task of upholding the identity of local communities and safeguarding the irreplaceable natural and cultural resources that form the bedrock of their territory.

SDG 7 focuses on ensuring universal, secure, sustainable, and modern access to energy for all. The goal aims to achieve a substantial shift in energy production and consumption, seeking to provide accessible, reliable, and clean energy for all while addressing the challenges of climate change, pollution, and energy poverty (UNDP, 2020).

Identity, Territories, and Sustainability: Challenges and Opportunities for Achieving the UN Sustainable Development Goals, 71–79
Copyright © 2024 by Salvatore Monaco
Published under exclusive licence by Emerald Publishing Limited
doi:10.1108/978-1-83797-549-520241008

Energy poverty is a complex and widespread issue affecting millions of people worldwide. It refers to the situation where individuals or entire communities lack access to reliable and affordable energy sources to meet their basic needs (González-Eguino, 2015; Sy & Mokaddem, 2022). According to data reported in the "Tracking SDG 7: The Energy Progress Report" (IRENA, 2023), in 2010, 84% of the global population had access to electricity. This percentage has increased over time, reaching 91% in 2021. This means that over the course of 10 years, more than a billion people gained access to electricity. However, the pace of growth in access slowed down between 2019 and 2021 compared to previous years. Efforts in rural electrification have contributed to this progress, but a significant territorial gap remains. Energy poverty is particularly critical in low-income countries and rural and remote regions, where access to electricity and other forms of energy is often limited or absent. In 2021, 567 million people in sub-Saharan Africa lacked access to electricity, accounting for over 80% of the global population without access. The access deficit in the region has remained nearly unchanged since 2010. Energy poverty profoundly affects people's lives, influencing their health, well-being, and social and economic development. Those living in energy poverty face daily challenges in meeting basic needs such as heating their homes during cold seasons, cooking meals, and providing household lighting. These challenges can have severe health consequences, with exposure to extreme temperatures leading to respiratory and cardiovascular diseases, especially among the most vulnerable, such as the elderly and children. Energy poverty is often linked to the lack of energy infrastructure in rural and remote areas, where extending electrical grids is difficult and economically costly. The lack of energy access also has significant impacts on local economies and socio-economic development. Without reliable access to electricity, opportunities for work and entrepreneurial development are limited.

Some sustainable development programs and initiatives are contributing to improving access to electrical energy in areas afflicted by energy poverty. As for sub-Saharan Africa and Southeast Asia, for instance, the "Sustainable Energy for All (SE4ALL)" initiative was launched by the UN Secretary-General. "SE4ALL" established three global objectives to be achieved by 2030: Ensuring universal access to modern energy services, doubling the global rate of improvement in energy efficiency, and doubling the share of renewable energy in the global energy mix (Hagumimana et al., 2021; Sugathapala, 2020). The initiative has implemented a range of interventions, including installing electrical grids in rural communities, promoting renewable sources like solar and wind energy, and supporting the development of microgrid systems and batteries for decentralized energy.

A successful example of the "Energy for All" initiative is the project carried out in the village of Kribi, in Cameroon, where a solar power plant was installed to provide clean and accessible energy to a previously unelectrified community (Bruce et al., 2018). Before the project's implementation, Kribi's residents relied on traditional and polluting energy sources like wood and coal to meet their daily energy needs. This not only contributed to air pollution and the greenhouse effect but also limited economic and social development opportunities in the community.

With the installation of the solar power plant, the village gained continuous and sustainable access to electrical energy, significantly impacting residents' daily lives by improving their quality of life. Electric energy has provided a safe and reliable source of lighting, creating a safer and more comfortable environment, reducing the risk of domestic accidents, and improving people's health and well-being. Furthermore, the introduction of electrical energy deeply influenced the community's territorial identity, reinforcing a sense of belonging. Indeed, the presence of electrical energy enhanced productive activities like processing agricultural products and manufacturing, expanding the production of typical goods and thereby increasing income opportunities for local families. Indirectly, the initiative also contributed to preserving and valuing local traditions and knowledge, which are integral parts of the community's cultural identity. Electrical energy also exerted a profound influence on the dietary and culinary habits of communities. The electrical appliances revolutionized cooking and food preservation methods, reshaping the culinary landscape in multifaceted ways. The utilization of electric stoves, microwaves, ovens drastically reduced the time required for cooking, and streamlining meal preparation processes. This newfound efficiency not only catered to the fast-paced modern lifestyle but also provided individuals with more leisure time to engage in other productive activities or spend quality moments with their families. Moreover, the precision and consistency offered by electrical cooking devices contributed to elevated culinary outcomes. Temperature control and automated features ensured that dishes were faster and better cooked, leading to the creation of dishes that echoed the essence of the community's identity. The introduction of electrical refrigerators and freezers presented another dimension of transformation. Preservation techniques evolved beyond traditional methods, and communities could now help to access a wider range of ingredients regardless of seasonality. This expansion of ingredient availability facilitated the conservation of traditional recipes and techniques. By bridging the gap between past and present, electrical energy can be defined as an instrument of cultural preservation and evolution, enabling the transfer of the local culinary culture to future generations.

Another example of a sustainable development initiative to combat energy poverty is the "Lighting Africa" project, launched in 2015 by the World Bank Group. It has been developed in order to promote access to clean and sustainable lighting in rural regions of Africa, where millions of people still lack electricity access (Ockwell et al., 2021). "Lighting Africa" is based on the installation of LED solar lamps and microgrid systems in rural communities, providing a safe and affordable alternative to traditional lighting sources like candles and kerosene lamps. The project played a significant role in encouraging the development of local markets for solar lamps and sustainable lighting technologies. It also created new job and business opportunities in local communities, promoting economic and social development. The initiative also demonstrated the importance of collaboration among various stakeholders, including governments, the private sector, non-governmental organizations, and local communities, to develop sustainable and long-term solutions for ensuring energy access for all.

SDG 7 also aims to promote energy efficiency and increase the share of renewable energy in the global energy mix, as up to 2.3 billion people still use polluting fuels and technologies for cooking, especially in sub-Saharan Africa and Asia. There, the use of traditional biomass also means that families spend up to 40 hours per week collecting firewood and cooking, preventing women from seeking employment or participating in local decision-making and children from attending school. Millions of premature deaths each year are attributable to domestic air pollution created using polluting fuels and cooking technologies (Lelieveld et al., 2019; Torjesen, 2021).

Numerous countries have already made progress in increasing renewable energy production capacity and expanding electricity access in rural and remote communities. The use of renewable electricity in global consumption grew from 26.3% in 2019 to 28.2% in 2020, marking the largest single-year increase since SDG progress monitoring began (UNDP, 2020). Morocco is an example of a country that has made remarkable progress in the development of wind and solar parks. The country has undertaken significant initiatives to harness the abundant renewable energy resources. With extensive solar and wind potential, Morocco has invested in the construction of wind and solar parks across the nation (Taoufik & Fekri, 2021). These initiatives have helped reduce the previous dependence on fossil fuel sources and promote the use of clean and renewable energy. Among them there is the Tarfaya Wind Farm, situated on the Atlantic coast of Morocco. It is one of Africa's largest wind parks, with a production capacity of 301 MW (Hochberg, 2016). These efforts have significantly contributed to lowering greenhouse gas emissions and preserving the country's environment and biodiversity. Additionally, Morocco has expanded electricity access in many rural areas, bringing electric power to communities that previously lacked this vital resource. This has positively impacted people's lives, enabling the establishment of better-equipped schools and healthcare facilities. These interventions ultimately have strengthened Morocco's territorial identity, promoting sustainable development and prosperity in local communities.

India stands as an example of a country that has achieved significant progress in the field of renewable energy too. India boasts one of the world's most ambitious solar energy development programs and has emerged as a leading producer of solar energy globally (Yenneti, 2016; Pandey et al., 2022). Through government efforts and private investments, India has witnessed a remarkable increase in solar energy production capacity, bringing substantial benefits to millions of people. Electrification of rural communities has been a priority for the Indian government, and significant strides have been made in recent years in bringing electricity to remote and disadvantaged areas of the country. Access to electrical energy has brought about transformative impacts on rural Indian communities, creating new economic opportunities. For instance, electric energy has facilitated the use of electric irrigation pumps, enhancing agricultural production and reducing reliance on seasonal rains. This has significantly contributed to food security and improved living conditions, reducing poverty and enhancing overall quality of life.

However, renewable energy sources do not always have a uniformly positive impact on territorial contexts. While wind and solar installations can contribute to clean electricity production, positive socio-territorial outcomes may be constrained due to various challenges and resistance from local populations. Wind farms, for instance, can pose a threat to the territorial identity and cultural landscape of local communities. In many cases, the construction of large wind installations can involve the expropriation of agricultural lands or areas considered culturally or spiritually valuable to local communities. Such a practice may lead to tensions and conflicts between local residents and renewable energy developers, hindering the acceptance and implementation of such projects (Bridge et al., 2013; Pepermans & Loots, 2013). This is applied to structures that could be called as "eco-blind projects." This neologism suggests that despite these infrastructures being designed with environmental considerations, they have overlooked the importance of considering and preserving territorial identity and the surrounding landscape. Thus, these initiatives could be termed "eco-blind" because they fail to fully see or understand the value of territorial identity and lack the respect for the local context, focusing their attention exclusively on environmental aspects.

"Eco-blind projects" challenge the increasingly widespread notion that green is always universally "good" for communities (Angelo, 2021). In other words, the search for environmental-friendly solutions often forms part of a growth-oriented policy that paves the way for territorial transformations and new projects that are not always beneficial for local communities (Anguelovski et al., 2022).

An example is the wind farm project in Oaxaca, Mexico. Its construction sparked protests from Zapotec indigenous communities who believed that the project would threaten their land rights and cultural identity. Local communities have emphasized that the wind farm was imposed without their consent and that land expropriation has harmed their traditions and connection to the land (Dunlap, 2017). Such protests align with several environmental and social impact studies (Child et al., 2018; Liao et al., 2023; Miller et al., 2013) that have identified potential ecosystem harm resulting from transforming territories in the name of energy transition.

Similarly, in 2021, the installation of new offshore wind parks off the coasts of the Netherlands led Dutch fishermen to organize protests, urging the governments in The Hague and Brussels to recognize the consequences of such wind parks on fishing. According to the fishermen, offshore wind parks force an increasing number of fishermen to operate in increasingly restricted areas, leading to overcrowding and reduced attention to sustainable fishing. Dutch fishermen have deemed government interference excessive.

In 2022, similar protests emerged in La Guajira, a department of Colombia, involving various Afro-descendant and indigenous communities, including the country's largest indigenous population, the Wayúu people (Schwab & Diaz, 2023; Vega-Araujo & Heffron, 2022). Due to its rich natural resources, La Guajira plays a central role in the country's energy transition. It is expected to become a major center for "green hydrogen" production in the coming years. La Guajira region ranks first nationwide in terms of solar radiation, and its plains experience consistent and strong winds almost throughout the year. In the next few years, 19 Colombian and foreign companies plan to build 65 wind parks on Wayúu lands (Barney, 2023). Wind measurement towers are being installed based on a narrative that conceptualizes La Guajira as a desert territory suitable for concentrating "clean" energy production. However, the vast tracts of land considered "uninhabited" are integral to a complex social and productive network that allows the distribution of lands according to Wayúu ancestral tradition, thereby enabling the grazing of goat herds, the main source of livelihood. Despite the arid landscape and dry climate, the local ecosystem is rich in shrubs, critical for goat farming survival. The "desert" ideology could potentially become a self-fulfilling prophecy. Environmental damage, which is likely caused by new wind parks, could accelerate desertification. The wind parks will be located along the migratory paths of certain bird species, and the pressure change generated by the wind turbine blades may repel bats, which are responsible for pollinating the shrubs that constitute La Guajira's only vegetation. All this will not only hurt the ecosystem but will have negative impacts on the identity of the territory. Furthermore, the dust raised by turbines and trucks transporting materials risks polluting the region's few water sources. Wind projects are primarily located in Wayúu indigenous areas. These regions are under specific jurisdiction prohibiting, among other things, the sale of land. Consequently, companies cannot buy or lease community lands but can only enter use agreements in exchange for compensation. According to International Labour Organization Convention 169, signed by the Colombian government, indigenous populations have the right to choose whether or not to cede their lands for extractive and logistic projects. This translates to a requirement for free and informed prior consultations. Despite this, communities have reported several challenges in conducting consultations. One of the key issues among them is the absence of an external and impartial representative to assist residents in understanding and negotiating the economic terms of agreements and environmental impact studies (Ulloa, 2023).

Even the construction of large solar installations can have significant territorial implications and pose challenges to sustainability and the identity of affected territories. An example is the Noor Solar Power Complex project in the Sahara Desert, Morocco (Fares & Abderafi, 2018). This is one of the world's largest solar complexes, encompassing three separate solar installations. Although the project has significantly contributed to the country's renewable energy production capacity, its construction required extensive land use, leading to impacts on local biodiversity and agricultural activities of surrounding communities.

In some cases, the acquisition of extensive land for construction can result in the expropriation of agricultural lands or areas considered of cultural or historical value to local communities, with adverse effects on local territorial identity. This can lead to tensions and conflicts between plant developers and local communities, undermining social cohesion and people's connection to their land (Chan et al., 2020; Horcea-Milcu, 2022). An example is the Ivanpah Solar Power Facility project in the Mojave Desert, California (Grodsky et al., 2021). This infrastructure is one of the world's largest solar installations, covering an area of approximately 14 square kilometers. While the facility offers the advantage of producing a significant amount of renewable energy, its construction resulted in the destruction of extensive tracts of natural desert habitat, endangering local biodiversity. The "eco-blind" project negatively impacted migratory bird species inhabiting the desert and populations of desert tortoises, both of which are protected species. Additionally, the construction of this facility involved the expropriation of lands historically used by indigenous tribes for cultural and spiritual purposes. The tribes protested, asserting the solar plant construction would threaten their cultural identity and connection to the land.

When projects are carried out by actively involving local communities at an early stage, the output can be positive, and they can become territorially desirable. This is, for example, the case with the Nyngan Solar Plant project, which was carried out in Australia. It included a participatory decision-making process, allowing citizens to express their concerns and provide input on plant-related decisions. This involvement helped identify and mitigate potential negative impacts related to the construction of a solar installation on local agricultural activities and contributed to improving the socio-economic conditions of the local community (Kean & Clark, 2015).

Synthesizing, while renewable energy is essential for energy sustainability, an inclusive and participatory approach involving local communities in the planning and implementation of alternative energy initiatives is imperative. This involvement is crucial for identifying and mitigating negative impacts on local ecosystems and traditional activities, as well as preserving the cultural identity of the involved communities. Community involvement can also promote a greater sense of responsibility toward alternative energy initiatives.

One of the ways to actively engage local communities is through dialogue and consultation with stakeholders. This process enables communities to voice their concerns, needs, and aspirations regarding alternative energy initiatives and provide meaningful input into project design and implementation. It is important to remember that each local community has a connection to the land and often possesses traditional knowledge and sustainable practices regarding natural resource use. Actively engaging each community in alternative energy projects can help ensure an environmentally respectful approach that considers territorial identity, minimizing negative impacts on biodiversity and local traditions.

Another way to actively engage local communities is through training programs and job opportunities related to alternative energy initiatives. By providing community members with access to such programs, they can acquire the expertise needed to actively participate in the design, implementation, and maintenance of renewable energy projects. Moreover, the integration of training programs ensures that local communities are equipped to harness the benefits of technological advancements in the renewable energy sector. As innovations continue to emerge, individuals trained in the latest technologies will be better positioned to contribute to the development and optimization of sustainable energy solutions. This not only enhances the overall competence of the community but also fosters a sense of innovation and adaptability, vital traits in the rapidly evolving landscape of alternative energy. In parallel, the creation of job opportunities in renewable energy-related sectors can serve as a key driver of economic growth too.

References

Angelo, H. (2021). *How green became good: Urbanized nature and the making of cities and citizens.* University of Chicago Press.

Barney, J. (Ed.) (2023). *Por el mar y la tierra guajiros vuela el viento Wayúu.* Instituto de Estudios para el Desarollo y la Paz.

Bridge, G., Bouzarovski, S., Bradshaw, M., & Eyre, N. (2013). Geographies of energy transition: Space, place and the low-carbon economy. *Energy Policy, 53*, 331–340.

Bruce, N., de Cuevas, R. A., Cooper, J., Enonchong, B., Ronzi, S., Puzzolo, E., Mbatcou, B., & Pope, D. (2018). The Government-led initiative for LPG scale-up in Cameroon: Programme development and initial evaluation. *Energy for Sustainable Development, 46*, 103–110.

Chan, K. M., Boyd, D. R., Gould, R. K., Jetzkowitz, J., Liu, J., Muraca, B., & Brondízio, E. S. (2020). Levers and leverage points for pathways to sustainability. *People and Nature, 2*(3), 693–717.

Child, M., Koskinen, O., Linnanen, L., & Breyer, C. (2018). Sustainability guardrails for energy scenarios of the global energy transition. *Renewable and Sustainable Energy Reviews, 91*, 321–334.

Dunlap, A. (2017). Wind energy: Toward a "Sustainable Violence" in Oaxaca: In Mexico's wind farms, a tense relationship between extractivism, counterinsurgency, and the green economy takes root. *NACLA Report on the Americas, 49*(4), 483–488.

Fares, M. S. B., & Abderafi, S. (2018). Water consumption analysis of Moroccan concentrating solar power station. *Solar Energy, 172*, 146–151.

González-Eguino, M. (2015). Energy poverty: An overview. *Renewable and Sustainable Energy Reviews, 47*, 377–385.

Grodsky, S. M., Campbell, J. W., & Hernandez, R. R. (2021). Solar energy development impacts flower-visiting beetles and flies in the Mojave Desert. *Biological Conservation, 263*, 109336.

Hagumimana, N., Zheng, J., Asemota, G. N. O., Niyonteze, J. D. D., Nsengiyumva, W., Nduwamungu, A., & Bimenyimana, S. (2021). Concentrated solar power and photovoltaic systems: A new approach to boost sustainable energy for all (Se4all) in Rwanda. *International Journal of Photoenergy, 2*, 1–32.

Hochberg, M. (2016). *Renewable energy growth in Morocco.* Middle East Institute.

Horcea-Milcu, A. I. (2022). Values as leverage points for sustainability transformation: Two pathways for transformation research. *Current Opinion in Environmental Sustainability, 57*, 101205.

IRENA. (2023). *Tracking SDG7: The energy progress report 2023.* https://www.irena.org/Publications/2023/Jun/Tracking-SDG7-2023

Kean, A., & Clark, T. (2015). Race to renewables: New south wales. *AQ-Australian Quarterly, 86*(4), 12–14.

Lelieveld, J., Klingmüller, K., Pozzer, A., Burnett, R. T., Haines, A., & Ramanathan, V. (2019). Effects of fossil fuel and total anthropogenic emission removal on public health and climate. *Proceedings of the National Academy of Sciences, 116*(15), 7192–7197.

Liao, J., Liu, X., Zhou, X., & Tursunova, N. R. (2023). Analyzing the role of renewable energy transition and industrialization on ecological sustainability: Can green innovation matter in OECD countries. *Renewable Energy, 204*, 141–151.

Miller, C. A., Iles, A., & Jones, C. F. (2013). The social dimensions of energy transitions. *Science as Culture, 22*(2), 135–148.

Ockwell, D., Byrne, R., Atela, J., Chengo, V., Onsongo, E., Fodio Todd, J., Kasprowicz, V., & Ely, A. (2021). Transforming access to clean energy technologies in the Global South: Learning from lighting Africa in Kenya. *Energies, 14*(14), 4362.

Pandey, A., Pandey, P., & Tumuluru, J. S. (2022). Solar energy production in India and commonly used technologies–An overview. *Energies*, *15*(2), 500.

Pepermans, Y., & Loots, I. (2013). Wind farm struggles in flanders fields: A sociological perspective. *Energy Policy*, *59*, 321–328.

Schwab, J., & Diaz, N. C. C. (2023). The discursive blinkers of climate change: Energy transition as a wicked problem. *The Extractive Industries and Society*, *15*, 101319.

Sugathapala, T. (2020). Progression of renewable energy development for electricity in South Asia: Drivers and challenges. In S. Narayan, C. Len, & R. Kapur (Eds.), *Sustainable Energy Transition in South Asia: Challenges and Opportunities* (pp. 69–88). World Scientific.

Sy, S. A., & Mokaddem, L. (2022). Energy poverty in developing countries: A review of the concept and its measurements. *Energy Research & Social Science*, *89*, 102562.

Taoufik, M., & Fekri, A. (2021). GIS-based multi-criteria analysis of offshore wind farm development in Morocco. *Energy Conversion and Management: X*, *11*, 100103.

Torjesen, I. (2021). Fossil fuel air pollution blamed for 1 in 5 deaths worldwide. *BMJ*, *372*(406).

Ulloa, A. (2023). Aesthetics of green dispossession: From coal to wind extraction in La Guajira, Colombia. *Journal of Political Ecology*, *30*(1), 166–190.

UNDP (UN Development Report). (2020). *Human development report 2020: The next frontier: human development and the Anthropocene.* http://hdr.undp.org/en/2020-report

Vega-Araujo, J., & Heffron, R. J. (2022). Assessing elements of energy justice in Colombia: A case study on transmission infrastructure in La Guajira. *Energy Research & Social Science*, *91*, 102688.

Yenneti, K. (2016). The grid-connected solar energy in India: Structures and challenges. *Energy Strategy Reviews*, *11*, 41–51.

Chapter 8

SDG 8. Promote Sustained, Inclusive and Sustainable Economic Growth, Full and Productive Employment, and Decent Work for All

Abstract

The chapter explores the intricate relationship between the pursuit of decent work and economic growth and the reinforcement of territorial identities. Through illustrative case studies, it showcases community-based initiatives that have effectively empowered local groups, igniting entrepreneurship and innovation as drivers of economic expansion and job generation. Conversely, the chapter examines the opposing influence of identity-driven discrimination and social exclusion, underscoring their adverse effects on accessing opportunities for decent work and economic progress. In response to these challenges, the chapter offers a comprehensive array of practical recommendations, equipping stakeholders with strategies to address and surmount such obstacles. Finally, the chapter extends its exploration to the pivotal role of championing social justice within the framework of the sustainable territorial development.

SDG 8 centers around promoting decent and sustainable work for all, along with inclusive economic growth. This goal aims to achieve an equitable and sustainable society in which individuals have access to decent work opportunities, fair wages, and safe working conditions. Moreover, it aims to create an environment conducive to entrepreneurship, innovation, and sustainable economic growth. Key indicators of SDG 8 include employment rates, the share of workers earning wages below the poverty threshold, access to training and education to enhance professional skills, gender equality in access to employment and career opportunities, as well as the protection of workers' rights, including workplace safety and health.

Identity, Territories, and Sustainability: Challenges and Opportunities for Achieving the UN Sustainable Development Goals, 81–86
Copyright © 2024 by Salvatore Monaco
Published under exclusive licence by Emerald Publishing Limited
doi:10.1108/978-1-83797-549-520241009

To achieve this goal, the promotion of technological innovation and entrepreneurship appears imperative. Innovation is considered as a key driver of economic development, aiding societies in finding low-impact environmental solutions to global problems and challenges. A green economy, based on renewable energy sources and sustainable production, can contribute to reducing the environmental impact of human activities and preserving ecosystems for future generations. The development of a green economy is closely tied to the implementation of processes and business models aimed at reducing environmental impact, assuming a role of social responsibility. It is achievable with the support of professionals with a strong background in ecological transition issues.

As the sustainable digitalization advances, the recruitment of the talents is becoming increasingly central to addressing companies' innovation and restructuring needs. However, while technological evolution opens the door to emerging professions, it is also exacerbating disparities between workers, both in terms of employability and wages (Adalet McGowan & Andrews, 2017; Autor, 2014). Over the past 20 years, skills disparities have increased in all sectors in OECD countries, particularly in markets with heavy investments in digital technologies (IMF, 2021). On average, around a quarter of workers report a gap between their skills and those demanded by the market (OECD, 2020). In a rapidly changing technological and economic landscape, many people may perceive themselves at a disadvantage due to lacking the skills and knowledge required to meet market demands or adapt to new challenges. This situation can evoke a sense of insecurity and inadequacy, driving many individuals to fear exclusion or marginalization.

In such circumstances, there is a risk that only a selected group or specific areas may benefit from the advantages of digitization (Bridge et al., 2018; Bulkeley, 2010; York, 2012). The transition to digital work increases the potential for widening the digital divide both among groups of people and between territories, in terms of differential access to infrastructure and competencies, motivation, and the ability to use new technologies (Calderón-Gómez et al., 2020; Monaco & Sacchi, 2023; Vasilescu et al., 2020). Imbalances between skills supply and demand play a significant role in perpetuating and exacerbating income inequality in various parts of the world. Income inequality in many advanced economies has been driven by the lack of adequate skills to meet the evolving demands of the labor market.

Individuals possessing the required skills have gained access to more profitable and secure job opportunities, whereas those without have experienced stagnant or declining incomes (Hanushek et al., 2015; Lindsey & Teles, 2017). Emerging economies have not been exempted from this trend either. Many developing countries face similar challenges in adapting to technological changes and ensuring that their workforce is equipped with the necessary skills (Khan et al., 2022; Topcu & Tugcu, 2020; Zhang & Zhang, 2022). For instance, in India's coal-mining regions, the transition to renewable energies has led to job losses for coal miners (Majid, 2020). Furthermore, informal sector workers appear particularly vulnerable to the negative consequences of transition due to the lack of social protection and access to training programs. In South Africa, informal waste pickers collecting recyclable materials risk being excluded from the formal waste management system, resulting in income loss and job insecurity (Schenck et al., 2019). In Brazil, the transition to a green economy has been criticized for prioritizing highly skilled jobs while neglecting the need for investment in education and training for low-skilled workers (Bastos Lima & Da Costa, 2022).

Another significant aspect is the exacerbation of gender disparities in the current scenario. Women's representation in the workforce is already low in Europe, with women constituting only 39% of the workforce (Eu-Ansa, 2022), and their representation in key transition sectors such as energy, transportation, water, waste, agriculture, forestry, and fisheries is even lower than the global average (Walk et al., 2021). This gap could be further widened by the transition to a green economy, with potential negative consequences for women's economic empowerment and livelihoods. For instance, potential changes in land use to accommodate shifting agricultural workers and impact their livelihoods could disproportionately affect women farmers who already have limited access to education and resources, making it harder for them to adapt to the changing agricultural landscape (Cooper & Nagel, 2022; Leach, 2016). In Ethiopia, the expansion of industrial agriculture for biofuel production has led to land grabbing and displacement of small farmers, with women often disproportionately affected (Konte & Tirivayi, 2020).

Technological progress and automation are significantly impacting most sectors. This has led to reduced labor demand in some occupations, resulting in layoffs and heightened competition for remaining jobs. One sector particularly affected by this transformation is the manufacturing industry. The automation of production lines has reduced the need for human labor, leading to job losses. A similar situation has occurred in the retail sector, where the rise of online shopping and app-based purchases has led to the closure of numerous traditional brick-and-mortar stores and reduced demand for salespeople and other retail staff. Even in the services sector, the introduction of new technologies is driving significant changes. For example, in the hospitality industry, the use of automated devices and systems to manage orders and serve food is reducing the need for waitstaff and kitchen staff. Similarly, artificial intelligence is revolutionizing customer support, with chatbots and automated support systems partially replacing traditional call center operators.

The impact of technological progress and automation on the identity of territories is profound and multifaceted. The transformations in the labor market caused by the introduction of new technologies and automation have social and economic consequences that can influence the identity and culture of local communities. First, the loss of jobs and the reduction in labor demand in certain traditional occupations can lead to significant economic instability in the affected communities. Individuals who have lost their jobs may face financial difficulties and issues of livelihood. Moreover, changes in the labor market can bring about shifts in the economic and social structure of communities. For example, the closure of traditional physical stores due to the rise of online commerce can affect the vibrancy and identity of urban centers and local commercial areas. The disappearance of traditional activities can result in the loss of meeting places and social exchanges, undermining social cohesion and community identity.

Furthermore, the introduction of new technologies and automated systems to pursue sustainability can impact local culture and traditions. For instance, the use of automated devices and systems in the catering industry can alter the customer experience and the quality of service (Mauracher et al., 2016). This can lead to a loss of authenticity and a change in the experience and perception of traditional places and activities.

Considering the other side of the coin, it is possible to argue that technological innovation can also create new opportunities and promote the development of new industries and economic activities, contributing to a redefinition and revitalization of territorial identity in terms of innovation. For instance, the adoption of green and sustainable technologies can establish a positive reputation for the territory as a hub for experimenting and promoting innovative solutions to address climate change and environmental challenges. Similarly, training and professional requalification of workers can also play a key role in preserving or strengthening territorial identity in a green context. Investing in skill training and entrepreneurship promotion can help retain local skills and traditions, enabling communities to adapt to new labor market challenges without compromising their identity and culture.

In light of these considerations, it is safe to argue that to address the challenges posed by SDG 8 entails the investment in worker training and requalification. Governments and educational institutions must collaborate to develop training programs that provide the skills needed to meet new labor market challenges. These programs should focus on both technical and vocational training, as well as the cultivation of transferable skills such as problem-solving, communication, and adaptability. The main political challenge is to enable people to acquire the new skills demanded by the labor market, improving access to affordable and quality education through facilitation and provision of scholarships for economically disadvantaged individuals (Turner, 2017). In order to prevent an exodus of workers not yet ready for the new socio-cultural scenario, supporting policies are needed during the adaptation process. Traditional formal education must be supplemented with new models for requalification and lifelong learning, capable of fostering a dynamic adaptation of old jobs to new professions (Acemoglu & Restrepo, 2018). The challenges presented by social and technological changes can be approached as opportunities for continuous learning and skill upgrading. Continuous learning and open-mindedness towards innovation are fundamental keys to overcoming the fear of being left behind and embracing change as a development opportunity. Such an approach, adopted in all economic sectors, and territories, can successfully support the dual transition towards a just, green, and digital economy.

Encouraging self-employment and the establishment of new businesses can also create job opportunities for those who are in precarious situations due to job losses in obsolete occupations.

It is also essential to adopt policies that promote a more equitable distribution of job opportunities and reduce social and economic inequalities. In many countries, the increasing automation and digitization of work have led to an increase in inequality between highly skilled workers and those with obsolete or inadequate skills for new market demands. Policies of social inclusion and support for the most vulnerable segments of the population can help ensure that no one is left behind in the labor market transformation process (Galgóczi, 2020; Petmesidou & Guillén, 2022; van der Ree, 2019).

At the present state, prevailing market conditions and the absence of policies aimed at capitalizing on human capital have contributed to an increase in income inequality in a fairly widespread manner. In this aspect, interventions are possible by implementing targeted and more responsive welfare policies that encourage requalification, placement services, and reemployment, including innovative mechanisms of unemployment insurance. Policymakers should understand the time needed to allow citizens, workers, and communities to absorb information, accept new circumstances, and prepare for the future. Long-term planning is indeed crucial to ensure that governments and states do not bear unnecessary costs. While comprehensive governmental interventions are necessary, the issues related to transition, extending from the individual to the global, require targeted efforts based on coordination between multiple actors and different levels of government. It is not coincidental that some virtuous examples are demonstrating the centrality of multilevel logic in decision-making processes to sustainably protect vulnerable groups without exacerbating social inequalities. In a forward-looking perspective, it is not far-fetched to suggest that cooperation between different levels of government and various institutional bodies, on the one hand, and between the public and private sectors, on the other, can facilitate the identification of proactive measures that help maximize long-term benefits and reactive measures aimed at minimizing the damages of transition (Monaco, 2023).

References

Acemoglu, D., & Restrepo, P. (2018). The race between machine and man: Implications of technology for growth, factor shares and employment. *American Economic Review, 108*(6), 1488–1542.

Adalet McGowan, M., & Andrews, D. (2017). Labor market mismatch and labor productivity: Evidence from PIAAC data. *Research in Labor Economics, 45*, 199–241.

Autor, D. H. (2014). Skills, education, and the rise of earnings inequality among the other 99 percent. *Science, 344*(6186), 843–851.

Bastos Lima, M. G., & Da Costa, K. (2022). Quo vadis, Brazil? Environmental malgovernance under Bolsonaro and the ambiguous role of the sustainable development goals. *Bulletin of Latin American Research, 41*(4), 508–524.

Bridge, G., Barr, S., Bouzarovski, S., Bradshaw, M., Brown, E., Bulkeley, H., & Walker, G. (2018). *Energy and society: A critical perspective*. Routledge.

Bulkeley, H. (2010). Cities and the governing of climate change. *Annual Review of Environment and Resources, 39*(1), 129–147.

Calderón-Gómez, D., Casas-Mas, B., Urraco-Solanilla, M., & Revilla, J. C. (2020). The labour digital divide: Digital dimensions of labour market segmentation. *Work Organisation, Labour and Globalisation, 14*(2), 7–30.

Cooper, D. H., & Nagel, J. (2022). Lessons from the pandemic: Climate change and COVID-19. *International Journal of Sociology and Social Policy, 42*(3/4), 332–347.

Eu-Ansa. (2022). *Gender equality in the EU*. EU Agencies Network on Scientific Advice.

Galgóczi, B. (2020). Just transition on the ground: Challenges and opportunities for social dialogue. *European Journal of Industrial Relations*, *26*(4), 367–382.

Hanushek, E., Schwerdt, G., Wiederhold, S., & Woessmann, L. (2015). Returns to skills around the world: Evidence from PIAAC. *European Economic Review*, *73C*, 103–130.

IMF. (2021). *World economic outlook*. International Monetary Fund.

Khan, S., Yahong, W., & Zeeshan, A. (2022). Impact of poverty and income inequality on the ecological footprint in Asian developing economies: Assessment of Sustainable Development Goals. *Energy Reports*, *8*, 670–679.

Konte, M., & Tirivayi, N. (Eds.) (2020). *Women and sustainable human development – Empowering women in Africa Gender, Development and Social Change*. Palgrave Macmillan.

Leach, M. (Ed.) (2016). *Gender equality and sustainable development*. Routledge.

Lindsey, B., & Teles, S. (2017). *The captured economy: How the powerful enrich themselves, slow down growth, and increase inequality*. Oxford University Press.

Majid, M. A. (2020). Renewable energy for sustainable development in India: Current status, future prospects, challenges, employment, and investment opportunities. *Energy, Sustainability and Society*, *10*(1), 1–36.

Mauracher, C., Procidano, I., & Sacchi, G. (2016). Wine tourism quality perception and customer satisfaction reliability: The Italian Prosecco District. *Journal of Wine Research*, *27*(4), 284–299.

Monaco, S., & Sacchi, G. (2023). Travelling the metaverse: Potential benefits and main challenges for tourism sectors and research applications. *Sustainability*, *15*(4), 3348.

Monaco, S. (2023). Climate (of) change: The promise and perils of technology in achieving a just transition. *International Journal of Sociology and Social Policy*, *43*(13/14), 129–145.

OECD (Organisation for Economic Co-operation and Development). (2020). *The productivity-inclusiveness nexus*. OECD.

Petmesidou, M., & Guillén, A. M. (2022). Europe's green, digital and demographic transition: A social policy research perspective. *Transfer: European Review of Labour and Research*, *28*(3), 317–332.

Schenck, C. J., Blaauw, P. F., Viljoen, J. M., & Swart, E. C. (2019). Exploring the potential health risks faced by waste pickers on landfills in South Africa: A socio-ecological perspective. *International Journal of Environmental Research and Public Health*, *16*(11), 2059–2071.

Topcu, M., & Tugcu, C. T. (2020). The impact of renewable energy consumption on income inequality: Evidence from developed countries. *Renewable Energy*, *151*, 1134–1140.

Turner, S. (2017). *Education markets: Forward-looking policy options*. Brookings Institution.

van der Ree, K. (2019). *Promoting green jobs: Decent work in the transition to low-carbon, green economies*. Brill Nijhoff.

Vasilescu, M. D., Serban, A. C., Dimian, G. C., Aceleanu, M. I., & Picatoste, X. (2020). Digital divide, skills and perceptions on digitalisation in the European Union – Towards a smart labour market. *PloS One*, *15*(4), e0232032.

Walk, P., Braunger, I., Semb, J., Brodtmann, C., Oei, P. Y., & Kemfert, C. (2021). Strengthening gender justice in a just transition: A research agenda based on a systematic map of gender in coal transitions. *Energies*, *14*(18), 5985.

York, R. (2012). Do alternative energy sources displace fossil fuels? *Nature Climate Change*, *2*(6), 441–443.

Zhang, J., & Zhang, Y. (2022). How emissions trading affects income inequality: Evidence from China. *Climate Policy*, *15*(7), 1–16.

Chapter 9

SDG 9. Build Resilient Infrastructure, Promote Inclusive and Sustainable Industrialization, and Foster Innovation

Abstract

While well-designed and environmentally conscious infrastructures are essential for economic growth and social progress, their implementation can sometimes neglect the unique characteristics of territories. The chapter explores the issues posed by eco-blind infrastructure projects, challenging the assumption that all forms of greening are universally beneficial. It delves into the implications of urban greening initiatives, showcasing instances where these projects, while aiming for sustainability, have inadvertently exacerbated issues of inequality, displacement, and social marginalization. Through critical analysis of cases, the chapter reveals the complex interplay among environmental improvement, territorial identity, and community involvement, underscoring the importance of community engagement in project planning and execution. This approach is described as a tool to balance environmental considerations with an appreciation for local identity, fostering projects that truly benefit communities while advancing the broader goals of environmental development.

SDG 9 focuses on the importance of building resilient infrastructure and fostering innovation. Well-designed infrastructure forms the foundation of a functional and prosperous society, facilitating the transfer of people and goods, improving access to resources, and enabling the development of vital economic activities. Roads, bridges, railways, ports, and airports are essential to ensure connectivity and accessibility in all areas of the world, especially the most remote ones. Ensuring robust and well-maintained basic infrastructure is crucial to promote adequate services and opportunities for all citizens. In the contemporary social context, it is essential for such infrastructures to be resilient and capable of

---

Identity, Territories, and Sustainability: Challenges and Opportunities for Achieving the UN Sustainable Development Goals, 87–93
Copyright © 2024 by Salvatore Monaco
Published under exclusive licence by Emerald Publishing Limited
doi:10.1108/978-1-83797-549-520241010

withstanding environmental shocks and stresses, as climate change and natural disasters pose an increasingly tangible threat to communities across the globe.

In implementing SDG 9, the importance of considering the aspect of innovation is also emphasized. Technology plays a key role in enhancing the efficiency and sustainability of infrastructure. For example, the use of intelligent and innovative technologies in the transportation sector can help reduce pollution and natural resource consumption while simultaneously improving citizens' quality of life.

Several institutions have already moved in this direction. For instance, in December 2021, the European Commission launched the Global Gateway initiative. This is a comprehensive global infrastructure project by the European Union aimed at promoting connectivity, trade, and economic growth on a global scale. The project aims to mobilize up to 300 billion euros by 2027 (Furness & Keijzer, 2022; Karjalainen, 2023). The Global Gateway strategy is based on four pillars: Infrastructure development for transportation, including the creation of ports, airports, roads, and railways; digital connectivity, such as the development of advanced telecommunications networks and IT connectivity; sustainable development, with reference to energy and environmental issues; simplification of trade, through the reduction of trade barriers and harmonization of regulations on cross-border trade. Approximately half of the project's budget is allocated to the Global Gateway Africa-Europe Investment Package, a supporting strategy for African countries to develop a strong, green, inclusive, and digital economy. Within this project, Africa holds a strategic centrality as African countries are considered by Brussels as key partners for economic cooperation and the achievement of sustainable development goals.

The Global Gateway initiative introduces a new approach, following the growing emphasis on cooperation and addressing the geopolitical risks stemming from projects of other global powers, such as the Chinese Belt and Road Initiative (BRI) (Huang, 2016; Hurley et al., 2019). The BRI aims to establish infrastructure to facilitate the transportation of Chinese products to Uganda, Rwanda, Burundi, and South Sudan while enabling the transport of African raw materials, especially South Sudanese and Ugandan oil, back to China. The Chinese action can be defined as soft power, as it adheres to the principle of non-intervention in the internal affairs of African states, disregarding the "moral" issues often considered conditional by Western powers for aid provision (Teo et al., 2019). On the one hand, through the realization of large infrastructure projects, China can boost the African local economy, facilitating trade, and creating new spaces for economic cooperation. On the other hand, the execution of projects is almost always managed by Chinese companies, limiting the positive impact as there are no jobs for local Africans. Nevertheless, it is equally true that the Chinese soft power system is complemented by the provision of scholarships and projects for African students who, through a period of study in China, can acquire the necessary knowledge to become "agents of their own development."

Infrastructures can have a significant impact on local communities, influencing their way of life and territorial identity. They cannot be designed and built uniformly for all regions and communities worldwide, as each territory has its own peculiarities and specific needs. It is necessary to take into account local specificities, cultural practices, and traditions during the design phase, in order to preserve and enrich territorial identity and cultural diversity.

There are numerous cases in which the design and implementation of infrastructure have considered territorial identity and the needs of local communities. When they have been environmentally respectful and have created social and economic opportunities while respecting local identities, they can be defined as sustainable in the real sense. One such example is the urban redevelopment project in Medellín, Colombia (Vilar & Cartes, 2016). The city had long been marked by violence and poverty, but through a series of urban regeneration policies, it has become more resilient and sustainable, thanks in part to new innovative and inclusive infrastructures. The infrastructure redevelopment project involved local communities from the beginning, listening to their needs and desires for the future of the area. Accessible and inclusive public spaces were created, such as parks and libraries, which fostered social cohesion and interaction among residents. Furthermore, efficient, and sustainable public transportation systems were developed, such as the metro system and rail transport (Furigo et al., 2020). In 2011, a series of six connected outdoor escalators were inaugurated, totaling 385 meters in length. These escalators provided citizens and visitors the opportunity to ascend the hill in about five minutes. Additionally, various public funds were used to pave the staircases and adjacent paths, and local and international artists painted murals on the walls of residents' homes. Under these circumstances, Medellín was awarded by the Urban Land Institute (ULI) and the Wall Street Journal (WSJ) as the most innovative city in the world in 2013, thanks to the urban transformation process implemented by the city's mayor. Building on these achievements, a Strategic Plan was developed in 2018, focusing more on the ecological and environmental dimensions. Its implementation involved planting over 8,000 trees and palms, with an investment of 49,000 million Colombian pesos. This activity is part of the more ambitious "Medellín Verde" project, which aims to create an environmental network connecting natural systems in the city – such as streams, hills, parks, and tree-lined streets – through pedestrian paths and bike lanes. Its goal is not only to promote green mobility but also to create areas that reduce temperatures, improve air quality, and enhance biodiversity conservation conditions.

Another virtuous example that can be placed within the framework of desired territorial development is the Anandaloy project, realized by the German architect Anna Heringer in Bangladesh (Charlesworth & Fien, 2022). In the local Bengali dialect, Anandaloy means "the place of deep joy." The project involved building a two-story multifunctional center made of mud and bamboo in the midst of rice paddies in the northern part of the country. Since mud is freely available and bamboo was sourced from local farmers, most of the budget allocated for the initiative remained within the community. The ground floor of the building hosts a therapy center dedicated to people with disabilities. The therapy center in the Rudrapur building serves a dual purpose: On one hand, it offers specific care and treatments tailored to the diverse needs of people with disabilities, enhancing their autonomy and quality of life. The center's staff provides physical therapy, rehabilitation, psychological support, and other forms of personalized assistance aimed at promoting the well-being and social integration of people with disabilities; on the other hand, the therapy center also plays a crucial role in educating the local community about disabilities. Through awareness initiatives and training programs, the center aims to remove prejudices and stereotypes associated with people with disabilities, promoting greater understanding and acceptance of these individuals within society, since disabilities in Bangladesh are often stigmatized and considered either divine punishment or a result of karma. These cultural beliefs may contribute to their exclusion from society and opportunities for social and economic participation. Additionally, the therapy center provides essential support for the families of people with disabilities. It is a place where families can access information, resources, and emotional support, contributing to improving their ability to care for their loved ones. On the upper floor of the building, a textile studio was created. This initiative was launched in response to the scarcity of job opportunities in rural areas of Bangladesh, where many women face a lack of prospects and poverty. In the countryside, women encounter many difficulties in accessing employment. Employment options are limited and often poorly paid. Faced with this situation, many of them are forced to seek opportunities in cities, moving away from their families and roots. This migration often leads to precarious working conditions, exploitation, and poor job security, especially for those employed in textile factories. The textile studio project in the Rudrapur building was also conceived as a way to address these challenges by supporting and promoting local textile traditions, enhancing the skills and craftsmanship of village women. This preserves an important cultural heritage and also provides new earning opportunities for women in the community, sparing them the need to seek work far from home. Thanks to the textile studio, women have the opportunity to work close to their homes and stay nearer to their families. This not only improves the quality of their lives but also contributes to strengthening social and familial bonds in the community. The project also plays a crucial role in promoting gender equality. Traditionally, many women in rural areas of Bangladesh have had few opportunities to develop their working skills and contribute economically to their families. The textile studio provides a platform where women can show and enhance their craft skills, enabling them to achieve greater economic and social autonomy. In addition to individual benefits, the textile studio also has positive impacts on the community as a whole. The promotion of local textile traditions helps preserve the village's cultural heritage and keeps it alive in the social fabric, reinforcing territorial identity and the sense of belonging to the community. For all these reasons, the structure won The Obel Award in 2020, the international architecture prize of the Henrik Frode Obel Foundation, which honors the most innovative and sustainable architectural contributions made in recent years.

These two cases demonstrate the possibility to design and implement sustainable infrastructure that respects territorial identity and meets the needs of local communities. In particular, the active involvement of communities in the decision-making process and the management of infrastructure represents an added value to ensure the success of projects and create an inclusive environment.

However, in the realm of sustainable development, it is important to remember that also certain large-scale green infrastructure projects, despite their ambitions, can inadvertently display "eco-blind" characteristics. These ambitious "eco-blind" infrastructures, ranging from the establishment of expansive transportation networks to the construction of energy facilities, are often conceived with the aim of advancing sustainability and propelling regions toward a more promising green future. A myopic approach to development can lead to unforeseen and undesirable outcomes. As anticipated in the previous chapter, this situation arises when such projects inflict adverse effects on both the intricate tapestry of territorial identity and the surrounding ecosystem. The dual nature of these endeavors becomes apparent when their roles in fostering modernity and sustainability on one hand coexist with the potential to pose threats to the intrinsic uniqueness of a territory on the other. As these extensive projects reshape landscapes and manipulate urban dynamics, they possess the unintended capability to disrupt the delicate equilibrium that sustains a community's distinct identity. Time-honored landmarks, deeply rooted traditions, and localized customs may find themselves imperiled or even eradicated, prompting a sense of detachment among residents whose connections to their rapidly transforming surroundings are set apart. This detachment has the potential to negate the positive intentions of the infrastructure project and conceivably impede the overarching progress it strives to accomplish.

The ramifications of these actions extend far beyond the construction phase, yielding enduring environmental repercussions that may undermine the very sustainability that such projects purportedly aim to enhance. In alignment with this perspective, a group of activists and scholars argues that initiatives centered around greening can lead to the esthetic enhancement of specific areas and an improvement in residents' quality of life, also entailing unforeseen risks (García-Lamarca et al., 2021; Triguero-Mas et al., 2021). This phenomenon emerges when infrastructure construction or improvement encourages gentrification processes, attracting new more affluent populations while displacing historic and low-income communities from their neighborhoods (Anguelovski et al., 2022; Immergluck & Balan, 2018). Consequently, speculation can arise, resulting in the loss of territorial identity for local communities who are compelled to leave their homes and traditional living spaces. The concepts of land grabbing and green grabbing, which were initially concentrated primarily in rural areas of the Global South and linked to energy projects, have in recent years expanded to peri-urban and urban geographical areas (Feola et al., 2019; Safransky, 2017; Zoomers et al., 2017). Critical literature on this subject underscores how various governance processes can trigger the accumulation of urban capital, exacerbate socio-spatial inequalities, and incite gentrification dynamics in the realm of urban land grabs (Steel et al., 2017).

For instance, in Colombo, Sri Lanka, the neoliberal era transformed extensive wetlands of the city into real estate assets. Real estate developers, urban development agencies, and the middle class benefited from the grab of wetland areas. They were transformed into properties characterized by new infrastructure such as parks, dams, and roads. At the same time, the poor urban populations living in those areas faced evictions and expropriations (Hettiarachchi et al., 2019).

The Detroit Future City (DFC), a long-term revitalization plan for the city of Detroit, represents another urban greening initiative that has critical implications for territorial identity and issues of social equity. The plan, made public in December 2013, envisioned a revitalization project for the city's most vacant neighborhoods, which were then identified as lacking "market value." The strategy proposed by the DFC involved the creation of blue and green infrastructure, including retention basins, carbon forests, urban farms, and green streets, to enhance the city's environmental sustainability and provide new development opportunities. The implementation of the actions outlined by the DFC had negative consequences for local communities. The goal of greening and revitalization, though seemingly noble and sustainable, ended up further marginalizing the people already residing in these neighborhoods. Local communities found themselves confronted with issues such as forced evictions and expropriations. This approach sparked social tensions and inequalities as greening actions were perceived as examples of appropriation and control of natural resources and green spaces to benefit privileged actors at the expense of the broader community (Fairhead et al., 2012). In this sense, greening initiatives led to the monetization and financialization of urban greenery, transforming green spaces into opportunities for profit and speculation. This financialization resulted in increased housing prices and rents, making it increasingly difficult for low-income families to remain in their original neighborhoods. A critical aspect to consider is that the vision of urban greening proposed by the DFC was largely determined by planners and elected officials, without significant involvement of local communities in formulating development strategies, which led to a lack of true understanding of the needs and aspirations of over 90,000 people living and working in these areas, thereby undermining the sustainability of greening initiatives.

The situation in Detroit reflects a broader issue concerning many projects. While green and blue infrastructure can bring significant improvements in terms of environmental sustainability, the lack of consideration for territorial identity can lead to negative outcomes in terms of equity and social justice. This reinforce the idea that the value of actions to requalify places through the implementation of new infrastructure depends on the level of territorial desirability, as well as the methods of implementation and the purposes for which they are introduced.

References

Anguelovski, I., Brand, A. L., Ranganathan, M., & Hyra, D. (2022). Decolonizing the green city: From environmental privilege to emancipatory green justice. *Environmental Justice*, *15*(1), 1–11.

Charlesworth, E., & Fien, J. (2022). *Design for fragility: 13 stories of humanitarian architects*. Taylor & Francis.

Fairhead, J., Leach, M., & Scoones, I. (2012). Green grabbing: A new appropriation of nature? *Journal of Peasant Studies*, *39*(2), 237–261.

Feola, G., Suzunaga, J., Soler, J., & Goodman, M. K. (2019). Ordinary land grabbing in peri-urban spaces: Land conflicts and governance in a small Colombian city. *Geoforum*, *105*, 145–157.

Furigo, R. D. F. R., Samora, P. R., & Tamayo, A. L. G. (2020). Right to the water, right to the city. The universalization of sanitation in precarious urban settlements of Medellin, Colombia. *Cadernos Metrópole*, *22*, 479–498.

Furness, M., & Keijzer, N. (2022). *Europe's Global Gateway: A new geostrategic framework for development policy?* German Development Institute.

García-Lamarca, M., Anguelovski, I., Cole, H., Connolly, J. J., Argüelles, L., Baró, F., Loveless, S., Pérez Del Pulgar Frowein, S., & Shokry, G. (2021). Urban green boosterism and city affordability: For whom is the 'branded' green city? *Urban Studies, 58*(1), 90–112.

Hettiarachchi, M., Morrison, T. H., & McAlpine, C. (2019). Power, politics and policy in the appropriation of urban wetlands: The critical case of Sri Lanka. *The Journal of Peasant Studies, 46*(4), 729–746.

Huang, Y. (2016). Understanding China's belt & road initiative: Motivation, framework and assessment. *China Economic Review, 40*, 314–321.

Hurley, J., Morris, S., & Portelance, G. (2019). Examining the debt implications of the belt and road initiative from a policy perspective. *Journal of Infrastructure, Policy and Development, 3*(1), 139–175.

Immergluck, D., & Balan, T. (2018). Sustainable for whom? Green urban development, environmental gentrification, and the Atlanta Beltline. *Urban Geography, 39*(4), 546–562.

Karjalainen, T. (2023). European norms trap? EU connectivity policies and the case of the global gateway. *East Asia, 1*, 1–24.

Safransky, S. (2017). Rethinking land struggle in the postindustrial city. *Antipode, 49*(4), 1079–1100.

Steel, G., van Noorloos, F., & Klaufus, C. (2017). The urban land debate in the global South: New avenues for research. *Geoforum, 83*, 133–141.

Teo, H. C., Lechner, A. M., Walton, G. W., Chan, F. K. S., Cheshmehzangi, A., Tan-Mullins, M., & Campos-Arceiz, A. (2019). Environmental impacts of infrastructure development under the belt and road initiative. *Environments, 6*(6), 72.

Triguero-Mas, M., Anguelovski, I., García-Lamarca, M., Argüelles, L., Perez-del-Pulgar, C., Shokry, G., Connoly, J., & Cole, H. V. (2021). Natural outdoor environments' health effects in gentrifying neighborhoods: Disruptive green landscapes for underprivileged neighborhood residents. *Social Science & Medicine, 279*, 113964.

Vilar, K., & Cartes, I. (2016). Urban design and social capital in slums. Case study: Moravia's neighborhood, Medellin, 2004–2014. *Procedia-Social and Behavioral Sciences, 216*, 56–67.

Zoomers, A., Van Noorloos, F., Otsuki, K., Steel, G., & Van Westen, G. (2017). The rush for land in an urbanizing world: From land grabbing toward developing safe, resilient, and sustainable cities and landscapes. *World Development, 92*, 242–252.

Chapter 10

SDG 10. Reduce Inequality Within and Among Countries

Abstract

The chapter underscores the urgency of creating an inclusive global society by comprehensively accommodating the intricate interplay among LGBTQ+ rights, territorial identity, and political dynamics. By recognizing the inherent connection between social acceptance and territorial profile, societies can build resilience by reducing inequality and creating environments where every individual's identity is respected. Comparative analysis reveals a sharp contrast between regions embracing diversity and those imposing discriminatory policies. While Pride Parades symbolize the celebration of identity and the integration of LGBTQ+ narratives into a place's essence, "LGBT-free zones" and restrictive legislations in certain countries starkly oppose this inclusive trajectory. The juxtaposition of these strategies highlights the fragile nature of equal rights and underscores the imperative of a global commitment to fostering an accepting society, emphasizing the significance of raising awareness and promoting understanding to foster a more inclusive environment.

Differences denote the absence of similarity or correspondence among individuals, who may vary from each other by nature or specific characteristic traits. These differences constitute an inherent element of humanity, contributing to diversity and the multitude of voices within societies. Differences often serve as the foundation for generating inequalities. These disparities manifest across multiple dimensions and can pertain to economic, social, political, and cultural aspects. Inequality is evident through the uneven distribution of resources, opportunities, and rewards within a society that are crucial for individual well-being. The concept

---

Identity, Territories, and Sustainability: Challenges and Opportunities for Achieving the UN Sustainable Development Goals, 95–105
Copyright © 2024 by Salvatore Monaco
Published under exclusive licence by Emerald Publishing Limited
doi:10.1108/978-1-83797-549-520241011

of inequality extends beyond mere differentiation. As articulated by Göran Therborn (2014):

> First, a difference may be horizontal, without anything or anybody being higher or lower, better or worse, whereas an inequality is always vertical, or involves ranking. Secondly, differences are matters of taste and/or of categorization only. An inequality, on the other hand, is not just a categorization; it is something that violates a moral norm of equality among human beings. Thirdly, for a difference to become an inequality it must also be abolishable. The greater physical prowess of the average 20-year-old in comparison with the average 60-year-old is not an inequality. But the different social life-chances of women as compared to men, or of black working-class boys in comparison with white bankers boys, have come to be seen as inequalities. In one sentence: inequalities are avoidable, morally unjustified, hierarchical differences.

Inequality is intertwined with the social and cultural context in which individuals reside. They can be deeply ingrained within the societal structure itself and perpetuated by systems of dominance that favor certain groups over others (Cotterell, 2008). This means that inequalities can be mitigated, as they result from political, economic, and social choices that influence the distribution of goods and opportunities within society.

In light of this, SDG 10 aims to reduce inequalities both within and among countries by urging the removal of barriers that restrict universal access to resources and opportunities, and dismantling discrimination, marginalization, and social exclusion. To achieve this goal, SDG 10 outlines a set of specific targets and indicators. Key objectives include the promotion of more inclusive fiscal, economic, and social policies aimed at supporting and safeguarding disadvantaged and vulnerable groups. This encompasses the adoption of income redistribution and social protection policies, ensuring more equitable access to essential resources and services such as education and healthcare. The goal also strives to foster social inclusion and equality of opportunity for all, regardless of ethnicity, gender, sexual identity, religion, or disability, which entails the promotion of a culture characterized by respect and diversity.

Among the various subjects experiencing forms of inequality across diverse contexts and circumstances, the focus of this chapter is on LGBTQ+ individuals. LGBTQ+, an acronym introduced in the early 20th century, encompasses all sexual and gender minorities. It serves as a semantic solution that unifies a plurality of subjectivities, each possessing distinct and specific characteristics, yet unified by their deviation from stereotypes associated with "masculinity" and "femininity" (Wood, 1997). Each letter in the acronym not only describes membership within an identity category but also metaphorically represents the social and cultural struggles undertaken to assert the right to be oneself in all aspects of existence (Monaco, 2021).

The first three letters of the acronym (LGB) refer to lesbian, gay, and bisexual individuals. Lesbians are women who experience romantic and/or sexual attraction toward other women; gay men experience romantic and/or sexual attraction toward other men; finally, bisexual individuals are those who experience romantic and/or sexual attraction to both men and women. According to the American Psychological Association (APA, 2008), discussing sexual orientations refers to something far more complex than a continuum from heterosexuality to homosexuality, including bisexuality. The LGBTQ+ acronym incorporates also the mathematical-scientific symbol "+" to indicate that the list of non-mainstream sexual identities is richer and more diverse. Recent studies (Corbisiero et al., 2021; Parker et al., 2019; Risman, 2018) have demonstrated that younger generations perceive their sexual identities as more fluid and constantly evolving. Within this framework, "demisexuality" emerges, characterized as a "gray" sexual orientation where emotional or sexual attraction is intermittent, activated solely in relationships with strong emotional bonds, irrespective of the partner's sexual identity (Buyantueva & Shevtsova, 2019). "Pansexuality" is another orientation characterized by emotional or physical attraction to individuals regardless of their sex or gender (Cavendish, 2010). Another orientation is labeled as "abrosexuality," referring to a fluid and mutable sexual interest. Even asexuality exists as a sexual orientation. Asexual individuals experience little to no sexual attraction to any gender (Bogaert, 2015). Asexuality must not be confused with sexual abstinence, chastity, or hyposexuality, as the former are voluntary actions or cultural influences, whereas the latter constitutes a diagnosable disorder.

Within the more inclusive acronym, the letter Q represents both Questioning and Queer. The former pertains to individuals who question their sexual orientation, gender, or gender identity, temporarily or permanently refraining from adhering to one or more identity categories while seeking a better understanding of their sexual identity. Queer is a politically charged term primarily used by those opposing binary thinking, advocating the uniqueness of each human being beyond stereotypes (de Lauretis, 1991; Leap & Boellstorff, 2003). The queer perspective suggests abandoning a stereotypical and dichotomous view of sexes, genders, identities, and sexual orientations in favor of less crystallized and more fluid and unstable forms, subject to reorganizations that may occur throughout individuals' lives due to social, psychological, cultural, and biological factors. Queer studies have promoted the deconstruction of the "gender-polarized world" (Connell, 2002), which represents a distinctly dichotomous conception of a gendered society, proposing instead an innovative perspective that considers ways of experiencing the body, erotic or sexual desire, femininity, and masculinity. From this analytical standpoint, it can be argued that sexual orientation can effectively be defined as a multidimensional construct encompassing various factors, with key elements including self-identification, sexual behavior, physical attraction, emotional involvement, and social preferences.

The inclusion of the letter "T" in the acronym refers to transgender people, a diverse group facing unique challenges in their journey of exploring and affirming their gender identity. Transgender individuals are those who do not identify with the gender assigned to them at birth based on physical characteristics. For instance, a transgender man, often referred to as FtM (Female to Male), identifies as a man despite being biologically assigned female at birth. Similarly, a transgender person MtF (Male to Female) identifies as a woman, even though biologically male (Levitt & Ippolito, 2014). The misalignment between biological sex and gender identity can, in certain circumstances, lead to a process of transitioning to the opposite gender, which may involve various surgical procedures and hormone therapies. However, it is crucial to underline that this is not the only possible path. The transgender identity is highly diverse and individualized. The ways in which transition takes place are deeply personal and influenced by factors such as gender identity perception, legal frameworks, socio-cultural context, personal beliefs, and economic opportunities. Some individuals may feel more comfortable with significant physical changes, while others can choose to not change anything in their gender expression or to modify their appearance through non-medical means or hormone therapies. Such transitions can involve changes in clothing, hairstyle, language, and social interactions to reflect the desired gender identity. The central aspect of this transition is the individual's self-determination in defining how they wish to be seen and perceived by others, without necessarily altering their physical traits (Stryker & Whittle, 2013).

It is worth noting that there are also individuals who do not identify with either the male or female gender (non-binary), feeling that they belong to both genders simultaneously (bigender) or alternating between them (genderfluid or genderqueer) (Monaco, 2024).

According to various authors (Bancronft, 2009; Weeks, 1981), individuals belonging to sexual or gender minorities experience differential treatment depending on the prevailing level of heteronormativity in their living area. The concept of heteronormativity was introduced in the field of social sciences in the early 1990s by Michael Warner (1993) as part of the early works of queer theory. This term refers to an ideological-cultural system that not only assumes a natural subordination of women to men but also considers only relationships between individuals of different sexes as the norm to follow. Heteronormativity is based on the idea that only two genders, male and female, exist in nature, aligning perfectly with the two biological sexes, and that only relationships between men and women are socially permissible (Gilbert, 2009). The male hegemony upon which heteronormativity is built has effectively produced a social model that does not aim to be better or superior to other ideologies but imposes itself as the sole and unquestionable norm. The resulting "straight mind" (Wittig, 1990) generates a dogmatic division among people, making it difficult for the mind to conceive of a society where heterosexuality does not govern all human relationships and social processes.

Assuming this principle has significant empirical consequences. Not only is it taken for granted that everyone should be heterosexual (Myers & Raymond, 2010), as heterosexuality is considered the natural trait (Kitzinger, 2005), but relationships are also hierarchically ordered based on heterosexist principles. Even today, in many countries, only identities and social relationships that fall within the boundaries of heteronormativity enjoy social and legal legitimacy. All other relationships, such as same-sex partnerships, are often either differently regulated or, in some cases, condemned to secrecy (Monaco & Corbisiero, 2022).

This scenario sets the stage for another phenomenon and a direct consequence: Homophobia (Habarth, 2015; Scandurra et al., 2021). The term was coined by George Weinberg (1972) to define the intolerance and hatred toward gay people in heterosexist society. The discourse extends to other sexual and gender minorities as well. In the case of bisexual individuals, for example, the term biphobia is used, while the intolerance toward transgender individuals is called transphobia. Sometimes the all-encompassing phrase homo-bi-transphobia is used.

Despite the "-phobia" suffix invoking the concept of fear, homophobia (as well as biphobia and transphobia) is not characterized by irrational phobia. On the contrary, it is based on conscious prejudice. Consequently, the negative effects of this aversion do not fall on the homophobic subject (as is usually the case with individuals experiencing any form of phobia), but rather on gay individuals, who are the true victims of prejudice. For this reason, some researchers have proposed alternative terms to "homophobia," capable of describing prejudice and discrimination against LGBTQ+ people without evoking the clinical concept of "phobia." One of the most widespread terms is "homonegativity," based on the neologism "homonegativism," used by Walter Hudson and Wendell Ricketts in an article in 1980. However, in common language, the label "homophobia" continues to be most used and widespread.

Homophobia involves certain individuals judging homosexuality hierarchically, mostly delegitimizing it even in areas of life where sexual orientation is seemingly irrelevant (Alden & Parker, 2005). More specifically, individuals belonging to or appearing to belong to a sexual minority are often negatively characterized and stigmatized for deviating from the heterosexual norm. In everyday life, homo-bi-transphobia manifests into repulsion, disgust, or avoidance of LGBTQ+ individuals, which in extreme cases can lead to physical or verbal violence (Herek, 2004).

In a public speech in 1998, author, activist, and civil rights leader Coretta Scott King defined homophobia as a form of fanaticism that, like racism and anti-Semitism, dehumanizes a large group of people, denying their dignity and individuality. Some theorists (Brod & Kaufman, 1994) argue that individuals expressing homo-bi-transphobic thoughts and feelings do so not only to convey their beliefs about LGBTQ+ individuals but also to distance themselves from this social group, implicitly emphasizing their belonging to the majority of the population. In other words, this form of violence serves to reinforce the dominance of heterosexuality and heteronormative culture.

Homophobia, biphobia, and transphobia can also take institutional form, particularly within legal systems that criminalize LGBTQ+ ideologies and individuals. This form of discrimination is still prevalent, with a staggering 71 countries and political entities enforcing anti-LGBTQ+ laws. In some instances, the consequences are severe, reaching the extreme of imposing the death penalty to condemn same-sex partner relationships in five states in Africa and Asia (ILGA, 2023). Moreover, in many countries, laws against discrimination based on sexual orientation and gender identity are still inadequate or even absent. As a consequence, in some states, LGBTQ+ individuals may face workplace discrimination without any specific legal protection (Martel, 2018). This results in situations where competent and qualified people are excluded or treated unfairly due to their gender identity or sexual orientation (Cech & Rothwell, 2020; Hossain et al., 2020; Monaco & Pezzella, 2022). Education systems can also become breeding grounds for institutional discrimination, with LGBTQ+ students often facing hostile environments devoid of inclusive policies. Many educational institutions lack specific anti-bullying measures or awareness programs that address the challenges confronted by LGBTQ+ students. Healthcare, a domain that should prioritize inclusivity and non-discrimination, is not immune to institutional bias. LGBTQ+ individuals may encounter obstacles in accessing adequate healthcare, with some healthcare professionals displaying prejudices. The lack of legal recognition and protection for LGBTQ+ couples is another facet of institutional discrimination that permeates some societies. In numerous jurisdictions, same-sex couples are still denied the right to marry, depriving them of essential legal and financial benefits. This institutionalized inequality can impact various aspects of life, from healthcare decisions to adoption processes (Mezey, 2015; Monaco & Nothdurfter, 2023; Moore & Stambolis-Ruhstorfer, 2013; Shapiro, 2012).

Discrimination and the lack of legal protections for sexual or gender minorities represent a serious threat to territorial identity and the sustainability of territories themselves. LGBTQ+ individuals are citizens equal to everyone else, and recognizing their identity and their needs is essential to preserve and enrich the diversity and authenticity of places. A concrete example of how LGBTQ+ equality and territorial identity are closely interconnected is the celebration of Pride Parades (Paternotte & Tremblay, 2016). Taking place in many cities around the world, these events not only provide an opportunity for LGBTQ+ individuals to express their identity with pride but also become an integral part of the city's identity itself. Pride Parades celebrate diversity, promote acceptance, and often actively involve the local community, fostering a sense of belonging and shared identity that goes beyond sexual orientation and gender identity.

In March 2021, the European Parliament declared the European Union a zone of LGBTQ+ freedom, symbolically condemning countries where discriminatory policies are in place. Despite this admonishment, Poland continues to have so-called "LGBT-free zones," areas free from LGBTQ+ ideologies and individuals. Although Poland decriminalized homosexuality in 1932, well before most other European countries, over a hundred Polish municipalities – roughly a third of the total – and some voivodeships have adopted resolutions against the LGBTQ+ community. These initiatives have been promoted by local authorities that have voiced support for traditional family values and opposition to what they consider a dangerous ideology. Swidnik, a city in eastern Poland with just over 40,000 inhabitants, was the first to declare itself an "LGBT-free zone." These attitudes have compelled many gay, lesbian, bisexual, and transgender individuals to emigrate to escape this social persecution.

Poland is often hailed as one of the most successful examples of achieving sustainability (Perović & Kosor, 2020; Sadłowski et al. 2021; Widawski et al., 2023). Over the past decade, Poland has shown a consistent commitment to an optimal ecological transition process, with strengthened efforts in environmental protection, focusing on the conservation of natural resources, waste management, and biodiversity preservation (Serowaniec, 2021). The country has adopted policies that encourage the use of renewable energies, setting a positive example in the European context

(Paska et al. 2020). For instance, in 2020, Poland exceeded the minimum target of 15% renewable energy usage set by the European Union, reaching 16.1% (Brodny et al., 2020). Nowadays, Poland is concentrating on developing all types of renewable energy, forming the foundation for sustainable development and the potential to create a stable and reliable energy system based on green sources (Marks-Bielska et al., 2020). In relation to SDG 10, Poland has taken an active role in the past several years in mitigating income inequality by implementing a number of welfare programs designed to give economically disadvantaged residents financial support. Interestingly, in this respect, Poland performed significantly better than other EU countries (Ambroziak et al., 2022). Despite these significant efforts, the persistent discrimination against LGBTQ+ individuals raises doubts about the evolution toward sustainable development. The introduction of "LGBT-free zones" represents a dramatic manifestation of this contradiction. These zones not only violate the fundamental principle of equality but also create an environment where the variety of identities and sexual orientations is openly rejected. The condemnation of the LGBTQ+ minority's silence deeply undermines the identity of the territory in various ways. Firstly, the silencing of a significant portion of the population contributes to creating a divided and alienated society. When diversity in identity and sexual orientations is opposed, if not openly rejected, an invisible wall is erected among the population, undermining the social cohesion that is essential for building a robust community fabric. This imposed silence creates an emotional and psychological barrier for LGBTQ+ individuals, preventing them from fully participating in the social and cultural life of the community. The fear of judgment, discrimination, and rejection forces many to hide their identities, contributing to an environment where the truth of who they are is constantly suppressed. Furthermore, silencing the LGBTQ+ community creates an atmosphere of forced conformity, where the authentic expression of people is stifled. This situation limits cultural and social diversity, preventing the emergence of unique perspectives and contributions derived from the LGBTQ+ experience. The community loses the opportunity to enrich itself through a plurality of voices and worldviews, living in a situation of partial citizenship, as they do not enjoy the same protections and rights as others (Corbisiero & Monaco, 2020; Monaco, 2022; Taylor, 2011; Valelly, 2012). Studies on citizenship have revealed that full citizenship confers a sense of collective belonging that qualifies individuals as members of the community (Nussbaum, 2010). Citizenship is not just a set of rights and duties but also a set of representations that politically, culturally, and sexually legitimize individuals in the public sphere (Puar, 2007). In this sense, full citizenship can only be guaranteed when all identity profiles are given the equal possibility of being recognized, protected, and politically, culturally, and sexually legitimized in the public sphere. At the same time, a lack of inclusion and acceptance can discourage LGBTQ+ individuals from establishing roots in places that are perceived as unsafe or oppressive, resulting in a drain of talent and resources. This exodus weakens the identity of territories, as a portion of their citizens seek to build their lives elsewhere. This phenomenon diminishes the overall territorial identity of a place, depriving it of the richness and diversity to that everyone can contribute (Florida, 2003).

In order to reduce inequalities both within and between countries, the importance of addressing the specific challenges that LGBTQ+ individuals face on a daily basis has emerged. Numerous initiatives at local, national, and international levels have been put into action. One of the key strategies has been to raise awareness in society about the rights and challenges of LGBTQ+ individuals, promoting greater understanding and acceptance. This can be achieved through awareness campaigns, educational programs in schools, and cultural initiatives that highlight the voices and stories of LGBTQ+ individuals. In this way, efforts are made to promote a cultural shift that challenges discriminatory norms and contributes to creating a more inclusive territory.

In addition, in many countries, laws have also been enacted over time to combat gender-based discrimination and violence. In territories like these, individuals and interterritorial and intersectional communities share experiences, lifestyles, and cultures, facilitating cross-fertilization of diverse knowledge, ideas, and creativity (Ghaziani, 2017).

Symbolic policies also play a significant role in dismantling inequalities. When effectively implemented and supported by a broader cultural change, they can contribute to creating a more inclusive and respectful environment. A significant example in this regard is the initiative promoted in 2015 by the US government regarding "all-gender" bathrooms and facilities. Under the leadership of then-President Barack Obama, federal guidelines were issued allowing individuals to use bathrooms and changing rooms corresponding to their chosen gender identity. This initiative aimed to reduce the level of stress and discrimination experienced by transgender or gender-nonconforming individuals when using public restrooms. A study conducted by the Stonewall Center (2018) highlighted that these individuals plan their days considering the possibility of accessing public restrooms that align with their gender identity. Where this possibility is compromised or denied, alternative options are carefully evaluated to avoid situations of discomfort and discrimination. The lack of access to appropriate restrooms can pose a risk of urinary infections or other physical issues, as well as causing dysphoria and emotional distress. Furthermore, "people who do not appear traditionally male or female risk harassment and violence in segregated facilities" (Molotch & Noren, 2010, p. 195).

The period following the inauguration of President Donald Trump at the White House represented a turning point in policies regarding transgender rights in the United States. Trump announced the decision to delegate to individual states the authority to adopt or not the guidelines promulgated by the previous administration. This decision had significant consequences, with some states adopting restrictive measures against transgender individuals. A critical example is provided by the state of North Carolina, which passed a "bathroom bill" requiring the use of restrooms and changing rooms based on the sex recorded at birth rather than the gender individuals identify with.

This example offers two important considerations about socio-cultural barriers. On one hand, these barriers can be erected suddenly and forcefully, immediately showcasing their disruptive strength. In the case of the United States, changes in government policies challenged previously established principles of acceptance and inclusion. This demonstrates the close link between inclusion and ideological positions, rendering the ground of inequalities vulnerable and easily mutable. Policies concerning the rights of LGBTQ+ individuals can undergo significant shifts depending on dominant political views, jeopardizing the protection of gender rights and identities. On the other hand, the example of North Carolina highlights that even if socio-cultural barriers may be invisible, they can create deep divisions within the population. Discriminatory policies toward LGBTQ+ individuals can have a devastating impact on their lives, forcing them to contend with laws, policies, and initiatives that deny their right to express and live their identity.

All of these highlights emphasize that the journey toward cultivating a globally inclusive and respectful society, embracing all identities, is both lengthy and riddled with challenges.

References

Alden, H. L., & Parker, K. F. (2005). Gender role ideology, homophobia and hate crime: Linking attitudes to macro-level anti-gay and lesbian hate crimes. *Deviant Behavior*, *26*(4), 321–343.
Ambroziak, A. A., Kawecka-Wyrzykowska, E., Schwabe, M., & Menkes, J. (Eds.) (2022). *Poland in the European Union: Report 2022*. SGH Publishing House.
APA (American Psychological Association). (2008). *Sexual orientation*. http://www.apa.org/helpcenter/sexual-orientation.aspx
Bancronft, L. (2009). *Human sexuality and its problems* (3rd ed.). Elsevier.
Bogaert, A. F. (2015). *Understanding asexuality*. Rowman & Littlefield.
Brod, H., & Kaufman, M. (Eds.) (1994). *Theorizing masculinities*. Sage.
Brodny, J., Tutak, M., & Saki, S. A. (2020). Forecasting the structure of energy production from renewable energy sources and biofuels in Poland. *Energies*, *13*(10), 2539.
Buyantueva, R. & Shevtsova, M. (2019). *LGBTQ+ activism in Central and Eastern Europe: Resistance, representation and identity*. Springer Nature.
Cavendish, M. (2010). *Sex and society* (Vol. 2). Marshall.
Cech, E. A., & Rothwell, W. R. (2020). LGBT workplace inequality in the federal workforce: Intersectional processes, organizational contexts, and turnover considerations. *ILR Review*, *73*(1), 25–60.
Connell, R. W. (1987). *Gender and power: Society, the person and sexual politics*. Polity Press.
Corbisiero, F., & Monaco, S. (2020). The right to a rainbow city: The Italian homosexual social movements. *Society Register*, *4*(4), 69–86.
Corbisiero, F., Monaco, S., & Ruspini, E. (2021). *Millennials, generation Z and the future of tourism*. Channel View.
Cotterell, G. (2008). Inequalities of the world: New theoretical frameworks, multiple empirical approaches. *Capital & Class*, *1*(96), 177–189.
de Lauretis, T. (1991). Queer theory: Lesbian and gay sexualities. An introduction. *Differences*, *3*(2), 3–18.
Florida, R. (2003). Entrepreneurship, creativity, and regional economic growth. In D. M. Hart (Ed.), *The emergence of entrepreneurship policy* (pp. 39–59). Cambridge University Press.
Ghaziani, A. (2017). *Sex cultures*. John Wiley & Sons.
Gilbert, M. A. (2009). Defeating bigenderism: Changing gender assumptions in the twenty-first century. *Hypatia*, *24*(3), 93–112.

Habarth, J. M. (2015). Development of the heteronormative attitudes and beliefs scale. *Psychology & Sexuality*, 6(2), 166–188.

Herek, G. M. (2004). Beyond "homophobia": Thinking about sexual stigma and prejudice in the twenty-first century. *Sexuality Research and Social Policy*, 1(2), 6–24.

Hossain, M., Atif, M., Ahmed, A., & Mia, L. (2020). Do LGBT workplace diversity policies create value for firms? *Journal of Business Ethics*, 167, 775–791.

Hudson, W. W., & Ricketts, W. A. (1980). A strategy for the measurement of homophobia. *Journal of Homosexuality*, 5(4), 357–372.

ILGA. (2023). *Annual Review 2023*. International Lesbian and Gay Association.

Kitzinger, C. (2005). Heteronormativity in action: Reproducing the heterosexual nuclear family in afterhours medical calls. *Social Problems*, 52, 477–498.

Leap, W. L., & Boellstorff, T. (2003). *Speaking in queer tongues: Globalization and gay language*. University of Illinois Press

Levitt, H. M., & Ippolito, M. R. (2014). Being transgender: The experience of transgender identity development. *Journal of Homosexuality*, 61(12), 1727–1758.

Marks-Bielska, R., Bielski, S., Pik, K., & Kurowska, K. (2020). The importance of renewable energy sources in Poland's energy mix. *Energies*, 13(18), 4624.

Martel, F. (2018). *Global gay: How gay culture is changing the world*. MIT Press

Mezey, N. J. (2015). *LGBT families*. Sage.

Molotch, N., & Noren, L. (2010). *Toilet: Public restrooms and the politics of sharing*. New York University Press

Monaco, S. (2021). Being bisexual in contemporary Italy: Between stigma and desire of visibility. *International Journal of Sociology and Social Policy*, 41(5/6), 673–688.

Monaco, S. (2022). Practicing urban citizenship in contemporary Italy: Policies, practices and spaces for same-sex parent families. *Fuori Luogo. Rivista di Sociologia del Territorio, Turismo, Tecnologia*, 11(1), 63–76.

Monaco, S. (2024). Breaking the binary: self-narratives of young people in Italy. *Journal of Youth Studies*, 1, 1–15.

Monaco, S., & Corbisiero, F. (2022). Urban sexuality across Europe. Do LGBT neighborhoods matter? *Polish Sociological Review*, 219, 351–366.

Monaco, S., & Nothdurfter, U. (2023). Discovered, made visible, constructed, and left out: LGBTQ+ parenting in the Italian sociological debate. *Journal of Family Studies*, 29(2), 471–488.

Monaco, S., & Pezzella, A. (2022). Coming out in the workplace: A comparative study between Italy and England. *Journal of Gay & Lesbian Mental Health*, 1, 1–20.

Moore, M. R., & Stambolis-Ruhstorfer, M. (2013). LGBT sexuality and families at the start of the twenty-first century. *Annual Review of Sociology*, 39, 491–507.

Myers, K., & Raymond, L. (2010). Elementary school girls and heteronormativity. *Gender & Society*, 24, 167–188.

Nussbaum, M. C. (2010). *From disgust to humanity: Sexual orientation and constitutional law*. Oxford University Press

Parker, K., Graf, N., & Igielnik, R. (2019). *Generation Z looks a lot like millennials on key social and political issues*. Pew Research. Center of Social and Demographic Trends.

Paska, J., Surma, T., Terlikowski, P., & Zagrajek, K. (2020). Electricity generation from renewable energy sources in Poland as a part of commitment to the polish and EU energy policy. *Energies*, 13(16), 4261.

Paternotte, D., & Tremblay, M. (2016). *The Ashgate research companion to lesbian and gay activism*. Routledge.

Perović, L. M., & Kosor, M. M. (2020). The efficiency of universities in achieving sustainable development goals. *Amfiteatru Economic*, 22(54), 516–532.

Puar, J. K. (2007). *Terrorist assemblages: Homonationalism in queer times*. Durham.

Risman, B. J. (2018). *Where the millennials will take us: A new generation wrestles with the gender structure*. Oxford University Press

Sadłowski, A., Wrzaszcz, W., Smędzik-Ambroży, K., Matras-Bolibok, A., Budzyńska, A., Angowski, M., & Mann, S. (2021). Direct payments and sustainable agricultural development – The example of Poland. *Sustainability, 13*(23), 13090.

Scandurra, C., Monaco, S., Dolce, P., & Nothdurfter, U. (2021). Heteronormativity in Italy: Psychometric characteristics of the Italian version of the heteronormative attitudes and beliefs scale. *Sexuality Research and Social Policy, 18*, 637–652.

Serowaniec, M. (2021). Sustainable development policy and renewable energy in Poland. *Energies, 14*(8), 2244.

Shapiro, J. (2012). The law governing LGBT-parent families. *LGBT-Parent Families: Innovations in Research and Implications for Practice, 1*, 291–304.

Stonewall Center. (2018). *Trans report*. YouGov.

Stryker, S., & Whittle, S. (Eds.). (2013). *The transgender studies reader*. Routledge.

Taylor, Y. (2011). Queer presences and absences: Citizenship, community, diversity–or death. *Feminist Theory, 12*(3), 335–341.

Therborn, G. (2014). *The killing fields of inequality*. John Wiley & Sons.

Valelly, R. M. (2012). LGBT politics and American political development. *Annual Review of Political Science, 15*, 313–332.

Warner, M. (1993). *Fear of a queer planet: Queer politics and social theory*. University of Minnesota Press

Weeks, J. (1981). *Sex, politics and society: The regulation of sexuality since 1800*. Longman.

Weinberg, G. (1972). *Society and the healthy homosexual*. Anchor Press Doubleday & Co.

Widawski, K., Krzemińska, A., Zaręba, A., & Dzikowska, A. (2023). A sustainable approach to tourism development in rural areas: The example of Poland. *Agriculture, 13*(10), 2028.

Wittig, M. (1990). *The straight mind and other essays*. Beacon Press.

Wood, J. T. (1997). *Gendered lives: Communication, gender and culture* (2nd ed.). Wadsworth.

Chapter 11

SDG 11. Make Cities and Human Settlements Inclusive, Safe, Resilient, and Sustainable

Abstract

The increasing urbanization has prompted governments and civil society actors worldwide to explore innovative approaches to create sustainable and desirable cities. In this context, the concept of U-cities, or ubiquitous cities, has emerged as a promising model to achieve social, economic, and environmental sustainability while also contributing to the preservation of territorial identity. U-cities represent advanced urban models characterized by the seamless integration of cutting-edge technologies into the urban scenario. Alongside their potential benefits, U-cities also present challenges. The digital divide, which stems from unequal access and usage of digital technologies, can magnify existing societal disparities. Moreover, ensuring the privacy and security of citizens' data in an era of extensive data collection and sharing poses ethical and technical dilemmas. Additionally, the delicate balance between technological advancement and the preservation of cultural identity must be addressed to avoid eroding the authenticity of urban communities. Achieving genuine sustainability requires careful consideration of these challenges and the implementation of policies that empower citizens, promote equitable access to technology, and maintain the intrinsic identity of urban landscapes.

The rapid urbanization of the 21st century is a socio-historical phenomenon of global magnitude that has radically transformed the face of many cities and posed significant challenges to contemporary societies. This process has been driven by various factors, including improved transportation infrastructure, industrialization, economic globalization, and the pursuit of better employment and living opportunities.

The roots of urbanization can be traced back to the social and economic changes of the 19th century. The industrial revolution was one of the main drivers of urbanization, encouraging a swift migration of people from rural areas to cities in search of job opportunities and improved living conditions (Ogburn, 1938). The expansion of factories and manufacturing industries made many cities hubs of production and trade. For example, in the United Kingdom, the city of Manchester was a major center of the textile industry (Lees, 1998). The same situation unfolded in other industrial cities like Birmingham, Liverpool, and London. The industrial urbanization of the 19th century had profound social implications. On one hand, it helped improve living conditions for some workers, by increasing employment opportunities and access to new services and goods (Hobsbawm, 1999). On the other hand, it also brought about serious social problems such as exploitation and precarious working conditions for the proletariat, housing overcrowding, lack of sanitation facilities, and the spread of diseases (Engels, 1845).

New industries and factories required large spaces and infrastructures, leading to the expansion of cities and the transformation of the urban landscape, resulting in the demolition of old structures and the creation of new industrial areas, causing fragmentation and transformation of the urban fabric (Boyer, 1994). In many cities, factories were concentrated in specific areas, creating a clear division between industrial and residential zones. This spatial division contributed to social segregation and the formation of ghettos (Wirth, 1938). It also led to the creation of poor and degraded neighborhoods where living conditions were extremely precarious (Nairn, 1964).

19th-century urbanization also had a significant environmental impact. The growth of cities led to an increased demand for natural resources such as coal and water to power factories and provide energy for homes (Morris, 1983). There were instances of deforestation and destruction of natural ecosystems, and air and water pollution intensified (Cronon, 1991). Moreover, the rapid population growth in cities resulted in the production of large amounts of waste and industrial refuse, posing disposal problems.

Over the succeeding centuries, urbanization has continued with great momentum, fueled by economic growth and population increase. Rural-urban migration has become a global phenomenon, with many countries witnessing an unprecedented expansion of their cities and megalopolises. Many urban centers have developed in a disorganized and chaotic manner, without a long-term vision and the consideration of the social and environmental impacts of new infrastructure and real estate developments. This has led to problems of traffic congestion, air pollution, urban degradation, and poor quality of life for many citizens (Batty, 2008; Lee, 2006). Accelerated urbanization has contributed to social fragmentation and spatial segregation too. While some urban areas thrive with appropriate infrastructure and quality services, others are left behind with outdated infrastructure, deficiencies in public services, and poor housing conditions. In some cases, accelerated urbanization has also resulted in the loss of territorial and cultural identity. Large influxes of people have often accelerated processes of globalization and standardization of cultures, leading to the homogenization of practices (Brunn et al., 2003; White, 2008). According to several authors, the inherent risk in the process of cultural homogenization is the gradual loss of specificity and the marginalization of local traditions (Harvey, 1989). Gentrification and urban revitalization often involve the restructuring of old neighborhoods and the transformation of public spaces into places of consumption and entertainment for tourists and foreigners, at the expense of daily life and the culture of local communities (Sassen, 2011; Zukin, 1987). Urbanization has frequently generated social inequalities and divisions within cities as well. Urban areas have often become sites of contrast between wealthy and impoverished neighborhoods, where access to opportunities and services can vary significantly. This has created social divisions and contributed to issues of marginalization and urban poverty.

In light of these circumstances, addressing the challenges of urbanization has become a key objective for governments and actors in civil society worldwide. SDG 11 aims to make cities and human settlements inclusive, safe, resilient, and sustainable. This can be achieved through the promotion of planning policies that take into account the environmental, social, and economic needs of cities and their inhabitants. This entails promoting social justice and citizen well-being through innovative and ethical solutions.

Within this framework, the concept of U-cities, or ubiquitous cities, emerged. They represent advanced and ambitious city models that are arising as exemplars in contemporary urban literature for pursuing a sustainable urban model. Characterized by a "ubiquitous computing environment" (Jang & Suh, 2010), these cities aim for a radical transformation of urban space through the pervasive integration of cutting-edge technologies such as the Internet of Things (IoT), artificial intelligence (AI), and big data. U-cities foster active citizen participation, promoting inclusion and accessibility through digital platforms and enhanced services.

In terms of environmental sustainability, these cities emphasize energy efficiency and optimized resource management. Indeed, IoT and AI technologies enable citizens to monitor and optimize energy use in real-time, reducing waste and lowering greenhouse gas emissions. With the aid of the collection and analysis of big data, U-cities can optimize water resource management, waste collection, and other activities, contributing to an overall reduction in the environmental impact.

U-cities also have the potential to promote sustainable mobility through intelligent transportation systems, encouraging car and bicycle sharing, and promoting electric vehicles to reduce air pollution and traffic congestion.

On the economic front, U-cities can attract investments and stimulate innovation through state-of-the-art technological infrastructure, improving administrative efficiency and preparing the city for future development. At the same time, U-cities can leverage digital platforms to promote local products and crafts, creating business opportunities for residents and promoting local sustainable development.

U-cities can also be socially sustainable. In fact, they not only represent technological and infrastructural innovation but also offer the opportunity to create more desirable communities by fostering inclusive public spaces, cultural diversity, and universal accessibility. Information and communication technologies are used to facilitate citizen participation in urban planning, so that they can express opinions and needs. Furthermore, the integration of technologies into the social fabric can lead to new forms of engagement, such as participatory digital art and digital storytelling initiatives that reflect local identity and history. Last but not least, digital infrastructure and access to services such as telemedicine, online education, and improved public services can contribute to reducing inequalities and enhancing accessibility for all segments of the population, including the elderly and people with disabilities.

U-city can also act as a driving force to enhance territorial identity, preserving and promoting the unique features that distinguish one place from another. This can be achieved through the thoughtful use of technology to document and share local history, preserve cultural traditions, and celebrate distinctive elements of the territory. For instance, the use of interactive mobile APP can guide citizens and visitors through cultural itineraries that highlight significant historical and artistic sites. Adopting digital architecture and urban design can be in line with existing architectural styles and landscape characteristics, creating a fusion of innovation and authenticity. Territorial identity can also be expressed through projects that use technologies like Augmented Reality (AR) and Virtual Reality (VR) to transform and enhance space utilization. These initiatives not only can engage the community but also have the potential to attract visitors from other places, contributing to the city's economic vitality. Evidently, U-cities represent an advanced perspective compared to the traditional concept of a digital city, as they seek to create an environment where digital technologies are seamlessly integrated into all aspects of urban life. This approach allows continuous and immediate access to information, services, and resources, radically transforming the daily urban experience.

The concept of U-cities emerged in the early 1990s when Mark Weiser proposed an experimental project of this kind at the Xerox Palo Alto Research Center in the United States. The Republic of Korea was the first country to develop national strategies for the development of an urban environment in which digital networks enabled communication among citizens and facilitated easy and immediate access to goods and services (Weiser, 1993). For this reason, Seoul is often considered as one of the most advanced cities in terms of ubiquitous technologies (Anttiroiko, 2013). The city has implemented a smart public transport system, with buses and subways equipped with sensors that allow citizens to monitor real-time schedules, book tickets, and plan routes with ease. Seoul has also developed an intelligent lighting system that adapts to environmental conditions and pedestrian movement, reducing energy consumption and improving street safety.

Similarly, Singapore is considered as one of the best examples of U-cities in the world (Yoo et al., 2016). This achievement has been reached through a holistic approach to the integration of digital technologies and through the adoption of innovative policies to improve citizen quality of life and urban sustainability. One of the fundamental pillars of Singapore's strategy to become a smart city has been the implementation of a vast network of sensors and connected devices that constantly monitor the urban environment and collect real-time data. This sensor infrastructure has been deployed throughout the city to gather information on various aspects of city life. This data is then processed and analyzed to provide valuable insights for urban management. One sector where IoT technology has had a significant impact is traffic management. Thanks to intelligent sensors placed on roads and real-time traffic data, Singapore is able to monitor and manage traffic flow efficiently. This has led to reduced travel times and inconveniences for citizens, as well as a decrease in greenhouse gas emissions from congested traffic. Another area where technology has brought significant benefits is waste collection. Singapore has introduced a fleet of intelligent vehicles equipped with sensors that allow monitoring of waste bin fill levels. This system optimizes waste collection operations, reducing costs and environmental impact. The use of intelligent sensors for waste management has helped reduce the number of overflowing bins, thus avoiding the onset of urban degradation. The city has adopted a range of measures to reduce energy consumption too. The use of intelligent sensors and IoT technology made homes and buildings "smart," allowing citizens to monitor and control the energy consumption of their household devices via smartphones or tablets, thereby optimizing electricity usage, reducing costs, and contributing to carbon emission reduction. Beyond advanced technologies, another key element in Singapore's success as a U-City has been the multi-level governance approach. The Singaporean government has played an active role in encouraging the adoption of smart technologies and in creating an innovation-friendly environment. The private sector has invested in technological innovation and collaborated with the government to implement pilot projects and experimentation initiatives. The Singaporean community has been involved in the decision-making process and priority setting, ensuring that technological solutions address the real needs of citizens.

Over time, collaborative technologies have significantly evolved worldwide. In line with the principles of "hybrid urbanism" (De Lange, 2013), urban space today can be defined not only as an architectural place but also as a setting where social actors interact and engage with urban resources. Specifically, urban space is expanded beyond the confines of cities by models and flows of goods and information that are constantly expanding and transforming (Graham & Aurigi,1997). In recent years, the proliferation of maps, virtual tours, digital squares, and online services has greatly enhanced the public dimension of territorial contexts. "Digital places" extend the space of cities beyond the material dimension, promoting additional forms of solidarity and sociability, and providing alternative public services that facilitate an expanded context of usability.

In this scenario, the COVID-19 pandemic has also brought about positive changes out of expectation. Specifically, an interesting impact brought about by the pandemic on the lives of social actors pertains to the redefinition of the utilization of urban spaces. As a result of forced quarantines, this utilization has unavoidably been largely mediated by new communication technologies. While the virus has compromised the traditional enjoyment of urban centers, it has simultaneously encouraged citizens to engage with digital places. In a period of global emergency, various administrations have initiated the creation or enhancement of digital ecosystems capable of ensuring visits to territories while also stimulating civil and intellectual debates, fostering more active participation in public life, bringing people closer to public administration, and generating a significant shift in the ways urban space is conceived and practiced. In this context, technological innovation has emerged as a useful tool to give full play and help revitalize urban spaces, not only for economic survival but also, and especially, for social and identity-related purposes. In other words, this transformation has not solely been technological. Rather, it has underpinned a different cultural approach that has imparted new forms and meanings to the construction of self-identity, social interactions, the perception of urban spaces, and ways of accessing territorial resources (Monaco, 2021).

Despite the achievements, there are also challenges and critical aspects associated with U-cities.

Digital divides represent one of the primary challenges in implementing intelligent technologies in urban settings. A considerable body of literature on the digital divide highlights how access to and use of digital technologies are unevenly distributed among different income groups and urban communities. Certain citizens may benefit more from intelligent technologies due to broader access to digital devices and services, while others may remain excluded or have only limited access. Studies conducted by authors like Pippa Norris (2001) and Jan van Dijk (2006) have demonstrated that the digital divide is closely related to socioeconomic inequalities. Individuals with higher incomes and greater education are more likely to possess digital devices such as computers and smartphones, and enjoy stable and fast internet connections. Those with lower incomes or limited education may be disadvantaged in terms of access to digital technologies. These digital inequalities can have significant repercussions on civic and political participation. The automation of certain public services, for instance, might reduce the opportunity to interact with public institutions. This could lead to the marginalization of people lacking digital skills or facing difficulties in accessing such services. The digital divide can also influence how intelligent technologies are utilized and adopted by different urban communities. Some neighborhoods or ethnic groups may receive less attention and investment in the implementation of intelligent technologies, so that they would experience greater marginalization and inequality. To overcome these challenges, it is crucial to adopt policies and strategies aimed at reducing the digital divide and ensuring fair access to intelligent technologies. This could involve implementing accessible digital infrastructures in disadvantaged areas, providing training and support to enhance citizens' digital skills, and adopting inclusive policies that consider the needs and desires of all urban communities.

The importance of digital skills becomes particularly evident in light of the "second-level digital divide," a concept referring to inequalities in use of digital technologies among individuals and communities that already have access to basic technological infrastructure (van Deursen & van Dijk, 2019; Van Dijk, 2020). While the traditional digital divide primarily focused on access to internet connections and technologies, the second-level digital divide goes beyond, highlighting differences in the effective and meaningful use of digital technologies. Individuals with advanced digital skills have greater opportunities to actively participate in the digital society, access resources and information, enhance their productivity, and make more informed decisions. Conversely, those with limited or absent digital skills are at risk of being marginalized and disadvantaged in an increasingly connected and digitized world. The second-level digital divide can be caused by various factors, including a lack of access to adequate digital skills training, a lack of awareness of the opportunities and benefits of digital technologies, and insecurity in using technologies due to a lack of familiarity or experience.

Concerns related to citizens' privacy also exist. With the enormous proliferation of sensors and connected devices in the urban environment, an unprecedented collection of personal data is taking place, making secure and responsible management of this sensitive information crucial. The vastness and variety of collected data necessitate sophisticated security measures to avoid breaches, hacking, or unauthorized access. The vulnerability of computer systems and the possibility of cyberattacks can also jeopardize the security of personal data and urban systems, creating major risks for citizens and the infrastructure itself. Furthermore, the sharing and use of data among different public and private entities can raise ethical concerns. It is essential to ensure that collected data are used only for legitimate purposes and they are adequately anonymized to protect individuals' identities. Transparency regarding data usage and the opportunity for citizens to provide informed consent on the collection and processing of their information are still open challenges and represent areas where further reflection is needed to ensure trust in data management in cities (Yu, 2016). Awareness and information campaigns can help citizens understand the risks and benefits of intelligent technologies and make them aware of their rights in personal data management. Citizens should be involved in the decision-making process regarding data usage in smart cities and they should gain the opportunity to express their opinions and concerns.

The final critical aspect concerns the balance between technological development and the preservation of cultural identity and the urban environment. The unsustainable introduction of advanced and innovative technologies in cities can lead to significant changes in urban appearance and structure. These changes may bring advantages such as greater efficiency, accessibility, and sustainability, but they can also pose the risk of losing authenticity and the distinctive characteristics of urban communities. When discussing new technologies for cities, attention is often focused on technological aspects, without giving due consideration to the impacts that technologies can have on territorial identity. Cities are the result of a development and growth process that has taken place over centuries. Each city has its own history, culture, and unique identity. Historical buildings, streets, places of worship, parks, and monuments are all elements that contribute to defining a city's identity and passing its history and culture to future generations. The development of U-cities must not underestimate the risk that these elements may be sacrificed in favor of uniform and homogeneous modernization.

A positive example of how cities can balance technological development with the preservation of cultural identity is the city of Amsterdam. Amsterdam has been recognized as one of the most advanced smart cities in the world, while at the same time, it succeeds in preserving its rich history and culture. The city has invested in innovative technologies to improve mobility, energy efficiency, and air quality, but it has also preserved its architectural heritage and promoted local culture and traditions. This balanced approach has allowed Amsterdam to become a technological leader while remaining a unique and charming place to visit (Baron et al., 2012).

In cities located in disadvantaged areas of the world, characterized by rapid population growth, political and economic instability, poverty, and vulnerability, different challenges arise in improving quality of life and urban development. These cities often suffer from inadequate infrastructure, lack of resources, and are vulnerable to extreme weather events and natural disasters. Technological solutions, while potentially helpful, may be inaccessible or inapplicable due to high costs, lack of technical skills, and inadequate infrastructure. An example of a city facing such challenges is Mumbai, India. It is one of the largest and most densely populated cities in the world, with over 20 million inhabitants. The metropolis grapples with serious issues such as air pollution, traffic congestion, housing shortages, and limited access to clean water. These issues present limitations to the implementation of advanced technologies that could enhance citizens' quality of life and the efficiency of urban infrastructure (Kar et al., 2017).

In situations like these, the adoption of sustainable urban development policies and strategies becomes essential to address the challenges of population growth and poverty. These policies should encompass targeted investments not only in infrastructure improvement but also in the provision of environmental and social policies and essential services. Furthermore, effective and inclusive governance is crucial to ensure that policies and initiatives respond to the needs and aspirations of the local population.

References

Anttiroiko, A. V. (2013). U-cities reshaping our future: Reflections on ubiquitous infrastructure as an enabler of smart urban development. *AI & Society*, *28*, 491–507.

Baron, G., Brinkman, J., & Wenzler, I. (2012). Supporting sustainability through smart infrastructures: The case for the city of Amsterdam. *International Journal of Critical Infrastructures*, *8*(2–3), 169–177.

Batty, M. (2008). The size, scale, and shape of cities. *Science*, *319*(5864), 769–771.

Boyer, M. C. (1994). *The city of collective memory: Its historical imagery and architectural entertainments*. MIT Press.

Brunn, S. D., Williams, J. F., & Zeigler, D. J. (Eds.) (2003). *Cities of the world: World regional urban development*. Rowman & Littlefield.

Cronon, W. (1991). *Nature's metropolis: Chicago and the Great West*. W. W. Norton & Company.

De Lange, M. (2013). The smart city you love to hate: Exploring the role of affect in hybrid urbanism. In D. Charitos, I. Theona, D. Dragona, & H. Rizopoulos (Eds.), *The Hybrid City II* (pp. 77–84). University Research Institute of Applied Communication.

Engels, F. (1845). *The condition of the working class in England*. Panther Edition.

Graham, S., & Aurigi, A. (1997). Virtual cities, social polarization and the crisis in urban public. *Journal of Urban Technology*, *4*(1), 19–52.

Harvey, D. (1989). From managerialism to entrepreneurialism: The transformation in urban governance in late capitalism. *Geografiska Annaler: Series B, Human Geography*, *71*(1), 3–17.

Hobsbawm, E. J. (1999). *Industry and Empire: From 1750 to the Present Day*. The New Press.

Jang, M., & Suh, S. T. (2010). U-city: New trends of urban planning in Korea based on pervasive and ubiquitous geotechnology and geoinformation. In *AA.VV. Computational Science and Its Applications–ICCSA 2010: International Conference*, Fukuoka, Japan, March 23-26, 2010, Proceedings, Part I 10. Springer Berlin Heidelberg.

Kar, A. K., Gupta, M. P., Ilavarasan, P. V., & Dwivedi, Y. K. (Eds.) (2017). *Advances in smart cities: Smarter people, governance, and solutions*. CRC Press.

Lee, R. L. (2006). Reinventing modernity: Reflexive modernization vs liquid modernity vs multiple modernities. *European Journal of Social Theory*, *9*(3), 355–368.

Lees, L. H. (1998). *The solidarities of strangers: The English poor laws and the people, 1700-1948*. Cambridge University Press.

Monaco, S. (2021). *Tourism, safety and COVID-19: Security, digitization and tourist behaviour*. Routledge.

Morris, R. J. (1983). Voluntary societies and British urban elites, 1780–1850: An analysis. *The Historical Journal*, *26*(1), 95–118.

Nairn, T. (1964). The English working class. *New Left Review*, *24*, 43–57.

Norris, P. (2001). *Digital divide: Civic engagement, information poverty, and the Internet worldwide*. Cambridge University Press.

Ogburn, W. F. (1938). Technology and sociology. *Social Forces*, *17*(1), 1–8.

Sassen, S. (2011). *The global city: New York, London, Tokyo*. Princeton University Press.

van Deursen, A. J., & van Dijk, J. A. (2019). The first-level digital divide shifts from inequalities in physical access to inequalities in material access. *New Media & Society*, *21*(2), 354–375.

Van Dijk, J. (2020). *The digital divide*. John Wiley & Sons.

Van Dijk, J. A. (2006). Digital divide research, achievements and shortcomings. *Poetics*, *34*(4-5), 221–235.

Weiser, M. (1993). Hot topics-ubiquitous computing. *Computer*, *26*(10), 71–72.

White, E. R. (2008). *Cities of the world: World regional urban development*. Rowman & Littlefield.

Wirth, L. (1938). Urbanism as a way of life. *American Journal of Sociology*, *44*(1), 1–24.

Yoo, J. S., Min, K. J., Jeong, S. H., & Shin, D. B. (2016). Inter-ministerial collaboration to utilize CCTV video service operated by U-City center of South Korea. *Spatial Information Research*, *24*, 389–400.

Yu, S. (2016). Big privacy: Challenges and opportunities of privacy study in the age of big data. *IEEE*, *4*, 2751–2763.

Zukin, S. (1987). Gentrification: Culture and capital in the urban core. *Annual Review of Sociology*, *13*(1), 129–147.

Chapter 12

SDG 12. Ensure Sustainable Consumption and Production Patterns

Abstract

This chapter explores how the dominance of a profit-oriented "take-use-dispose" economic model presents challenges to sustainable development. Globalization's role in accelerating consumerism is analyzed, along with its potential to exacerbate social inequalities, concentrating economic power within multinational corporations. The environmental consequences of globalization include overexploitation and resource depletion, highlighting the need for balanced and responsible approaches to global governance. The chapter also investigates the impact of globalization on territorial identities, ranging from the risk of cultural homogenization to the emergence of hybrid cultural forms. Finally, it considers diverse perspectives on managing globalization and consumerism's effects.

The culture of consumerism has deep roots, dating back to the era of the industrial revolution and the economic boom of the 20th century. During this period, the production of consumer goods has exponentially increased, leading to greater availability and accessibility of products for people. This phenomenon has fueled the so-called culture of consumerism, wherein the possession of material goods is seen as a status symbol and a source of happiness and personal satisfaction (Kasser, 2003). This culture promotes a desire to constantly acquire new material possessions, driving individuals to buy, consume, and discard incessantly. Over time, advertising and media have taken on an increasingly central role in this process, employing persuasive strategies to create artificial desires and needs in consumers.

In recent decades, the culture of consumerism has spread and intensified worldwide due to the phenomenon of globalization. Globalization is a complex process that has transformed the world into a "global village" (McLuhan & Powers, 1992), facilitating the movement of people, goods, information, and ideas. This process has made consumer products from around the world easily accessible and desirable to a growing number of people, creating an interconnected and interdependent global market.

Manuel Castells (1989) has contributed to understanding the impact of globalization-induced consumerism on the social and economic sustainability of cities, starting from an analysis of changes in urban structure. The author highlighted how consumerism has increased inequality and amplified marginalization, affecting the most vulnerable individuals and endangering the sustainability of cities. Castells emphasized the importance of urban policies that promote democratic participation, social equity, and environmental protection, in order to create sustainable and more inclusive cities.

Several researchers have conducted in-depth analyses of consumption patterns, motivations driving consumer choices, and social dynamics influencing consumption behaviors. One of the leading contributors is Juliet Schor (2010), who has offered important insights into the culture of consumerism and the possibilities of transitioning to more sustainable forms of consumption. After underscoring how consumerism has contributed to environmental and social unsustainability, fueling a growing demand for material goods and a lifestyle based on accumulation and competitiveness, the author argued that a transition to more sustainable consumption forms has become necessary. Schor's work has encouraged a culture of responsible consumption, oriented towards quality rather than quantity of material goods. Her perspective suggests the importance of assessing well-being in terms of immaterial goods, such as leisure time, social relationships, and community engagement. Schor has also advocated for the adoption of economic models based on sharing and collaboration, such as collaborative consumption and resource sharing, which can reduce consumption and promote sustainability.

Other scholars have contributed to the field of sustainable consumption as well, exploring themes such as social influence on consumption behaviors and the role of public policies in promoting more sustainable consumption patterns. In this field, some studies (Higgs, 2015; Lee et al., 2009; Lin & Niu, 2018) have highlighted how people's consumption choices are often influenced by the expectations and practices of other members of society, underscoring the importance of promoting social norms that favor sustainable consumption on a broader societal level.

The analysis of sustainable consumption has also extended to the realm of public policies. Some scholars have examined the role of regulatory policies, economic incentives, and awareness campaigns in promoting more sustainable consumption behaviors. For instance, Tim Jackson (2009) investigated public policies that can facilitate a transition towards a low-impact environmental society. Jackson argued that public policies must address not only economic aspects but also social and environmental ones, in order to promote a sustainable development model.

Within the field of environmental sociology, which focuses on the interactions between humans and the natural environment, some studies have been conducted with the aim of investigating how social relationships, cultural practices, and power structures influence resource management and environmental impact. Within this framework, Allan Schnaiberg theorized the concept of the "treadmill of production" (1980), highlighting how economic and growth logics have contributed to unsustainable resource consumption. The concept of the "treadmill of production" refers to a vicious cycle in which industrial society continues to generate insatiable demand for goods, stimulated by the relentless pursuit of profit and the need to sustain the market economy. This critical approach underscores the importance of in-depth analysis of social and economic dynamics that guide our relationship with the environment.

This perspective partly aligns with the viewpoint of ecological economist Herman Daly (2014), who emphasized the need for a stable and sustainable economy operating within the planet's limits, promoting responsible resource utilization, and paying attention to intergenerational justice.

Significant contribution has also been provided by Elinor Ostrom (1990) through her analysis of common pool resources and her proposals of solutions based on collective resource management. Her work focused on the importance of understanding how local communities can sustainably manage common resources. The author challenged the prevailing idea that common resources would inevitably succumb to selfish individual interests. She demonstrated that communities can develop institutions and rules that promote sustainable resource management, avoiding degradation and collapse. Her research was based on empirical case studies conducted in various parts of the world, highlighting the effectiveness of collective management practices. Ostrom (2009) also explored the diversity of existing institutions to address the challenges of common resource management. She emphasized how institutions are a reflection of territorial identity when they are adapted to local conditions and reflect the experiences and knowledge of the involved communities. She underscored the importance of understanding institutional diversity to develop sustainable solutions suitable for specific contexts.

Joseph Stiglitz (2007) argued that the model of development based on unchecked consumption and profit-seeking at the expense of the genuine needs of the population and the environment has exacerbated economic and social inequalities. The culture of consumerism has had severe consequences on environmental sustainability and quality of life, as the growing consumption of natural resources to produce consumer goods has led to rapid exploitation of the planet's resources. Similarly, the production and transportation of consumer goods have significantly contributed to air, water, and soil pollution, with serious implications for the environment and human health. It is evident that the culture of consumerism has generated a society and an economy centered on accumulation and waste. The production and intensive use of consumer goods have resulted in massive waste production, much of which is non-biodegradable and ends up in landfills or oceans, damaging natural ecosystems.

SDG 12 aims to curb this trend, promoting more responsible and resource-efficient consumption and production practices, with a particular focus on valuing local resources. Achieving this goal entails a radical shift in patterns of industrial and agricultural production, energy supply, transportation, and household and business consumption. Concrete actions that can be taken to promote sustainable consumption and production models include adopting clean and low-impact environmental technologies, implementing energy efficiency policies, promoting responsible and circular consumption patterns, and educating citizens about sustainable practices.

Amid a growing recognition of the need to adopt policies and strategies that address the challenges posed by the dominant consumption and production model, many cities are demonstrating concrete commitment to sustainable development. These efforts are manifested through investments in waste sorting infrastructure, recycling, and composting. Recycling is a crucial practice for reducing the environmental impact of solid waste, as it allows for the recovery and reuse of valuable materials, preventing them from ending up in landfills or polluting the surrounding environment. Cities are implementing waste collection systems and dedicated collection points, promoting awareness campaigns to educate citizens about the importance of recycling, and offering incentives to encourage active participation in recycling practices.

A virtuous example of success in the recycling sector has been implemented in San Francisco, USA. The city initiated a recycling program in 2009 that actively engaged citizens through public education programs and the distribution of recycling and composting containers. As a result of these initiatives, San Francisco has maintained an 80% recycling rate since 2020 (Dorr et al., 2023). This success demonstrates how a combination of proactive policies and community involvement can lead to significant waste reduction and sustainability goals.

In addition to recycling, various measures to reduce the use of single-use plastics have been adopted, as it is one of the major environmental pollutants threatening marine and terrestrial ecosystems. In particular, after the pandemic crisis, the European Union introduced Directive EU 2019/904, known as the SUP (Single-Use Plastics) Directive, which bans the use of certain single-use plastic products for which alternatives are available in the market. The directive aims to reduce plastic waste, especially in water bodies, by at least 50% by 2025 and 80% by 2030 (Aristei et al., 2020). Outside of Europe, a successful example in the fight against single-use plastics has been recorded in Vancouver, Canada. The city banned the use of plastic straws and polystyrene containers in 2019, becoming the first Canadian city to adopt this policy. This ban has significantly reduced the amount of single-use plastic produced and discarded, decreasing the environmental impact on waterways and wildlife. Vancouver has also adopted policies to promote the use of reusable containers and has established water bottle refill stations throughout the city, encouraging citizens to opt for sustainable alternatives (Pettipas et al., 2016).

In addition to recycling and reducing single-use plastics, sustainable consumption and production models through circular economy initiatives are gaining momentum. The circular economy can be considered an alternative to the linear model of consumption and production. It is based on the reduction, reuse, recycling, and repair of materials and products, rather than their production and disposal. This approach aims to create a virtuous cycle in which materials and products are kept in use for as long as possible, thus reducing the need for new resources and waste production (Geisendorf & Pietrulla, 2018). Many companies are adopting circular economy strategies to reduce the environmental impact of their activities and meet the growing demand from environmentally conscious consumers. For instance, many companies are introducing the concept of "products as services," where consumers rent or share products instead of purchasing them, thereby reducing the need for new production and the amount of generated waste.

The proliferation of technologies and the use of social platforms have emphasized, consolidated, and made more visible a contemporary version of reciprocity, an economic model centered not so much on ownership but on sharing, less focused on the purchase of goods and services and more on their use (Hopkinson et al., 2018; Lüdeke-Freund et al., 2019; Urbinati et al., 2017). Online platforms, acting as digital intermediaries, over the course of a decade have contributed to the spread of a diverse range of services, enabling peer-to-peer exchange practices (Schor & Attwood-Charles, 2017), and extracting value from the resources made available by users.

According to Rachel Botsman (2017), younger generations have implicitly introduced a "culture of we" through their behaviors, which has complemented (and in part surpassed) a more individualistic way of thinking and acting that characterized previous generations. The author believes that the spread of the concept of sharing has been rapidly growing thanks to technology, which has made collaboration possible through constant network connectivity. The main difference between contemporary reciprocity and that of the past is precisely that the network within which gifts, exchanges, and loans occur is no longer limited to friends, relatives, neighbors, and acquaintances, but is much more global. Increasing connectivity, propagated by online social network platforms, allows people to share access to products and services among each other. Online platforms allow users to make a variety of arrangements, which are mostly entered into amongst individuals who do not know each other personally but share similar goals.

This phenomenon was defined in a Forbes article as "NOwnership" (Morgan, 2019), to emphasize the decreasing interest shown by younger generations in owning various consumer goods. This trend has even prompted jurists Aaron Perzanowski and Jason Schultz to speak of the "End of Ownership" (2016). Nowadays there is a subscription for everything, which can be shared with both known and unknown people: From sports to on-demand cinema. Tien Tzuo, CEO of Zuora, has defined this as the "Subscription Economy," where people increasingly prefer subscription or rental over purchase: What people own matters less than what people do, through a series of experiences.

Cities are also contributing to the spread of circular economy practices. A virtuous example has been established in Amsterdam, Netherlands. The city launched the Amsterdam Circular Strategy 2020–2025, with the goal of becoming a fully circular city by 2050 (Calisto Friant et al., 2023). The project involves companies, public institutions, and citizens in transitioning to a circular economy, promoting innovation and collaboration among different stakeholders. The municipal administration has encouraged the use of recycled materials and the design of modular and durable products, favoring reuse and recycling. The city is also exploring new performance-based business models, where companies sell services rather than products, promoting repair and product maintenance.

Even in disadvantaged regions of the world, where poverty and inadequate infrastructure pose significant obstacles to urban sustainability, there are examples of positive initiatives. For instance, in some cities in Sub-Saharan Africa, circular economy projects have been launched to reduce waste and maximize the use of available resources. These projects involve the local population in material recovery and recycling, creating employment and business opportunities for communities (Mutezo & Mulopo, 2021). Such endeavors not only contribute to environmental sustainability but also play a crucial role in fostering a sense of territorial identity in various ways. Firstly, by promoting recycling and responsible material recovery, these initiatives help minimize the environmental impact of waste disposal, reducing pollution and preserving natural resources. Additionally, the emphasis on maximizing the use of available resources aligns with principles of sustainable development, ensuring that communities can meet their present needs without compromising the ability of future generations to meet theirs. Moreover, these initiatives play a crucial role in fostering a sense of community. By actively involving the local population in material recovery and recycling processes, such projects empower community members to take ownership of their environmental responsibilities. This engagement creates a shared sense of purpose and pride, as individuals witness the positive impact of their collective efforts on the local environment. The creation of employment and business opportunities within the communities further strengthens the fabric of territorial identity. When residents are directly involved in sustainable practices, they gain economic benefits and simultaneously nurture a deep connection to the region. This connection forms the basis for a strong local identity, as community members become stewards of their environment and active participants in the sustainable development of their surroundings. The skills and knowledge acquired through participation in circular economy projects contribute to the overall resilience of the community too, fostering a spirit of cooperation and preparedness for future challenges. To promote sustainable policies and the circular economy in the Sub-Saharan area, regional financial institutions such as the African Development Bank and governments continue to fund more scalable technologies and adopt "intentional" regulations guided by circular principles and a just transition.

Despite some progress made in promoting sustainable consumption and production models in cities, there are still substantial challenges that need to be addressed for a true transformation towards sustainability. A key obstacle is the status quo of the dominant economic model, characterized by a production and consumption system based on a "take-use-dispose" mentality that tends to prioritize immediate profit and unsustainable exploitation of natural resources (Jackson, 2016). This model is strongly supported by entrenched economic interests and political powers, which often resist change and policies that threaten their profits and positions of power.

Furthermore, in the realm of science, several scholars argue that the culture of consumerism has provided in-depth analyses of how globalization, if not carefully managed, can compromise the pursuit of sustainable development goals in social, economic, and environmental realms (Dalby, 2021; Sabir & Gorus, 2019; Schor, 2005). From a social perspective, many theorists and scholars have extensively analyzed how the process of globalization can influence the distribution of resources, opportunities, and power within societies (Białas, 2009; Yan & Jianqiao, 2019). This critical dimension of globalization is particularly relevant in the context of the sustainable development debate, as it directly impacts societies' ability to achieve a balance among economic well-being, social justice, and environmental respect. Furthermore, the concept of "surveillance capitalism," introduced by Shoshana Zuboff (2015), provides additional insights into the relationship between globalization and social inequalities. In her work, the author explored how large technology companies collect and exploit consumers' personal data for economic purposes, influencing the dynamics of economic and social power. This phenomenon can lead to increased inequalities, as technology companies amass immense wealth through data control, while consumers may be at risk of manipulation and exploitation.

Looking at the economic dimension, some scholars have highlighted how globalization has often led to the concentration of economic power in the hands of a few large multinational corporations (Cantwell & Janne, 2000; Yeganeh, 2019). This phenomenon can result in a lack of control and regulation, leading to resource and human exploitation for profit. Additionally, the race to lower production costs can lead to greater environmental degradation and a reduction in decent working conditions.

Environmentally, globalization can trigger competition for supplies and resources, leading to overexploitation and depletion of natural resources in the end. Global demand for goods and resources can drive nations to exploit their resources without adequately considering long-term environmental impacts. Large-scale production and the global supply chain can increase ecological impact through energy consumption, greenhouse gas emissions, and waste production (Spencer, 2014).

It is important to note that the described threats do not imply that globalization is inherently negative or should be avoided. There is a need for a balanced and responsible approach to globalization that takes into account its complex and multifaceted implications. Efforts to address these threats require more effective global governance and regulatory mechanisms that ensure globalization occurs in line with principles of equity, social justice, and ecological responsibility.

A similar reasoning can be applied to the discussion surrounding the preservation of territorial identities. One of the risks inherent in globalization is the potential loss of some distinctive elements. This perspective is based on the assumption that globalization processes are bringing about innovation on multiple levels, not only altering local cultures but also converging them toward a shared model. The more critical approach envisions the extreme consequence of erasing local traditions and differences in favor of a homogenized global culture (Scott, 2013). However, this radical view overlooks two elements: The first is the changeable nature of territorial identities, which are subject to transformation. Cultural identity transformation can occur when it is territorially desired. Therefore, change, even in the direction of globalization, is attainable as long as it is not imposed but embraced by the local population. The second is that each culture contains elements deeply rooted and distinctive, making them largely resistant to global processes. Globalization, therefore, should be viewed as a phenomenon that stimulates change but does not interfere with the internal structure of identity. A more moderate perspective suggests that globalization is fostering the development of cultural elements that are repeated across different civilizations, while also maintaining distinct characteristics that continue to exist. To clarify this process of cultural convergence, George Ritzer (1996) coined the term "McDonaldization," referring to how certain major chains (like McDonald's in America) have become globally widespread while originating from a different cultural context, presenting the same identical traits. The same can be applied to other fast-food giants, large shopping centers, or specific clothing or high-tech chains that, despite emerging from specific territorial and cultural contexts, replicate their formulas elsewhere without adapting to the identity traits of the territories in which they settle in. According to Ritzer, proposals that are more likely to spread globally are those that are "empty," meaning that they do not offer significant content but, on the contrary, lack substance and value. In this sense, globalization concerns products, goods, and services that neither add nor subtract anything from territory, representing elements that at most offer an alternative but do not truly make a difference.

In line with Samuel Huntington's perspective (1993), territorial identities which he refers to as "civilizations," are based on specific worldviews, reference values, customs, and ways of relating. These civilizations can span multiple states and are primarily founded on ethnic characteristics and shared religion. The history of the world can be seen as the sum of the histories of individual civilizations, each representing a distinct entity. According to Huntington's historical reconstruction, for about 3,000 years (from 1500 BCE to 1500 CE), each civilization lived without coming into contact with others. Improvements in navigation technology and the development of military power changed the whole situation, driving Western civilization to attempt to dominate others, eventually asserting global dominance in the 19th century. However, the movements of rebellion and self-determination that have occurred since the end of World War I, as well as the current conflicts among diverse cultures, even among territorially close peoples, testify to the enduring strength of local identities. Huntington suggests that the rejection of imposed modernization and Westernization by many civilizations will contribute to the decline of the West, that is yet evident in the United States. The growing multiculturalism in North American countries is described as an internal threat, diminishing Western civilization both in quantity and quality to accommodate other cultures. Looking ahead, the weakened Western civilization may be offset by the rise of the Eastern world, that is already demonstrating economic prowess, and a resurgence of Islam. Huntington argues that Islam, historically associated with violence, could become more assertive. If the West, which has employed various policies to control Islamic power, continues to decline, there may be a resurgence of violence from Islam, fueled by demographic growth expanding into new territories. The author suggests that the only effective strategy to prevent the decline of Western culture is a reaffirmation of its identity, achieved through a departure from openness and multiculturalism.

About globalization, another perspective is about cultural hybridization. It suggests that ongoing and enduring interactions among different cultures are leading to a blending that creates new, hybrid cultural forms emerging from intersections among diverse realities. This outlook views globalization positively, considering it a phenomenon capable of fostering dialogue, knowledge, and mutual integration. Mike Featherstone (1995), for instance, argued that the term "global" has often been incorrectly linked with homogenization. He emphasized that history has consistently shown that globalization can spark movements of resistance and opposition, illustrating that each culture decides whether, how, and to what extent they allow to be influenced by others or choose to build barriers against perceived foreign elements. Featherstone contended that when discussing globalization, one should not refer to the establishment of a single dominant cultural worldview extending globally. Instead, globalization should be seen as a continuous and ongoing set of exchanges and interconnections among different subjects, groups, and societies. At the core of this idea, there is the concept of "glocalization," which highlights the intertwining of global and local dimensions, producing specific forms in each social context based on the level of openness and willingness to change. It is marked by innovation, with key roles played by individuals and social groups (Robertson, 1992). These actors and groups don't just accept change, but they actively work together and may even promote it when needed. One effect of glocalization is "creolization," where a blend of languages or cultures from various sources emerges.

References

Aristei, L., Villani, L., & Ricciardi, W. (2020). Directive 2019/904/EU. The need to raise awareness on plastic misuse and consequences on health. *European Journal of Public Health*, 30(5), 166–138.

Białas, S. (2009). Power distance as a determinant of relations between managers and employees in the enterprises with foreign capital. *Journal of Intercultural Management*, 1(2), 105–115.

Botsman, R. (2017). *Who can you trust?: How technology brought us together–and why it could drive us apart*. Penguin UK.

Calisto Friant, M., Reid, K., Boesler, P., Vermeulen, W. J., & Salomone, R. (2023). Sustainable circular cities? Analysing urban circular economy policies in Amsterdam, Glasgow, and Copenhagen. *Local Environment*, 1, 1–39.

Cantwell, J., & Janne, O. (2000). The role of multinational corporations and national states in the globalization of innovatory capacity: The European perspective. *Technology Analysis & Strategic Management*, 12(2), 243–262.

Castells, M. (1989). *The informational city: Information technology, economic restructuring, and the urban-regional process*. Blackwell.

Dalby, S. (2021). Unsustainable borders: Globalization in a climate-disrupted world. *Borders in Globalization Review*, 2(2), 26–37.

Daly, H. E. (2014). *Beyond growth: The economics of sustainable development*. Beacon Press.

Dorr, E., Goldstein, B., Aubry, C., Gabrielle, B., & Horvath, A. (2023). Life cycle assessment of eight urban farms and community gardens in France and California. *Resources, Conservation and Recycling, 192*, 106921.
Featherstone, M. (1995). Undoing culture: Globalization, postmodernism and identity. *Undoing Culture, 1*, 1–192.
Geisendorf, S., & Pietrulla, F. (2018). The circular economy and circular economic concepts – A literature analysis and redefinition. *Thunderbird International Business Review, 60*(5), 771–782.
Higgs, S. (2015). Social norms and their influence on eating behaviours. *Appetite, 86*, 38–44.
Hopkinson, P., Zils, M., Hawkins, P., & Roper, S. (2018). Managing a complex global circular economy business model: Opportunities and challenges. *California Management Review, 60*(3), 71–94.
Jackson, T. (2009). *Prosperity without growth: Economics for a finite planet*. Routledge.
Jackson, T. (2016). *Prosperity without growth: Foundations for the economy of tomorrow*. Taylor & Francis.
Kasser, T. (2003). *The high price of materialism*. MIT Press.
Lee, R., Murphy, J., & Neale, L. (2009). The interactions of consumption characteristics on social norms. *Journal of Consumer Marketing, 26*(4), 277–285.
Lin, S. T., & Niu, H. J. (2018). Green consumption: Environmental knowledge, environmental consciousness, social norms, and purchasing behavior. *Business Strategy and the Environment, 27*(8), 1679–1688.
Lüdeke-Freund, F., Gold, S., & Bocken, N. M. (2019). A review and typology of circular economy business model patterns. *Journal of Industrial Ecology, 23*(1), 36–61.
McLuhan, M., & Powers, B. R. (1992). *The global village: Transformations in world life and media in the 21st century*. Oxford University Press.
Morgan, B. (2019). No ownership, no problem: An updated look at why millennials value experiences over owning things. *Forbes*, January, 2.
Mutezo, G., & Mulopo, J. (2021). A review of Africa's transition from fossil fuels to renewable energy using circular economy principles. *Renewable and Sustainable Energy Reviews, 137*, 110609.
Ostrom, E. (1990). *Governing the commons: The evolution of institutions for collective action*. Cambridge University Press.
Ostrom, E. (2009). *Understanding institutional diversity*. Princeton University Press.
Perzanowski, A., & Schultz, J. (2016). *The end of ownership: Personal property in the digital economy*. MIT Press.
Pettipas, S., Bernier, M., & Walker, T. R. (2016). A Canadian policy framework to mitigate plastic marine pollution. *Marine Policy, 68*, 117–122.
Ritzer, G. (1996). The McDonaldization thesis: Is expansion inevitable? *International Sociology, 11*(3), 291–308.
Robertson, R. (1992). *Globalization: Social theory and global culture*. Sage.
Sabir, S., & Gorus, M. S. (2019). The impact of globalization on ecological footprint: Empirical evidence from the South Asian countries. *Environmental Science and Pollution Research, 26*, 33387–33398.
Samuel, H. (1993). The clash of civilizations. *Foreign Affairs, 72*(3), 22–49.
Schnaiberg, A. (1980). *The environment: From surplus to scarcity*. Oxford University Press.
Schor, J. (2010). *Plenitude: The new economics of true wealth*. Penguin Press.
Schor, J. B. (2005). Prices and quantities: Unsustainable consumption and the global economy. *Ecological Economics, 55*(3), 309–320.
Schor, J. B., & Attwood-Charles, W. (2017). The "sharing" economy: Labor, inequality, and social connection on for-profit platforms. *Sociology Compass, 11*(8), e12493.
Scott, A. (Ed.). (2013). *The limits of globalization*. Routledge.

Spencer, J. H. (2014). *Globalization and urbanization: The global urban ecosystem*. Rowman & Littlefield.
Stiglitz, J. E. (2007). *Making globalization work*. WW Norton & Company.
Urbinati, A., Chiaroni, D., & Chiesa, V. (2017). Towards a new taxonomy of circular economy business models. *Journal of Cleaner Production, 168*, 487–498.
Yan, B., & Jianqiao, L. (2019). Power distance: A literature review and prospect. *Management Review, 31*(3), 178.
Yeganeh, H. (2019). A critical examination of the social impacts of large multinational corporations in the age of globalization. *Critical Perspectives on International Business, 16*(3), 193–208.
Zuboff, S. (2015). Big other: Surveillance capitalism and the prospects of an information civilization. *Journal of Information Technology, 30*(1), 75–89.

Chapter 13

SDG 13. Take Urgent Action to Combat Climate Change and Its Impacts

Abstract

While climate change mitigation policies are indispensable for addressing global environmental crises, the chapter prompts that their implementation should account for the intricate tapestry of territorial identities. The solution lies in a balanced approach that harmonizes emission reduction targets with the preservation of cultural heritage and local customs. The chapter concludes by warning against top-down imposition of policies, as this could jeopardize community autonomy and engender mistrust. Given the delicate balance between climate concerns and cultural preservation, a path forward emerges, that upholds the integrity of desirable territorial development.

Climate change has become one of the most urgent global challenges of our time, with serious implications for both the natural environment and human society (Beck, 1992; Giddens, 2009; Latour, 2018; Urry, 2011). As highlighted during COP28, 2023 marked the warmest year ever recorded. Parts of Southern Europe reached nearly 30°C in mid-December, underscoring the increasing significance of climate adaptation. The climate crisis is predominantly caused by the increase in greenhouse gas emissions primarily due to human activities such as the use of fossil fuels, industry, and intensive agriculture. These greenhouse gases, by trapping heat in the atmosphere, contribute to rising global temperatures and changes in weather and climate patterns.

Climate change has a wide range of impacts on various sectors and systems. They can manifest through extreme weather events like storms, floods, droughts, and wildfires, but also through long-term changes such as sea level rise, glacier melting, and biodiversity loss. These impacts can vary significantly from region to region and can affect different human activities such as agriculture, fishing, tourism, and food security.

Vulnerable and less developed communities and territories are often the victims most affected by the impacts of climate change, as they have fewer resources to adapt and address the challenges. This can lead to a vicious cycle where climate change exacerbates existing social and economic inequalities, further endangering the identity and resilience of the most fragile territories. For example, local communities heavily reliant on natural resources, such as those in coastal areas or rural regions, may face greater challenges due to climate alterations and natural resource erosion. Additionally, territories with fewer financial resources or technological capabilities might face greater challenges in mitigating the negative effects of climate change and engaging actively in the transition toward a more sustainable economy.

The emergence of scientific consensus on climate change has led to an increasing recognition of the need for systematic change to address the root causes of this crisis. To ensure a sustainable future, the transition to sustainability must be guided by justice, aiming to ensure equity for all, especially for territories, economies, and people most vulnerable to the impacts of climate change (Billi et al., 2022; Galgóczi, 2020; Monaco, 2022; Yan, 2021). From a sociological perspective, justice refers to the fair distribution of resources, opportunities, and benefits within a society. This implies a critical evaluation of the social, economic, and political mechanisms that create and distribute advantages and disadvantages among individuals and groups (Rawls, 1971). Sociologists conceive a range of methods and dimensions to measure the degree of achieved or threatened justice in a society, including the analysis of economic inequalities, political power, social inclusion, cultural identity, among others (Fraser, 1995).

Building upon these considerations, SDG 13 aims to combat climate change and its impacts, committing to take urgent and concrete actions to limit global temperature rise and adapt to the effects of climate change in a just manner. The main goal of SDG 13 is to address climate change through mitigation and adaptation measures. Mitigation refers to efforts aimed at reducing greenhouse gas emissions into the atmosphere, responsible for global temperature increase. This is essential to limit planetary warming to an acceptable level and avoid catastrophic impacts on life on Earth. Mitigation efforts include transitioning to renewable energy sources, energy efficiency, forest protection, and adopting sustainable agricultural practices. Adaptation, on the other hand, refers to actions aimed at protecting communities and ecosystems from the damages and impacts of ongoing or inevitable climate change. This is crucial because even though mitigation actions are effective, climate change is already underway and will have lasting effects on our planet. Adaptation action includes enhancing climate-resilient infrastructure, implementing early warning systems for extreme weather events, promoting climate-resilient agricultural and management practices, and protecting natural ecosystems that play a key role in mitigating the impacts of climate change. SDG 13 also recognizes the fundamental role of technologies and innovation in fighting against climate change. New technologies and innovative solutions can play a key role in reducing greenhouse gas emissions and adapting to climate change. As a result, there is an encouragement for research and development of low-carbon emission technologies.

Some virtuous solutions have already been implemented. Recent articles have explored the potential benefits of new technologies in addressing climate change and improving environmental quality (Francisco Ribeiro & Camargo Rodriguez, 2020; George et al., 2021; Panepinto et al., 2021). Approaches range from satellite image monitoring to assess the impact of environmental disasters at a local level, to efforts to combat carbon dioxide emissions, and long-term weather forecasting to mitigate the impacts of climate change. Carbon removal technologies provide another globally implementable measure to mitigate climate change. For instance, Negative Emissions Technologies (NET), such as bioenergy with carbon capture and storage (BECCS) and direct air capture of carbon using chemicals (Direct Air Carbon Capture and Storage, or DACCS), already exist as processes to separate carbon dioxide from other particles (Suleman et al., 2022). Some countries have developed solar geoengineering systems that release reflective particles into the stratosphere to enhance cloud reflectivity, thus lowering the planet's temperature (McLaren & Corry, 2021; Parson & Reynolds, 2021).

Moreover, integrating modern technologies such as big data analysis, artificial intelligence (AI), 5G networks, and blockchain technology into environmental monitoring and management can lead to significant improvements in the collection, analysis, and use of environmental data. With the help of these technologies, it is now possible to gather large amounts of environmental data from various sources and analyze them more efficiently and accurately. For example, AI algorithms can help identify patterns and trends in data that might otherwise be overlooked by humans, leading to better predictions and decision-making processes. In the UK, for instance, Vodafone, together with Defra and Forest Research, has launched an experimental project to monitor the condition of English forests through sensors.

However, while significant resources can be identified within new technologies, the ecological footprint of the digital sector is a concern. Digital infrastructures, such as data centers, communication networks, and electronic devices, require a considerable amount of energy to operate. This results in increased greenhouse gas emissions, especially related to energy production from fossil sources. Additionally, the extraction and production of materials necessary for electronic device manufacturing require limited natural resources and can lead to negative environmental impacts such as habitat destruction and soil and water contamination.

The increased energy and resource consumption by the digital sector directly impact the environment and territorial identity. First, greenhouse gas emissions threaten not only the survival of unique ecosystems, and plant and animal species but also alter the natural and landscape identity of territories. Additionally, the high energy consumption of the digital sector can cause an increased demand for electricity, potentially leading to the expansion of power plants and facilities near local communities. This could degrade or modify the natural environment, leading to a greater local population's exposure to air pollutants, thereby jeopardizing their health and quality of life.

Among virtuous initiatives aimed at mitigating climate change while respecting territorial identities, there are energy communities. These represent an innovative form of energy organization and management that actively involves citizens and local communities in energy production, distribution, and consumption. This new energy management approach has emerged in response to growing awareness of climate change and the need for transitions toward more sustainable energy sources. Energy communities offer a decentralized and participatory approach to addressing climate change, allowing people to become key actors in combating pollution and adopting more sustainable energy practices (Charokopos, 2013). The first experiences of energy communities emerged in Europe, particularly in northern countries like Denmark and Germany, in the 2000s. These nations promoted policies to incentivize renewable energies and created opportunities for citizens to participate in energy production and management through cooperatives and sharing projects. This led to the birth of the first energy communities, where citizens come together to develop renewable energy facilities, such as wind farms and solar installations, and share the benefits of clean energy production (Koirala et al., 2016). The functioning of energy communities is based on a collaborative production and consumption model, where multiple actors come together to create an integrated and sustainable energy system. These actors can be individuals, families, businesses, cooperatives, local authorities, and nonprofit organizations. Each member of the community can participate in renewable energy production, for example by installing solar panels on their roofs or participating in a shared wind farm. The produced energy is then fed into the electricity grid and shared among all community members. Energy communities not only focus on energy production but also integrate smart technologies for energy management and optimization. This can include the installation of energy storage systems, such as batteries, to store excess electricity for future use. Furthermore, the use of digital technologies and smart grids allows for real-time monitoring and control of energy production and consumption, improving system efficiency and reducing waste. A key element of energy communities is the sharing of economic benefits. Community members share the costs and revenues of energy production and can benefit from more favorable energy tariffs and prices. This sharing model democratizes energy, making it accessible to a greater number of people and reducing dependence on large energy companies. Energy communities can operate at a local level, involving neighborhoods or villages, but they can also be extended to encompass different geographic areas. This model of energy management is particularly suited to rural areas, where the availability of natural resources like sunlight and wind can be harnessed for renewable energy production. Energy communities represent a significant opportunity to address the challenges of climate change and promote sustainable and participatory energy development. This model can facilitate the transition to cleaner energy sources and reduce the environmental impact of human activities. Furthermore, energy communities promote citizen empowerment and active involvement of local communities in managing energy resources, thereby enhancing community resilience and the adoption of sustainable practices.

The adoption of sustainable agricultural practices can also significantly contribute to climate change mitigation while respecting territorial identities. Sustainable agriculture can be defined as a responsible and environmentally conscious approach to food production and the use of agricultural resources. These practices emphasize environmental conservation, protection of biodiversity, animal welfare, and the social inclusion of agricultural communities. One of the key features of sustainable agricultural practices is the adoption of environmentally friendly farming techniques. This can include the use of organic cultivation methods – avoiding the use of pesticides and chemical fertilizers – and promoting natural methods to control infestations and maintain soil fertility. Organic farming has been shown to be more resilient to the effects of climate change and to reduce the environmental impact of agriculture on water resources and biodiversity (Chown et al., 2016; Thornton et al., 2014). Another important aspect of sustainable agricultural practices is the conservation and efficient use of natural resources. This can involve responsible water use, promoting biodiversity through the protection of natural areas, and advocating for diversified farming systems that reduce pressure on agricultural land and preserve soil fertility. For example, conservation farming practices, such as no-till farming and crop rotation, can contribute to reducing soil erosion, increasing biodiversity, and improving carbon sequestration capacity. Sustainable agricultural practices also promote local and circular food systems. This implies reducing long and complex supply chains, favoring the consumption of local and seasonal products. This approach reduces greenhouse gas emissions associated with transportation and promotes support for local farming communities too. Sustainable agricultural practices also encourage the recovery and reuse of agricultural waste and the promotion of low-impact production and consumption practices.

A concrete example of sustainable agricultural practice is agroforestry. This technique combines the cultivation of trees or shrubs with the cultivation of crops or livestock grazing on the same area of land. Trees can provide shade, protect the soil from erosion, increase biodiversity, and contribute to carbon capture from the atmosphere. Additionally, agroforestry can improve crop yields and reduce pressure on deforestation (IPCC, 2019; Newaj et al., 2013; Raj et al., 2020).

In most cases, sustainable agricultural practices are adapted to specific local conditions and the needs of agricultural communities, including factors such as climate, soil type, and local farming traditions. By actively involving local communities in the design and implementation of these practices, they promote a sense of ownership and responsibility toward the environment and their territory (Pretty, 2018; Vanlauwe et al., 2014).

However, there are initiatives and policies aimed at combating climate change that paradoxically may conflict with the preservation of the cultural and identity heritage of territories. As an illustrative example, reference can be made to concerns regarding the impact of the livestock industry on the climate.

Both the FAO and WWF agree in supporting that the livestock sector produces more greenhouse gases than the global transportation system. While the livestock industry contributes to providing meat and dairy products for a global population that will reach 10 billion people by 2050, its impact on the climate crisis is worrisome. In Europe, intensive livestock farming accounts for 14.5% of the total greenhouse gas emissions, uses 20% of land as pasture, and requires 40% of cultivated land for feed production. Consequently, the European Union has mandated European countries to commit to reducing the number of cows to lower CO_2 emissions by 2030. In France, the French Court of Auditors raised a critique regarding the quantity of cows in the country, as cattle farming significantly contributes to greenhouse gas emissions. According to the report, the livestock industry is responsible for over 11% of total greenhouse gas emissions in France. The request to reduce the number of cows on farms triggered a series of protests by farmers.

A similar situation occurred in the Netherlands in 2019, where the government introduced a measure aimed at reducing the number of cows in the country by 30%. To achieve this goal, the government allocated 25 billion euros to buy (and close) certain farms and to help others in adopting innovative approaches to reduce emissions. In addition to the protests, in the Netherlands, farmers and their representatives formed a dedicated party for defense, called BoerBurgerBeweging (Meijers, 2023). In 2023, the party participated in provincial elections for the first time and won.

Similarly, in Ireland, where approximately 2.5 million cattle are distributed throughout the country for dairy and meat production, the government has declared its intention to withdraw nearly 200,000 cows from the market by 2030. The sector has grown exponentially in recent years. In fact, between 2013 and 2022, dairy cows in the country increased by about 40%. To incentivize this process, farmers should receive compensation of around 3,000 euros per culled cow. However, industry associations began to protest, as they would rather make voluntary decisions about the extent to which they reduce their herds of cows.

These examples highlight how initiatives to reduce livestock herds have stirred a deep sense of threat in the professional and cultural identity of farmers. For many of them, cattle farming goes beyond mere economic activity. It represents a mission and a legacy to be preserved for future generations. Cattle farming practices are closely linked to land stewardship and agricultural sustainability, as herds can contribute to maintaining ecosystem balance through grazing and fertilizing the land. Furthermore, rural and agricultural traditions are deeply intertwined with the identity of local communities, defining their way of life, work, and relationship with the land. The demand to reduce livestock farming challenges this cultural and identity heritage, generating a sense of uncertainty and threat for the future of farming communities.

Another aspect is the importance of appreciation of traditional knowledge and local agricultural practices. Farming communities have developed a wide range of knowledge and skills over centuries related to sustainable natural resource management and adaptation to climate change. This knowledge can provide valuable input for defining sustainable agricultural and climate mitigation policies and initiatives. Involving rural communities in the planning and implementation of these initiatives is essential to ensure that policies are effective and respectful of territorial identities.

In conclusion, addressing the challenges posed by climate change requires a holistic approach that takes into account both the goals of greenhouse gas emissions mitigation and the needs and traditions of rural communities. Imposing top-down decisions can contribute to increasing the sense of vulnerability of individuals and communities, threatening their autonomy and their sense of territorial identity. When policies or initiatives are imposed without considering local needs and specificities, tensions and conflicts can arise between communities and institutions responsible for decision-making. Imposition can lead to a lack of trust in institutions and the decision-making process, undermining democratic participation and the empowerment of local communities.

References

Beck, U. (1992). *Risk society: Towards a new modernity*. Sage.
Billi, M., Zurbriggen, C., & Morchain, D. (2022). Discussing structural, systemic and enabling approaches to socio-environmental transformations: Stimulating an interdisciplinary and plural debate within the social sciences. *Frontiers in Sociology*, 7, 968018.
Charokopos, M. (2013). Energy community and European common aviation area: Two tales of one story. *European Foreign Affairs Review*, 18(2), 1–12.
Chown, S. L., Hodgins, K. A., & Griffin, P. C. (2016). Biological invasions, climate change, and genomics. *Crop Breeding*, 1, 59–114.
Francisco Ribeiro, P., & Camargo Rodriguez, A. V. (2020). Emerging advanced technologies to mitigate the impact of climate change in Africa. *Plants*, 9(3), 381–402.
Fraser, N. (1995). From redistribution to recognition? Dilemmas of justice in a 'post-socialist' age. *New Left Review*, 212, 68–93.
Galgóczi, B. (2020). Just transition on the ground: Challenges and opportunities for social dialogue. *European Journal of Industrial Relations*, 26(4), 367–382.
George, G., Merrill, R. K., & Schillebeeckx, S. J. (2021). Digital sustainability and entrepreneurship: How digital innovations are helping tackle climate change and sustainable development. *Entrepreneurship Theory and Practice*, 45(5), 999–1027.
Giddens, A. (2009). *The politics of climate change*. Polity.
IPCC. (2019). *Climate change and land: An IPCC special report on climate change, desertification, land degradation, sustainable land management, food security, and greenhouse gas fluxes in terrestrial ecosystems. intergovernmental panel on climate change*. https://www.ipcc.ch/srccl/
Koirala, B. P., Koliou, E., Friege, J., Hakvoort, R. A., & Herder, P. M. (2016). Energetic communities for community energy: A review of key issues and trends shaping integrated community energy systems. *Renewable and Sustainable Energy Reviews*, 56, 722–744.
Latour, B. (2018). *Down to earth: Politics in the new climatic regime*. Polity.
McLaren, D., & Corry, O. (2021). The politics and governance of research into solar geoengineering. *Wiley Interdisciplinary Reviews: Climate Change*, 12(3), e707.
Meijers, A. (2023). Wat gaat de overheid doen? *Vakblad Sociaal Werk*, 24(4), 41–42.
Monaco, S. (2022). Energy transition and its societal challenges. Themes, gaps and possible developments in sociology, Fuori Luogo. *Rivista Di Sociologia Del Territorio, Turismo, Tecnologia*, 10(2), 137–147.
Newaj, R., Chavan, S., & Prasad, R. (2013). Agroforestry as a strategy for climate change adaptation and mitigation. *Indian Journal of Agroforestry*, 15(2), 41–48.

Panepinto, D., Riggio, V. A., & Zanetti, M. (2021). Analysis of the emergent climate change mitigation technologies. *International Journal of Environmental Research and Public Health, 18*(13), 6767–6785.

Parson, E. A., & Reynolds, J. L. (2021). Solar geoengineering: Scenarios of future governance challenges. *Futures, 133*, 102806.

Pretty, J. (2018). Sustainable intensification: Innovation in agricultural systems. *International Journal of Agricultural Sustainability, 17*(1), 6–8.

Raj, A., Jhariya, M. K., Yadav, D. K., & Banerjee, A. (Eds.) (2020). *Climate change and agroforestry systems: Adaptation and mitigation strategies*. CRC Press.

Rawls, J. (1971). *A theory of justice*. Harvard University Press.

Suleman, H., Fosbøl, P. L., Nasir, R., & Ameen, M. (Eds.) (2022). *Sustainable carbon capture: Technologies and applications*. CRC Press.

Thornton, P. K., Ericksen, P. J., Herrero, M., & Challinor, A. J. (2014). Climate variability and vulnerability to climate change: A review. *Global Change Biology, 20*(11), 3313–3328.

Urry, J. (2011). *Climate change and society*. Polity.

Vanlauwe, B., Coyne, D., Gockowski, J., Hauser, S., Huising, J., Masso, C., & Van Asten, P. (2014). Sustainable intensification and the African smallholder farmer. *Current Opinion in Environmental Sustainability, 8*, 15–22.

Yan, L. (2021). Climate action and just transition. *Nature Climate Change, 11*(11), 895–897.

Chapter 14

SDG 14. Conserve and Sustainably Use the Oceans, Seas, and Marine Resources for Sustainable Development

Abstract

Through a comprehensive examination of the significance of conserving and sustainably using oceans, seas, and marine resources, this chapter sheds light on how such endeavors contribute to sustainable development across social, economic, and environmental realms. Drawing on a plethora of case studies and analyses, the chapter also underscores the central role of marine ecosystems in supporting livelihoods, cultural identities, and economic growth. It showcases how tailored conservation strategies, rooted in the unique territorial identities of places, can yield better outcomes. By recognizing the intrinsic value of marine ecosystems and their interconnectedness with human well-being, the chapter underscores the urgency of collaborative efforts to achieve SDG 14, which seeks to establish a harmonious coexistence between humanity and the oceans for present and future generations.

The ocean is a precious ecosystem that plays a vital role in sustaining life on Earth. However, the sustainability of marine resources and the conservation of aquatic ecosystems are at risk due to multiple anthropogenic factors, including overfishing, pollution, ocean acidification, and climate change. Excessive fishing, both legal and illegal, has exerted significant pressure on fish populations, endangering the survival of many marine species. Unsustainable fishing methods like trawling have damaged marine habitats, leading to the destruction of coral reefs and seaweed meadows (Kumar & Deepthi, 2006). Trawling involves dragging a fishing net along the sea floor using a weighted bottom portion made of chain or steel cables and an upper mesh portion. Fishing vessels tow the net through the sea, capturing fish and other marine creatures in their path.

Identity, Territories, and Sustainability: Challenges and Opportunities for Achieving the UN Sustainable Development Goals, 137–143
Copyright © 2024 by Salvatore Monaco
Published under exclusive licence by Emerald Publishing Limited
doi:10.1108/978-1-83797-549-520241015

Marine pollution is another severe issue that threatens the health of marine ecosystems and biodiversity (Bergmann et al., 2017). The introduction of chemicals and waste into the ocean has negatively impacted marine species and coastal habitats. Plastics, in particular, have become a significant menace to marine fauna, causing suffocation and poisoning. Additionally, industrial and agricultural runoff has led to the emergence of marine dead zones where oxygen depletion makes it impossible for marine life to survive. Some of the largest and persistent dead zones are found in the Gulf of Mexico, the Bay of Bengal, the Black Sea, and the western coast of North America. Marine dead zones have been reported in many other parts of the world, including the Baltic Sea, the North Sea, the East China Sea, and the Adriatic Sea.

Ocean acidification (Gattuso & Hansson, 2011), resulting from the increasing absorption of carbon dioxide from the atmosphere, poses a threat to shell-forming organisms and coral reefs. It weakens the shells of certain mollusks and will have severe implications for marine ecosystems. Climate change, including rising water temperatures and sea levels, has devastating effects on coastal ecosystems and the marine species dependent on them.

Under these circumstances, SDG 14 emphasizes the critical need to conserve and sustainably use oceans, seas, and marine resources. This goal recognizes the intrinsic value of marine ecosystems and their significance in fostering sustainable development across social, economic, and environmental dimensions of sustainability.

Conservation and sustainable use of oceans contribute significantly to social well-being. Coastal and island communities often depend on marine resources for their livelihoods. By adopting sustainable practices, such communities can ensure the longevity of their traditional ways of life. Furthermore, marine ecosystems provide recreational activities and esthetic value, enhancing the quality of life for both residents and visitors. The preservation of marine biodiversity has broader social implications as well. Healthy marine ecosystems support food security, as fish and seafood are critical protein sources for many populations. Sustainable fishing practices and marine protected areas help maintain stable fish populations, reducing the vulnerability of communities to food shortages and economic instability. Additionally, fostering marine conservation can create opportunities for education and awareness campaigns, empowering people to become advocates for the environment and encouraging responsible behavior.

Conserving and sustainably using marine resources can also stimulate economic growth and ensure long-term prosperity. Fisheries and aquaculture industries generate substantial economic value, providing job opportunities and livelihoods for millions of people worldwide. By implementing sustainable management practices, nations can enhance the resilience of these industries and secure their economic profits. Marine ecosystems play also a crucial role in supporting other sectors, such as tourism and pharmaceuticals. Coastal tourism, which relies on pristine beaches and marine biodiversity, generates substantial revenue for many economies. The appeal of ecotourism and marine-based activities like snorkeling and diving reinforces the economic importance of maintaining healthy marine environments.

Conserving oceans and marine resources are essential for maintaining environmental integrity. Healthy marine ecosystems regulate climate and weather patterns, absorbing and storing significant amounts of carbon dioxide. This helps mitigate the impacts of climate change and contributes to global climate stability. Marine conservation also protects valuable natural habitats. These ecosystems act as buffers against coastal erosion, storm surges, and tsunamis, shielding coastal communities from natural disasters. By preserving these habitats, nations can diminish vulnerability and enhance resilience when confronting climate-related challenges.

Integrating some reflections about territorial Identity into SDGs can further contribute to achieving a desirable territorial development, since marine resources hold a crucial place in shaping the identity of coastal and island territories around the world. In many areas, fishing is not only a source of food and income but also a fundamental element of local culture and the identity of fishing communities (Jackson, 1995; Pita et al., 2018). Maritime routes have not only facilitated trade but also the movement of people and goods, enabling the exchange of ideas and cultures across different regions of the world. These flows of people and commodities have forged connections among coastal communities and influenced their traditions and social practices. For instance, many port cities have a rich history of interaction with foreign cultures, evident in their architecture, cuisine, and cultural traditions. Moreover, the ocean serves as a wellspring of inspiration for the traditions, beliefs, and ways of life of coastal communities. Coastal populations often form deep bonds with the sea and marine activities such as fishing and navigation. These activities are often passed down through generations and constitute a core element of the identity of these communities. In the Pacific Islands, for example, the ocean holds a profound connection to the culture and spirituality of local communities (Nunn et al., 2016). Beliefs and practices linked to the sea vary from island to island, but generally, the ocean is frequently associated with deities and protective spirits. Pacific Islanders regard the sea as a source of life and blessings. Fishing is viewed as a form of sacred ritual through which fishermen show respect and gratitude to the sea and its riches. In some islands, specific deities linked to the sea are invoked for protection and to ensure a successful catch. Inhabitants may hold ceremonies and make offerings to appease these deities and gain their favor. Fishing can also be seen as a collaborative and communal practice, where fishermen work together to provide food for the entire community. This profound connection with the sea is also reflected in the oral traditions and mythological narratives of Pacific communities. Many legends and traditional stories revolve around the sea and its creatures, passing down through generations and reinforcing the people's bond with the sea and nature. Thus, fishing also serves as a means of conserving cultural and spiritual traditions.

SDG 14 encapsulates a range of specific objectives aimed at safeguarding oceans, seas, and marine resources for achieving overall sustainability. Notably, within the framework of SDG 14, there are instances where a nuanced focus on the territorial identity of distinct locales has yielded remarkable outcomes. The following case studies exemplify how tailoring conservation efforts to the unique cultural, social, and economic contexts of specific regions can yield better results.

In order to reduce marine pollution from terrestrial and marine sources, in Italy, the Center for Juvenile Justice in the city of Naples initiated the Bust Buster project in 2023. The project aims to engage young individuals in the external penal area in an educational journey guided by values of eco-sustainability and green living. The initiative targets vulnerable subjects placed on probation by social services or residing in educational communities. They are provided the opportunity to undergo training to become technical diving operators. The Bust Buster trainees, under the supervision of a group of skilled diving professionals, thus acquire the necessary skills to obtain certification and join the ranks of certified divers, should they wish to do so. This initiative guides minors in social care toward employment, offering a concrete path to redemption. The initiative, in collaboration with the naval divers and raiders group of the Italian Navy in Naples and Marenostrum Archeoclub of Italy, is doubly virtuous. On one hand, it aims to cleanse marine waters, contributing to the safeguarding of a delicate and compromised environment. On the other hand, it represents a chance for rejuvenation and personal growth for youths facing adversity. The environmental action originated in a seafaring settlement near Castel dell'Ovo in Naples and has expanded to other contexts within and beyond the Gulf embraced by the Neapolitan city, in cooperation with the naval divers of the Italian Navy and instructors from Marenostrum Archeoclub. The Bust Buster team has carried out beach and underwater clean-up operations in the Naples area, from Marina di Meta in Sorrento to the Bourbon Pier in Naples. They free beaches from waste and dive into the sea to recover surface contaminants. More experienced youths dive deeper, removing waste that risks sinking to the seafloor, such as glass bottles, worn-out tires, and fishing nets. For the city of Naples, safeguarding its Gulf is translated to protecting a significant part of its territorial identity. The relationship between Naples and its sea has shaped the city's history, culture, and heritage over millennia. Since ancient times, the Gulf of Naples has been a vital center for trade and culture. Its waters have been traversed by merchants, explorers, and conquerors who contributed to making Naples a crossroads of cultures and traditions. Its strategic location facilitated trade with other Mediterranean cities, fostering the development of a vibrant maritime and port economy (Amaturo & Zaccaria, 2019). The Gulf of Naples also played a pivotal role in the city's history during the Roman era. Naples, then known as Neapolis, became one of the principal cities of the Roman Empire. The port of Naples was one of the most important in the Mediterranean, serving as a departure point for trade with other Roman provinces and military expeditions. The strategic significance of the Gulf of Naples was so great that Emperor Augustus decided to construct a powerful naval fleet at Misenum, on the opposite coast of the city. Yet, the bond between Naples and its Gulf is not solely historical and economic but also artistic. The Gulf of Naples has inspired artists, writers, and poets throughout the centuries. The breathtaking landscape, with its crystal-clear waters, picturesque beaches, and majestic mountains, has been painted and sung about by numerous artists, including the renowned 18th-century landscape painter Gaspar Van Wittel, also known as Vanvitelli. Writers and poets have also drawn inspiration from the Gulf of Naples, such as the celebrated Romantic poet Giacomo Leopardi, who penned verses extolling the beauty of the Neapolitan landscape. Beyond its historical and cultural importance, the Gulf of Naples plays a crucial role in the daily life of Neapolitans. Fishing has always been a primary economic activity of the city, and the Gulf offers a rich variety of marine species used in traditional Neapolitan cuisine. The flavors of the sea are present in many of Naples' delicacies, such as the famous "pasta with clams" or the "fried small fish" (De Sanctis, 2002).

SDG 14 also aims to preserve marine ecosystems, including coral reefs and mangroves, and protect endangered marine species. To achieve this goal, marine protected areas have been established worldwide.

A significant example is the historic agreement reached within the United Nations for the creation of an extensive marine reserve in the Pacific Ocean. In September 2016, the world's largest marine protected area, the Papahānaumokuākea Marine National Monument, was established, covering an area of over 1.5 million square kilometers in the northwest Hawaiian Islands, USA (Kikiloi et al., 2017). This vast protected area was established to preserve a unique marine ecosystem and protect endangered marine species such as sea turtles and Hawaiian monk seals.

The strengthening of marine protected areas has garnered the attention of various international organizations. For instance, in 2019, the UNESCO Intergovernmental Oceanographic Commission adopted new guidelines for the establishment and management of marine protected areas, aiming to enhance their effectiveness in conserving marine biodiversity and ecosystems (Maestro et al., 2019).

In 2020, Australia enacted legislation to establish an extensive marine protected area around Christmas Island in the Indian Ocean. Encompassing an expanse of over 740,000 square kilometers, this protected area includes various no-trawl zones aimed at preserving the unique ecosystems and vulnerable species of the region (Ali & Aitchison, 2020).

In parallel with the creation of marine protected areas, numerous initiatives have been undertaken to safeguard endangered marine species. An important example is the initiative carried out to protect populations of marine turtles. In 2016, the International Union for Conservation of Nature (IUCN) updated the conservation status of several species of marine turtles, acknowledging conservation efforts in various countries to safeguard turtles and their habitats (Rhodin et al., 2018). Initiatives such as monitoring and protecting nesting sites and promoting sustainable fishing practices, along with reducing accidental captures, have benefited marine turtle populations around the world.

Mangroves, as critical marine ecosystems, have been the focus of some conservation initiatives too. In 2018, UNESCO designated mangroves as globally significant ecological sites, recognizing their fundamental role in coastal protection, support of marine biodiversity, and carbon sequestration (Buot et al., 2022; Friess et al., 2016). International organizations like the Global Mangrove Alliance have championed mangrove conservation and restoration in various parts of the world, in close cooperation with governments and local communities to protect these valuable ecosystems (Friess et al., 2020).

SDG 14 also calls for sustainable management of marine resources, using appropriate fishing practices. In this regard, the European Union approved a reform of its Common Fisheries Policy in 2015, which included trawl fishing restrictions to protect marine ecosystems and mitigate negative impacts on biodiversity. The reform posed limits on trawling zones and introduced measures to reduce bycatch of non-target species (Dolman et al., 2016).

In 2017, the Canadian government announced a series of measures to protect vulnerable marine habitats, including a ban on trawl fishing in the waters of the Gulf of St. Lawrence. This decision was made in response to concerns about the decline of lobster populations in the area (Campbell et al., 2020). This intervention underscored the commitment to preserving the sea while simultaneously safeguarding elements of local identity. Lobster fishing provides employment and sustenance for coastal communities, creating a strong connection between people and the sea. Lobsters are also an icon of Canadian maritime identity and are celebrated in local culture and cuisine. Lobster festivals are popular events in these regions, where people gather to celebrate fishing and maritime heritage, reinforcing their territorial identity.

In 2019, the Food and Agriculture Organization of the United Nations (FAO) adopted the Voluntary Guidelines for Sustainable Trawl Fishing in High Seas, providing guidance to reduce the environmental impact of trawl fishing and improve marine resource management.

Lastly, SDG 14 recognizes the significance of scientific research and international cooperation. These two elements are crucial in addressing the challenges related to the conservation and sustainable management of oceans. Equally important is ensuring that these initiatives consider aspects related to the enhancement and preservation of the territorial identities of communities that rely on the seas for their sustenance and culture.

The challenges posed by the impact of climate change and human activities on the oceans are not only the threat to the health of marine ecosystems and species, but also social and cultural aspects tied to the maritime life of local communities. Local knowledge and traditional practices related to fishing, navigation, and sustainable use of marine resources can offer valuable insights for scientific research and ocean management. Involving local communities in research and defining conservation strategies is therefore essential to ensure that these strategies are tailored to the specific needs and cultures of people living along coastlines and on islands.

International cooperation is another fundamental element. Oceans have no borders, and the actions of one country can have global impacts. Thus, international collaboration is required to address issues such as illegal fishing, marine pollution, and climate change, which necessitate joint global actions (Ferraro & Failler, 2020). Even in this context, it is important for international cooperation to consider the needs and territorial identities of local communities. International policies and agreements should be inclusive and take into account the contributions of local communities in shaping conservation strategies. Coastal and island communities should be engaged in decision-making processes and in defining international policies concerning the oceans, ensuring that these policies are well-suited to the specific needs and cultures of people living in these regions.

References

Ali, J. R., & Aitchison, J. C. (2020). Time of re-emergence of Christmas Island and its biogeographical significance. *Palaeogeography, Palaeoclimatology, Palaeoecology, 537*, 109396.
Amaturo, E., & Zaccaria, A. M. (2019). *Napoli. Persone, spazi e pratiche di innovazione*. Rubbettino.
Bergmann, M., Tekman, M. B., & Gutow, L. (2017). Sea change for plastic pollution. *Nature, 544*(7650), 297–297.
Buot Jr, I. E., Origenes, M. G., & Obeña, R. D. R. (2022). Conservation status of native mangrove species in the Philippines. *Journal Wetlands Biodiversity, 12*, 51–65.
Campbell, C. E., MacDonald, E., & Payne, B. (Eds.). (2020). *The Greater Gulf: Essays on the environmental history of the Gulf of St Lawrence*. McGill-Queen's Press-MQUP.
De Sanctis, F. (2002). *Napoli un golfo per l'Europa* (Vol. 26). Guida Editori.
Dolman, S., Baulch, S., Evans, P. G., Read, F., & Ritter, F. (2016). Towards an EU action plan on cetacean bycatch. *Marine Policy, 72*, 67–75.
Ferraro, G., & Failler, P. (2020). Governing plastic pollution in the oceans: Institutional challenges and areas for action. *Environmental Science & Policy, 112*, 453–460.
Friess, D. A., Thompson, B. S., Brown, B., Amir, A. A., Cameron, C., Koldewey, H. J., Sasmito, S. D., & Sidik, F. (2016). Policy challenges and approaches for the conservation of mangrove forests in Southeast Asia. *Conservation Biology, 30*(5), 933–949.
Friess, D. A., Yando, E. S., Abuchahla, G. M., Adams, J. B., Cannicci, S., Canty, S. W., Cavanaugh, K. C., Connolly, R. M., Cormier, N., Dahdouh-Guebas, F., Diele, K., Feller, I. C., Fratini, S., Jennerjahn, T. C., Yip Lee, S., Ogurcak, D. E., Ouyang, X., Rogers, K., Rowntree, J. K., Sharma, S., Sloey, T. M., & Wee, A. K. (2020). Mangroves give cause for conservation optimism, for now. *Current Biology, 30*(4), R153–R154.
Gattuso, J. P., & Hansson, L. (Eds.) (2011). *Ocean acidification*. Oxford University Press.
Jackson, S. E. (1995). The water is not empty: Cross-cultural issues in conceptualising sea space. *The Australian Geographer, 26*(1), 87–96.
Kikiloi, K., Friedlander, A. M., Wilhelm, A., Lewis, N. A., Quiocho, K., 'Āila Jr, W., & Kaho'ohalahala, S. (2017). Papahānaumokuākea: Integrating culture in the design and management of one of the world's largest marine protected areas. *Coastal Management, 45*(6), 436–451.
Kumar, A. B., & Deepthi, G. R. (2006). Trawling and by-catch: Implications on marine ecosystem. *Current Science, 90*(8), 922–931.
Maestro, M., Pérez-Cayeiro, M. L., Chica-Ruiz, J. A., & Reyes, H. (2019). Marine protected areas in the 21st century: Current situation and trends. *Ocean & Coastal Management, 171*, 28–36.
Nunn, P. D., Mulgrew, K., Scott-Parker, B., Hine, D. W., Marks, A. D., Mahar, D., & Maebuta, J. (2016). Spirituality and attitudes towards nature in the Pacific Islands: Insights for enabling climate-change adaptation. *Climatic Change, 136*, 477–493.
Pita, P., Bolognini, L., & Villasante, S. (2018). Coastal fisheries: Emerging initiatives toward the sustainability objective. *Frontiers in Marine Science, 10*, 1268711.
Rhodin, A. G., Stanford, C. B., Van Dijk, P. P., Eisemberg, C., Luiselli, L., Mittermeier, R. A., et al. (2018). Global conservation status of turtles and tortoises (order Testudines). *Chelonian Conservation and Biology, 17*(2), 135–161.

Chapter 15

SDG 15. Protect, Restore, and Promote Sustainable Use of Terrestrial Ecosystems, Sustainably Manage Forests, Combat Desertification, Halt and Reverse Land Degradation, and Halt Biodiversity Loss

Abstract

The chapter contains an in-depth analysis of contemporary risks confronting terrestrial ecosystems and examines prominent strategies for biodiversity preservation, sustainable tourism, and ecological management. Agroforestry parks and ecological corridors emerge as central mechanisms for safeguarding biodiversity and enhancing habitat connectivity. The chapter delves also into the urgent task of combating desertification, exacerbated by climate change and unsustainable practices, with a particular emphasis on the challenges inherent in the realm of tourism. Within the context of tourism, the chapter identifies nature and adventure tourism as catalysts for fostering biodiversity conservation through emotive engagement, thereby stimulating visitor support for conservation policies. The imperative of sustainable tourism practices, underscored by a dedicated commitment to attenuating adverse impacts while optimizing positive outcomes, assumes paramount importance in this pursuit. The chapter underscores the strategic significance of managing visitor influxes, exemplified by techniques such as access limitations and temporal restrictions, as a key approach to mitigate issues of overcrowding and ecological deterioration.

Biodiversity, defined as the variety of living organisms on Earth and the complex interactions that characterize ecosystems, represents one of the fundamental pillars for human survival and planetary health. This concept extends well

---

Identity, Territories, and Sustainability: Challenges and Opportunities for Achieving the UN Sustainable Development Goals, 145–155
Copyright © 2024 by Salvatore Monaco
Published under exclusive licence by Emerald Publishing Limited
doi:10.1108/978-1-83797-549-520241016

beyond mere species diversity, encompassing genetic diversity within species and the diversity of ecosystems that constitute the natural habitat of these organisms. The organisms composing biodiversity fulfill a wide range of ecological roles, including species population regulation, seed dispersal, plant pollination, organic matter decomposition, and water purification. These processes contribute to ecosystem stability, biological balance, and the provision of essential ecosystem services for human life.

For instance, pollination plays a vital role in the global ecosystem and human food security. Bees and other pollinating insects, such as butterflies and beetles, play a central role in flower and plant reproduction, ensuring the formation of fruits, vegetables, and oil-rich seeds. Crops like apples, peaches, tomatoes, and zucchinis heavily depend on bee pollination for significant yields (Wurz et al., 2021). The wide variety of foods derived from this process underscores its indispensable role in providing essential nutrients and maintaining human dietary diversity. Furthermore, pollination is central in livestock feed production, indirectly influencing the food chain and the availability of meat and dairy products. The significance of pollination for food security becomes even more evident in the analysis of its impact on local and global economies. Agricultural sectors reliant on pollination significantly contribute to global GDP and rural employment (Murphy et al., 2022).

Biodiversity also serves as a valuable resource for medical and pharmaceutical research. Many living organisms, such as plants, fungi, and microorganisms, produce chemical compounds with therapeutic properties. These compounds can be utilized to develop drugs for treating diseases like cancer, heart disease, and bacterial infections (Cragg & Newman, 2013). For example, a substance called Taxol, extracted from the yew tree, has been used as a basis for developing chemotherapy drugs for breast cancer treatment (Howes et al., 2020; Austin et al., 2023).

Biodiversity serves not only as an essential ecological resource for human survival and planetary health but also plays a significant role in defining the identity of territories. Each ecosystem, characterized by a unique variety of plant, animal, and microbial species, contributes to creating a distinctive environment shaping the history, culture, and traditions of a region.

The presence of endemic species can become a source of pride for local communities, developing a deep connection with the surrounding nature and becoming an integral part of their identity. Endemism occurs when a species or subspecies is restricted to a limited geographical area and is not naturally found anywhere else in the world. This can result from various evolutionary processes, such as genetic divergence and natural selection, which develop in response to specific environmental conditions. Islands, with their geographic isolation, are among the places where endemism is most evident and pronounced. The lack of connections to the mainland restricts species migration and creates a conducive environment for the development of new populations and distinct adaptations. Geological age and distance from the mainland directly influence an island's endemic diversity. Older and more distant islands tend to host a greater amount of endemism, as time and isolation foster genetic divergence (Cartwright, 2019). Endemism is not limited exclusively to islands. Some particularly distinct environments, such as high mountain peaks, caves, deep lakes, and ocean trenches, can function as true refuges for endemic biodiversity. These habitats, characterized by unique climatic or ecological conditions, can create ecological enclaves where highly specialized species can evolve and persist (Kandoussi et al., 2021; Li et al., 2021). These unique species are often tied to the identity of territories and local communities, contributing to a sense of attachment and belonging. The presence of endemic species is frequently a source of pride for local communities, developing a deep bond with the surrounding nature and becoming an integral part of their identity.

In addition, it is safe to argue that biodiversity is often intertwined with cultural traditions and ways of life of local communities. Agricultural practices, traditional medicine, construction techniques, and art are just some facets of human culture that have been shaped by interaction with the natural environment. Traditional knowledge and skills are passed down from generation to generation and are closely linked to the conservation and sustainable use of biodiversity (Chaplin-Kramer et al., 2019). For example, indigenous populations have developed a profound understanding of medicinal plants and natural resources in their territory, contributing both to their health and the preservation of local ecosystems (Hill et al., 2020).

Biodiversity also represents an important resource in the context of tourism, creating opportunities for economic development for local communities. The interaction between biodiversity and tourism can create a virtuous circle in which the enhancement of a territory's natural wealth is translated into benefits for both the environment and the local economy. This deep connection between biodiversity and tourism is based on several factors that contribute to a positive synergy between the two realities (Bhammar et al., 2021). Territories characterized by a wide range of flora and fauna can be attractive destinations for travelers seeking authentic immersive experiences in nature. Biological diversity offers nature enthusiasts the opportunity to explore and discover unique ecosystems, rare species, and breathtaking landscapes. For instance, an ecological gem that enchants visitors from all corners of the world is the Vesuvius National Park (Brewer, 2021; Monaco, 2024). It embraces the majestic Somma-Vesuvius volcanic complex, a geological entity that has shaped the landscape and history of the surrounding region. The area has been recognized as a UNESCO World Heritage site for its ecosystem and millennial history. Attention to the conservation of this unique environment is essential to preserve both the ecosystem and the well-being of local communities. The park's mission is to reconcile the need for environmental protection with sustainable territorial development, ensuring the conscious enjoyment of its resources. The geological aspect is one of the most fascinating features of Vesuvius National Park. Traces of past volcanic activity are visible in every corner, with craters and remains of lava flows that reveal the volcano's millennial history. The opportunity to closely explore these geological testimonies offers visitors a unique chance to travel through time and understand the processes that have shaped the territory. This interactive learning experience is crucial for raising awareness about the importance of geodiversity and the conservation of volcanic ecosystems (Suhud & Allan, 2019). Amidst the dense Mediterranean scrub forests and grassy clearings, mammals like foxes, hedgehogs, as well as numerous species of birds and reptiles can be spotted. The adaptability of these creatures to live in such a dynamic and ever-changing territory is an extraordinary example of life's resilience and the interconnection between organisms and their environment. Tourism activities within the park, such as guided hikes, environmental education, and promotion of local products, provide economic opportunities for people living nearby (Canale et al., 2019).

However, global biodiversity is currently facing a complex and interconnected array of threats. SDG 15, dedicated to life on Earth, aims to preserve and restore biodiversity in all its forms, recognizing its crucial role in the health of the planet and future generations.

Deforestation is one of the main causes of biodiversity loss, as it involves the direct destruction of natural habitats, endangering numerous plant and animal species that depend on these areas for their survival. Despite the Glasgow Climate Pact, endorsed by 197 countries in 2021 during COP26, allocating $20 billion to achieve the "zero deforestation" goal by 2030, the ongoing advancement of deforestation continues to be alarming. According to data from the Global Forest Watch[1] satellite platform by the World Resource Institute, in 2022 alone, 4.1 million hectares of tropical virgin forest were destroyed worldwide, equivalent to the entire land area of the Netherlands, and the increase in destruction compared to 2021 was 10%. The greatest losses were recorded in Brazil (1.7 million hectares, that is 43% of the total), followed by Congo and Bolivia. In most cases, forests and woodlands are annihilated for timber production or to clear land for agriculture and pasture. Additionally, certain industries rely on raw materials derived from forests and tree felling, such as the cosmetics industry or palm oil producers, which are concentrated in vegetation-rich regions like Indonesia and Malaysia. In Africa, Asia, and South America, small-scale farmers often clear or occupy forested lands and strategically set fires to cultivate lands enriched by ashes. Cambodia holds the world record for illegal deforestation. According to Amnesty International, between 2001 and 2020, the country lost approximately 2.5 million hectares of forest.

A virtuous reforestation program has been the Green Legacy initiative (Jalleta, 2021; Tiruye et al., 2021) implemented in Ethiopia under the direction of the Ministry of Health and the Ministry of Innovation and Technology. With the participation of countless citizens from all regions of the country, over 353 million trees have been planted. The initiative is part of a government program that has allocated $6.2 billion to increase forest coverage to 95 million hectares by 2030. A similar initiative was carried out in 2017 in the Indian state of Uttar Pradesh. Approximately 800,000 individuals, including farmers, homemakers, students, and NGO volunteers, planted 50 million trees (Patel et al., 2021).

Habitat loss is further exacerbated by uncontrolled urbanization and the human alteration of natural areas. The expansion of urban areas involves the conversion of previously forested, grassland, wetland, and other natural habitat lands into anthropized spaces characterized by buildings, roads, parking lots, and infrastructure. This drastic transformation directly results in the loss of habitat for

---

[1] Global Forest Watch (GFW). https:// www. globalforestwatch. org/

many animal and plant species, forcing them to move, adapt, or, in the worst cases, disappear. Furthermore, urbanization can fragment remaining habitats, isolating species populations and reducing their migration and dispersal capacity.

An emblematic example of how urbanization can negatively impact biodiversity is the escalating cementing of wetland areas. These ecosystems, which play vital roles in the water cycle and host an extraordinary variety of species, are often drained and filled to make way for urban settlements and infrastructure. The loss of wetlands has disastrous consequences for species like aquatic birds, amphibians, and plants that rely on these habitats for their survival. Additionally, urbanization can increase the risk of floods and disrupt the ecological balance of surrounding ecosystems.

For instance, in Hungary, the Balaton Lake area, also a UNESCO World Heritage site, has been witnessing various cementing projects for years, despite protests from residents to save wetlands. Residential parks and lodging facilities are gradually replacing reed beds and parts of the rich fauna (Dudás et al., 2020).

Another threat comes from the increasing anthropization of many coastal areas worldwide, defined in geography and ecology as the conversion of open spaces, landscapes, and natural environments by human action. Beaches, dunes, and coastal marshes are habitats for numerous species such as sea turtles, migratory birds, and coastal vegetation. Transforming coastal areas to meet housing or tourism needs leads to the destruction of these areas to make room for real estate developments, tourist ports, and other infrastructure. This phenomenon not only endangers the survival of unique species but also increases vulnerability to flooding and coastal erosion.

Intensive agriculture, natural resource extraction, and other human activities can also result in direct habitat destruction and environmental pollution. For example, indiscriminate use of pesticides and chemical fertilizers can contaminate soil and natural resources, further damaging habitats (Zeraatpisheh et al., 2020). In this regard, various best practices and public policies have been developed worldwide. Many countries have adopted policies and incentives to promote sustainable agricultural practices that reduce environmental impact. For instance, the European Union has implemented the Common Agricultural Policy (CAP) that encourages farmers to use environmentally friendly methods, such as crop rotation, organic farming, and responsible pesticide use. Similarly, Japan has promoted organic farming and sustainable land use through its Ecological Agriculture program (Watari et al., 2021).

Promoting the use of sustainable agricultural product certifications is another approach to encouraging eco-friendly and sustainable farming practices, contributing to biodiversity conservation and improving social and environmental conditions in farming communities. One internationally recognized certification is the "Rainforest Alliance" label, which focuses on promoting responsible agricultural practices, protecting natural resources, and enhancing the well-being of rural communities (Gather & Wollni, 2022). Established in 1987, the non-profit organization "Rainforest Alliance" is committed to supporting sustainable farming practices through certification programs, while raising consumer awareness about the importance of purchasing products from sustainable sources. One of the main sectors where "Rainforest Alliance" has made a significant impact is coffee production. Over the years, many coffee-growing farms have been certified according to the organization's standards, demonstrating their commitment to paying attention to the environment. These farms adopt agricultural practices that promote biodiversity conservation, such as planting tall trees that serve as habitats for birds and other wildlife and prohibiting the use of harmful chemical pesticides. "Rainforest Alliance" works closely with farming communities to improve livelihoods by providing training in sustainable resource management and ecological farming practices. The organization also promotes social equity practices, such as respecting workers' rights and protecting indigenous communities.

Another example of a certification that promotes agricultural sustainability is the "Fair Trade" label, which focuses on creating economic and social opportunities for disadvantaged producers, including farmers in developing countries (Berry & Romero, 2021). The "Fair Trade" movement supports agricultural production based on principles of social and economic justice, working to ensure that producers receive fair compensation for their work and have access to dignified working conditions. The organization sets strict standards for fair trade, such as promoting organic cultivation and reducing the use of harmful chemicals. A concrete example of how the "Fair Trade" label has had a positive impact is in cocoa production. In many regions of West Africa and Latin America, cocoa growers are often underpaid and work under precarious conditions. The "Fair Trade" label works to address these issues by adopting fair trade practices that guarantee a minimum price for cocoa and promote the involvement of local communities in production and marketing decisions.

Promoting the use of these certifications not only fosters sustainable agricultural practices and biodiversity conservation but can also exert a positive impact on global markets. Increasingly conscious consumers are willing to pay more for products that have been produced sustainably and adhere to social and environmental standards. As a result, producers who obtain these certifications can enjoy a competitive advantage in the market and contribute to creating a virtuous circle of sustainability and responsibility.

Establishing agroforestry parks and ecological corridors represents another key strategy for biodiversity conservation and the promotion of functional natural habitats (Gonçalves et al., 2021). These parks and corridors act as "ecological highways," enabling animals to migrate between different areas and facilitating plant dispersal. This practice is particularly important in heavily anthropized areas, where habitat fragmentation due to urbanization and intensive agriculture can restrict organism mobility and put at risk their survival. A successful example of establishing ecological corridors comes from the Appalachian region in the United States (Kaup et al., 2021). The "Wildlife Corridor Action Plan" was developed in 2020 with the aim of connecting natural areas through ecological corridors, creating a more favorable environment for animal migration and plant movement. These corridors allow animals to move between different areas, seeking food, water, and nesting sites. This is crucial for the conservation of species that require large territories to meet their vital needs.

The implementation of agroforestry parks and ecological corridors requires a multidisciplinary approach involving various stakeholders, including local governments, non-governmental organizations, local communities, and researchers. It is important to consider the needs of the different species present in the ecosystem and understand the ecological dynamics that influence their mobility (Taïbi et al., 2019).

Desertification is another phenomenon that negatively impacts biodiversity (Huang et al., 2020). This phenomenon occurs when arid and semi-arid lands, often already vulnerable, become increasingly degraded due to natural and human factors, such as climate change, intensive agricultural practices, and inappropriate natural resource management.

An important contemporary anti-desertification project is the Great Green Wall initiative implemented in sub-Saharan Africa (Goffner et al., 2019). Established in 2007, the GGW received an additional $14.3 billion in funding through the World Bank and France in 2021. It aims to rehabilitate an area that had previously become almost uncultivable due to a combination of human activity and climate change. Similarly, Pakistan is implementing the Ten Billion Tree Tsunami program, following the completion of its first Billion Tree Tsunami in 2017 (Zaheer, 2023). Also, Saudi Arabia is investing in its Saudi Green Initiative and a regional plan called the Middle East Green Initiative (Hameed et al., 2022).

The adoption of targeted policies has become essential to balance the economic benefits of tourism with the need to preserve natural and cultural resources in the long term. One of the main policies is the promotion of sustainable tourism. This approach is based on responsibility toward the environment, resources, and local communities, to ensure that tourism activities have minimal impact on the territorial identity. Sustainable tourism seeks to maximize the economic benefits of tourism while minimizing negative impacts, promoting environmental conservation, community involvement, and respect for local cultures. Policies of sustainable tourism often involve promoting eco-friendly practices, educating visitors about conservation, and supporting initiatives that promote the sustainable development of tourist areas (Milano et al., 2019; Streimikiene et al., 2021).

A concrete example of success in promoting sustainable tourism is represented by Costa Rica (Herrero Amo & De Stefano, 2019; Molina-Murillo, 2019). This Central American country has become a reference point for ecological and sustainable tourism through a series of policies and initiatives aimed at preserving its identity. The Costa Rica Tourism Board has adopted an integrated approach to sustainability, encouraging accommodation facilities to adhere to rigorous environmental standards and promoting tourist activities that actively involve local communities. This vision has allowed Costa Rica to become one of the world's leading eco-tourism destinations, generating economic benefits for local communities and supporting environmental protection simultaneously.

Nature and adventure tourism can also play a crucial role in supporting biodiversity conservation (Novelli et al., 2022). When visitors develop an emotional connection with the natural environment through engaging experiences, they tend to gain greater awareness of the importance of ecosystem protection. This can translate into increased support for conservation policies and environmental protection initiatives. For example, travelers participating in African savanna observation tours can develop a greater understanding and sensitivity to the challenges faced by wildlife and free-ranging animals, such as lions, elephants, and zebras, thereby promoting conservation messages and active engagement in safeguarding territorial resources.

Another crucial policy in the tourism sector is the management of traveler flows (De Luca et al., 2020; Ribeiro de Almeida et al., 2020). In many tourist destinations, excessive overcrowding can lead to negative impacts on sensitive ecosystems and limited resources. Tourism flow management aims to regulate the number of visitors to avoid congestion, environmental degradation, and excessive pressure on local resources. This can be achieved through access limits, seasonal restrictions, or limits on daily access to certain sensitive areas. For example, in Italy, the city of Venice is constantly affected by tourist overcrowding, with an estimated average of around 20 million visitors per year and a long-standing issue of large cruise ships transiting through its lagoon. The crowds in its symbolic places, on the canals, among the calli (narrow streets), and labyrinthine streets have a burdensome impact on Venice's delicate environment and the surrounding lagoon (Bertocchi et al., 2020). Another side effect of overtourism in Venice is the gradual depopulation of homes with residents moving away from the city's chaos and converting their property into vacation rentals for tourists. To address this situation, the city administration has tried to regulate tourist influx with a combination of measures, including installing turnstiles on the two bridges that serve as entrances and exits, requiring advance online booking and payment of a €5 fee to enter, and restricting the entry of large cruise ships considered harmful to the lagoon ecosystem.

Similarly in Spain, cultural attractions, its Gaudí-designed architecture, the beach, favorable climate, and various entertainment have made Barcelona one of the top summer tourism destinations (Álvarez-Sousa, 2021; Gutiérrez et al., 2022). The massive influx of travelers has led the local government to impose restrictions on vacation rentals and to limit access to the historic center to small groups. To prevent its streets from becoming congested with crowds, one-way systems have been implemented on some streets and squares to keep people moving, and bus lines have been reinforced to transport visitors to the beaches, reducing traffic and emissions. The city council has also enacted new legislation banning the construction of new hotels in the city center and announced stricter regulation for residents wishing to use home-sharing platforms to rent out their accommodations, requiring them to register and obtain a permit.

In Peru, Machu Picchu is universally regarded as one of the world's most significant historical sites and has been dealing with a massive influx of tourists for decades (Schlauderaff et al., 2022). Before the global pandemic crisis, it was estimated that Machu Picchu received over 1.4 million visitors annually, and even though the tourist flow has not yet returned to those levels, the high number of visitors continues to pose a problem for delicate archaeological sites afflicted by excessive waste and soil compaction. To address this issue, a timed entry system was introduced at Machu Picchu, distributing visitors evenly so that they do not congregate in one place. It is also mandatory for all travelers to participate with a tour guide, with groups limited to 10 people per guide.

In Thailand, Maya Bay on Ko Phi Phi Island has managed to accommodate over 5,000 visitors per day (Koh & Fakfare, 2020). The beach, made globally famous by the movie "The Beach," regularly imposes access bans on tourists due to damage caused to the coral reef and boats docking in the bay during high season. Temporary closures of natural attractions are not new in Thailand. Each year, the Thai tourism authority closes several national parks for a certain period to allow for proper ecological recovery. The closure dates for the public are decided based on weather conditions and the location of the parks. The restrictions are mainly due to extreme weather conditions, especially during the annual rainy monsoon, which can create unsafe conditions.

Environmental protection policies often also focus on the creation and management of protected areas and national parks. These spaces are designated to preserve and conserve exceptional ecosystems, often rich in biodiversity, while allowing responsible enjoyment by visitors. Protected areas provide a controlled environment in which tourist activities can be regulated to minimize impacts on biodiversity.

References

Álvarez-Sousa, A. (2021). La percepción de los problemas del overtourism en Barcelona. *RECERCA: revista de pensament i anàlisi, 26*(1), 59–92.

Austin, A., Colyson, J. H., Rohmatulloh, F. G., Destriani, W., & Rosyati, M. M. (2023). Potential of Indonesian Medicinal Plant Biodiversity as CHK1 Inhibitor Agent for cancer treatment by bioinformatics and computational chemistry. *Indonesian Journal of Computational Biology, 2*(1), 1–10.

Berry, C., & Romero, M. (2021). The fair trade food labeling health halo: Effects of fair trade labeling on consumption and perceived healthfulness. *Food Quality and Preference, 94*, 104321.

Bertocchi, D., Camatti, N., Giove, S., & van der Borg, J. (2020). Venice and overtourism: Simulating sustainable development scenarios through a tourism carrying capacity model. *Sustainability, 12*(2), 512.

Bhammar, H., Li, W., Molina, C. M. M., Hickey, V., Pendry, J., & Narain, U. (2021). Framework for sustainable recovery of tourism in protected areas. *Sustainability, 13*(5), 2798.

Brewer, J. (2021). Visiting Vesuvius: Guides, local knowledge, sublime tourism, and science, 1760–1890. *The Journal of Modern History, 93*(1), 1–33.

Canale, R. R., De Simone, E., Di Maio, A., & Parenti, B. (2019). UNESCO World Heritage sites and tourism attractiveness: The case of Italian provinces. *Land Use Policy, 85*, 114–120.

Cartwright, J. (2019). Ecological islands: Conserving biodiversity hotspots in a changing climate. *Frontiers in Ecology and the Environment, 17*(6), 331–340.

Chaplin-Kramer, R., Sharp, R. P., Weil, C., Bennett, E. M., Pascual, U., Arkema, K. K., Brauman, K. A., Bryant, B. P., Guerry, A. D., Haddad, N. M., Hamann, M., Hamel, P., Johnson, J. A., Mandle, L., Pereira, H. M., Polasky, S., Ruckelshaus, M., Shaw,

M. R., Silver, J. M., Vogl, A. L., & Daily, G. C. (2019). Global modeling of nature's contributions to people. *Science*, *366*(6462), 255–258.

Cragg, G. M., & Newman, D. J. (2013). Natural products: a continuing source of novel drug leads. *Biochimica et Biophysica Acta (BBA)-General Subjects*, *1830*(6), 3670–3695.

De Luca, G., Shirvani Dastgerdi, A., Francini, C., & Liberatore, G. (2020). Sustainable cultural heritage planning and management of overtourism in art cities: Lessons from atlas world heritage. *Sustainability*, *12*(9), 3929.

Dudás, G., Kovalcsik, T., Vida, G., Boros, L., & Nagy, G. (2020). Price determinants of Airbnb listing prices in lake Balaton touristic region, Hungary. *European Journal of Tourism Research*, *24*, 2389–2410.

Gather, J., & Wollni, M. (2022). Setting the standard: Does Rainforest Alliance Certification increase environmental and socio-economic outcomes for small-scale coffee producers in Rwanda? *Applied Economic Perspectives and Policy*, *44*(4), 1807–1825.

Goffner, D., Sinare, H., & Gordon, L. J. (2019). The Great Green Wall for the Sahara and the Sahel Initiative as an opportunity to enhance resilience in Sahelian landscapes and livelihoods. *Regional Environmental Change*, *19*, 1417–1428.

Gonçalves, C. D. B. Q., Schlindwein, M. M., & Martinelli, G. D. C. (2021). Agroforestry systems: A systematic review focusing on traditional indigenous practices, food and nutrition security, economic viability, and the role of women. *Sustainability*, *13*(20), 11397.

Gutiérrez, V. P., Aguilera, D. S., & Ramis, M. À. C. (2022). Políticas públicas y overtourism en destinos urbanos: un análisis comparado entre Barcelona y Palma. *Cuadernos de Turismo*, *49*, 189–207.

Hameed, A., Jabeen, I., & Afzal, N. (2022). Towards an eco-friendly future: A corpus-based analysis of media discourse on" Saudi Green Initiative. *Lege Artis*, *7*(1), 84–119.

Herrero Amo, M. D., & De Stefano, M. C. (2019). Public–private partnership as an innovative approach for sustainable tourism in Guanacaste, Costa Rica. *Worldwide Hospitality and Tourism Themes*, *11*(2), 130–139.

Hill, R., Adem, Ç., Alangui, W. V., Molnár, Z., Aumeeruddy-Thomas, Y., Bridgewater, P., Tengö, M., Thaman, R., Adou Yao, C., Berkes, F., Carino, J., Carneiro da Cunha, M., Diaw, M., Díaz, S., Figueroa, V., Fisher, J., Hardison, P., Ichikawa, K., Kariuki, P., Karki, M., Lyver, P., Malmer, P., Masardule, O., Oteng Yeboah, A., Pacheco, D., Pataridze, T., Perez, E., Roué, M., Roba, H., Rubis, J., Saito, O., Xue, D., Tengö, M., Thaman, R., Adou Yao, C., Berkes, F., Carino, J., Carneiro da Cunha, M., Diaw, M., Díaz, S., Figueroa, V., Fisher, J., Hardison, P., Ichikawa, K., Kariuki, P., Karki, M., Lyver, P., Malmer, P., Masardule, O., Oteng Yeboah, A., Pacheco, D., Pataridze, T., Perez, E., Roué, M., Roba, H., Rubis, J., Saito, O., & Xue, D., (2020). Working with indigenous, local and scientific knowledge in assessments of nature and nature's linkages with people. *Current Opinion in Environmental Sustainability*, *43*, 8–20.

Howes, M. J. R., Quave, C. L., Collemare, J., Tatsis, E. C., Twilley, D., Lulekal, E., Farlow, A., Li, L.; Cazar, M.; Danna, J.; Prescott, T. A. K.; Milliken, W.; Martin, C., De Canha, M., Lall, N. Qin, H. Walker, B. E., Vásquez-Londoño, C., Allkin, B., Rivers, M. Simmonds, M. S. J., Bell, E., Battison, A., Felix, J., Forest, F., Leon, C., Williams, C., & Nic Lughadha, E. (2020). Molecules from nature: Reconciling biodiversity conservation and global healthcare imperatives for sustainable use of medicinal plants and fungi. *Plants, People, Planet*, *2*(5), 463–481.

Huang, J., Zhang, G., Zhang, Y., Guan, X., Wei, Y., & Guo, R. (2020). Global desertification vulnerability to climate change and human activities. *Land Degradation & Development*, *31*(11), 1380–1391.

Jalleta, A. K. (2021). The legal protection of forests: Ethiopian Green Legacy vs. International Environmental Regimes. *Beijing Law Review*, *12*, 725–749.

Kandoussi, A., Petit, D., & Boujenane, I. (2021). Morphologic characterization of the Blanche de Montagne, an endemic sheep of the Atlas Mountains. *Tropical Animal Health and Production*, *53*, 1–8.

Kaup, B. Z., Abel, M., & Sikirica, A. (2021). Individualized environments, individual cures: An examination of Lyme disease activism in Virginia. *Environment and Planning E: Nature and Space, 4*(2), 545–563.

Koh, E. & Fakfare, P. (2020). Overcoming "over-tourism": The closure of Maya Bay. *International Journal of Tourism Cities, 6*(2), 279–296.

Li, Y., Huang, K., Tang, S., Feng, L., Yang, J., Li, Z., & Li, B. (2021). Genetic structure and evolutionary history of *Rhinopithecus roxellana* in Qinling Mountains, Central China. *Frontiers in Genetics, 11*, 611914.

Milano, C., Cheer, J. M., & Novelli, M. (Eds.) (2019). *Overtourism: Excesses, discontents and measures in travel and tourism.* Cabi.

Molina-Murillo, S. A. (2019). Sustainable tourism certification and its perceived socioeconomic impacts in Costa Rican hotels. *PASOS: Revista de Turismo y Patrimonio Cultural, 17*(2), 363–372.

Monaco, S. (2024). The generational transition of Gen Z tourists behaviour: A sociological snapshot from the Vesuvius National Park. In S. Seyfi, M. Hall, & Strzelecka (Eds.), *Gen Z, Tourism, and Sustainable Consumption* (pp. 89–100). Routledge.

Murphy, J. T., Breeze, T. D., Willcox, B., Kavanagh, S., & Stout, J. C. (2022). Globalisation and pollinators: Pollinator declines are an economic threat to global food systems. *People and Nature, 4*(3), 773–785.

Novelli, M., Cheer, J. M., Dolezal, C., Jones, A., & Milano, C. (Eds.) (2022). *Handbook of niche tourism.* Edward Elgar Publishing.

Patel, R., Goswami, S., Sahoo, M., Pillai, S. S. K., Aggarwal, N., Mathews, R. P., Swain, R. R., Saxena, A., & Singh, K. J. (2021). Biodiversity of a Permian temperate forest: A case study from Ustali area, Ib River Basin, Odisha, India. *Geological Journal, 56*(2), 903–933.

Ribeiro de Almeida, C., Quintano, A., Simancas, M., Huete, R., & Breda, Z. (Eds.). (2020). *Handbook of research on the impacts, challenges, and policy responses to overtourism.* IGI Global.

Schlauderaff, S., Press, J., Huston, H., Su, C. H. J., & Tsai, C. H. K. (2022). Are we putting our favorite destinations in Peril? A no longer lost city-Machu Picchu case study. *Journal of Hospitality and Tourism Cases, 10*(1), 34–41.

Streimikiene, D., Svagzdiene, B., Jasinskas, E., & Simanavicius, A. (2021). Sustainable tourism development and competitiveness: The systematic literature review. *Sustainable Development, 29*(1), 259–271.

Suhud, U., & Allan, M. (2019). Exploring the impact of travel motivation and constraint on stage of readiness in the context of volcano tourism. *Geoheritage, 11*, 927–934.

Taïbi, A. N., Hannani, M. E., Khalki, Y. E., & Ballouche, A. (2019). The agroforestry parks of Azilal (Morocco): A centuries-old and still living landscape construction. *Journal of Alpine Research| Revue de géographie alpine, 3*, 107–123.

Tiruye, G. A., Besha, A. T., Mekonnen, Y. S., Benti, N. E., Gebreslase, G. A., & Tufa, R. A. (2021). Opportunities and challenges of renewable energy production in Ethiopia. *Sustainability, 13*(18), 10381.

Watari, Y., Komine, H., Angulo, E., Diagne, C., Ballesteros-Mejia, L., & Courchamp, F. (2021). First synthesis of the economic costs of biological invasions in Japan. *NeoBiota, 67*, 79–101.

Wurz, A., Grass, I., & Tscharntke, T. (2021). Hand pollination of global crops: A systematic review. *Basic and Applied Ecology, 56*, 299–321.

Zaheer, M. A. (2023). Ten billion trees tsunami program: Mitigating the non-traditional security threat of climate change and water crisis in Pakistan. *Insights of Pakistan, Iran and the Caucasus Studies, 2*(6), 1–11.

Zeraatpisheh, M., Bakhshandeh, E., Hosseini, M., & Alavi, S. M. (2020). Assessing the effects of deforestation and intensive agriculture on the soil quality through digital soil mapping. *Geoderma, 363*, 114–139.

Chapter 16

SDG 16. Promote Peaceful and Inclusive Societies for Sustainable Development, Provide Access to Justice for All, and Build Effective, Accountable, and Inclusive Institutions at All Levels

Abstract

SDG 16 is committed to reducing violence in all its forms and ensuring personal and collective security. Drawing several examples from all over the world, the chapter underscores the complexities and challenges faced in pursuing social justice. It highlights the role of peacebuilding and conflict prevention in preserving territorial identity, emphasizing the detrimental effects of violence on cultural heritage and social cohesion. Furthermore, it examines the ways in which access to justice, protection of rights, and responsible governance contribute to the fortification of territorial identity, enabling communities to uphold their distinct traditions and values. The chapter also delves into the analysis of obstacles such as corruption, human rights violations, and criminal activities that undermine the achievement of SDG 16. Through an analysis of these challenges in various contexts, it underscores the global significance of addressing these issues to create environments where territorial identities can thrive.

The core of SDG 16 is about the promotion of social justice and peaceful and inclusive societies for all. Social justice refers to the equitable distribution of resources, opportunities, and benefits within a society. This principle has attracted the attention of numerous authors and theorists.

One of the fundamental pillars of the approach to social justice was developed by Karl Marx (1867). His pioneering analysis shed light on the complex interconnection between economic structure and social dynamics. Marx placed particular emphasis on class struggle as the driving force behind socio-economic changes. In his approach, he deeply analyzed the intrinsic conflict between proletarians – the workforce – and capitalists – the holders of means of production. This dichotomy highlighted how exclusive control of means of production by a dominant class can trigger a cycle of social inequality and systematic exploitation of workers. Marx revealed how economic mechanisms can act as levers to perpetuate injustices, determining the asymmetric distribution of resources and differentiated access to opportunities. His vision highlighted the crucial role played by the economic system in shaping social dynamics, prompting reflection on the need for fair redistribution of resources and increased democratic control over production. The Marxist theory continued to serve as a conceptual foundation for the critical analysis of social and economic structures, stimulating debate on social justice and pathways for positive change.

During the 20th century, the work of Max Weber (1922) enriched the landscape of social justice through an in-depth exploration of social dynamics and their implications for equity. Weber introduced a perspective projected beyond purely economic boundaries, shedding light on a wide range of factors influencing social justice. His analysis emphasized how the concept of stratification is crucial for understanding how power, social class, and status interact to shape the distribution of resources within a society. Weber's theory introduced the concept of "rationalization" as a key element in the context of capitalism and social institutions. This rationalization, which concerns the efficient and calculated organization of human activities, can be both a factor that promotes equity and a tool to contribute to inequalities. Weber's analysis highlighted how complex social structures and bureaucratic institutions can have a significant impact on the distribution of resources and opportunities. In this regard, social justice cannot be understood solely from an economic perspective but requires a thorough consideration of the interconnected dynamics of power, stratification, and rationalization.

The conflict theory has highlighted how power and resource inequalities form the basis of social conflicts. This perspective has emphasized the dynamics of power struggles and underlined the role of institutions in establishing and maintaining inequalities (Dahrendorf, 1957). According to this approach, institutions represent the social, political, and economic structures that regulate the organization of society and the distribution of resources. These institutions are not neutral but rather reflect and perpetuate existing power dynamics and inequalities in various ways. First, institutional laws and policies can favor certain categories of people at the expense of others. For example, economic policies that favor large corporate conglomerates can contribute to concentrating economic power in the hands of a few, while leaving other segments of the population in a disadvantaged state. Additionally, labor laws and market regulations can influence working conditions, wages, and opportunities for economic growth, with direct impacts on social inequalities. Political institutions play a fundamental role in power distribution and access to resources. Electoral systems, decision-making processes, and government structures can determine who has a voice in political decisions and who is excluded. According to this perspective, if political institutions are designed to favor certain groups or interests, this can contribute to a cycle of inequality and a concentration of power in the hands of a few. Economic institutions, such as banks, businesses, and financial organizations, directly influence the distribution of economic resources. For instance, the financial system can favor access to credit and investment opportunities for some while excluding others due to structural barriers or discrimination. This can amplify economic inequalities and hinder socially and economically disadvantaged individuals from progressing.

In the realm of philosophical and political debate on justice, John Rawls (1971) presented an innovative approach based on the concept of "justice as fairness." According to Rawls, individuals should imagine themselves behind a "veil of ignorance" where they do not know their social, economic, or personal position in society. This imaginative exercise allows for the creation of an impartial starting point for designing a just society. Rawls enunciated two fundamental principles of justice. The first, known as the "principle of equal liberty," asserts that everyone should have the right to a set of basic liberties that cannot be violated. The second, called the "difference principle," states that socio-economic inequalities can be accepted only if they benefit the least privileged and are connected to positions and opportunities accessible to all. This latter position underlies the principle of rectification, wherein relative inequalities among society members are justified if they result in an absolute benefit, even for the less advantaged. This would lead to a fair outcome, as in such a society, no one would have too much or too little.

Rawls' philosophical position can thus be seen as a form of egalitarian liberalism, attentive to issues of equality and equal opportunities. His theory has sparked lively academic debate and has inspired multiple interpretations and criticisms. For example, Robert Nozick's (1974) critiques reflect a deep philosophical divergence regarding the role of the state and social justice. The author promoted a libertarian ideology, asserting that only market forces and individual choices should determine the distribution of resources, without external interference. Consequently, any attempt at coerced redistribution would violate the principle of individual autonomy, leading to unjust outcomes. From his perspective, it is not possible to define or achieve a perfectly just distribution of resources in a complex and diverse society.

Michael Sandel (1998) criticized Rawls' approach to justice for its excessive abstractness. His position is often associated with a more communitarian approach, which recognizes the importance of communities, shared values, and traditions in defining what is just. Specifically, he raised questions about the real-world applicability of the "veil of ignorance" and the ability of individuals to reach a fair consensus through this hypothetical position of ignorance, emphasizing the significance of cultural values and traditions in shaping notions of justice.

Another prominent figure in the social justice debate is Martha Nussbaum (1999), who is famous for her theory of "capabilities" and her approach to social justice based on the centrality of essential human functions. Nussbaum criticized theories of justice for their sole focus on the distribution of material resources, highlighting instead the importance of capabilities and opportunities that individuals have for leading a meaningful and fully realized life. According to Nussbaum, adequate justice must ensure not only the satisfaction of basic needs but also the possibility of developing human capabilities in areas such as knowledge, political participation, creativity, and personal achievement. Her approach has expanded the traditional focus of justice theories, encompassing both material and immaterial dimensions. Nussbaum also emphasized the significance of cultural diversity and individual choices in enriching the fabric of society and shaping justice, encouraging scholars to consider a broader range of factors in the analysis and promotion of equity in society.

SDG 16 is also broken down into several specific goals that largely echo the theorizing set forth so far. First, it aims to reduce violence in all its forms, ensuring personal and collective security. This includes reducing the incidence of homicides, robberies, sexual violence, and domestic violence, as well as the abolition of practices such as torture and summary executions. The goal also aims to end impunity for crimes against humanity and ensure access to fair and impartial justice for all, regardless of social or economic status.

Another fundamental element of SDG 16 is the promotion of accountability and transparency in government institutions and decision-making processes. This involves creating laws and policies that allow for meaningful citizen participation, access to public information, and the fight against corruption. The aim is to create an environment where institutions are accountable for the populations they serve and operate ethically and transparently.

A further specific objective of SDG 16 is the construction of effective institutions at all levels, capable of providing high-quality public services and responding to the needs of communities. This includes promoting strong local institutions capable of addressing the daily challenges of citizens and tackling issues such as access to clean water, education, and healthcare. At the same time, it involves strengthening national and international institutions to address complex challenges such as climate change, terrorism, and migration.

Implicitly, SDG 16 presents an intrinsic link to the safeguarding of territorial identity, as it aims to create inclusive, fair, and harmonious societies that respect and preserve the specificities of different localities. It seeks to address many challenges that can threaten territorial identity and social cohesion in various dimensions.

First and foremost, the goal promotes peace and conflict prevention. This is an essential purpose for preserving territorial identity. Conflicts can devastate the social and economic structures of communities, leading to forced migrations and the loss of deeply rooted cultural traditions.

The promotion of access to justice and the protection of rights represent another point of convergence between SDG 16 and the dimension of safeguarding territorial identity. Access to a fair and impartial judicial system for all, regardless of social or economic status, is crucial to ensuring the rights of communities and protecting their unique identity.

SDG 16 also addresses the importance of encouraging responsible, transparent, and participatory governance. It plays a fundamental role in safeguarding and promoting territorial identity, as it allows for the representation and visibility of all the identities that shape a territory, enabling different aspects to defend their own traditions and values. Notably, the protection of cultural rights and minorities is a key goal of SDG 16. Respect for human rights and fundamental freedoms, including those of minorities, is crucial to allowing all groups to preserve and pass their unique traditions, languages, and cultural practices to future generations.

Final, SDG 16 promotes active participation and involvement of local communities in endorsing peace, justice, and responsible governance, thus strengthening territorial identity. By involving citizens in the decision-making process and policy implementation, the goal establishes a direct link between communities and policies that influence their lives, enabling them to defend and enhance their unique identity.

In many countries, significant progress has been made toward achieving strong and just institutions. Examples from Rwanda and Colombia provide intriguing insights into the complex dynamics and challenges surrounding the concept of social justice within unique national contexts. Both countries have made significant efforts to address issues of justice and build more inclusive and equitable societies, demonstrating that the pursuit of social justice is not merely an abstract ideal but a tangible reality that requires commitment, leadership, and concerted action.

Rwanda, devastated by the 1994 genocide, faced a painful history of ethnic divisions and violence (Cossa, 2021). In the subsequent years, the country has made substantial efforts to strengthen its judicial system, aiming to build a more stable and prosperous society. Through legal and institutional reforms, Rwanda has worked to create an independent and efficient judicial system, ensuring access to justice for all citizens. The establishment of Gacaca courts to address genocide-related crimes exemplified community justice, seeking to promote reconciliation between victims and perpetrators (Clark, 2010). The country adopted policies to address gender inequalities, promoting women's empowerment and improving their educational and employment opportunities (Nyiransabimana, 2018). Despite ongoing challenges, the efforts made over time are contributing to a more equitable environment and the country's economic growth and demonstrating that social justice can be a driving force for sustainable development.

As for Colombia, the country has faced decades of armed conflict among the government, rebel groups, and criminal gangs, causing suffering and divisions within society (Pérez-Garzón, 2018). In recent years, the country has sought to address the wounds of the past and build lasting peace through transitional justice and reconciliation processes. The 2016 peace agreement between the Colombian government and the Revolutionary Armed Forces of Colombia (FARC) marked a significant step toward ending the armed conflict. This agreement included a commitment to address serious human rights violations committed during the conflict through the transitional justice system. This system includes the Special

Criminal Court, which investigates the most serious crimes and ensures accountability for those responsible, and the Truth Commission, which seeks to establish the truth about the events that occurred. On June 27, 2017, FARC ceased to be an armed group, disarming and handing over their weapons to the United Nations. A month later, FARC announced their transformation into a legal political party, in accordance with the terms of the peace agreement (Maher & Thomson, 2018). These efforts have contributed to promoting reconciliation and stabilizing the country, paving the way for a fairer and more peaceful society.

It is important to emphasize that both examples present significant and complex challenges in pursuing social justice. In the case of Rwanda, while the Gacaca courts sought to address genocide crimes, concerns have been raised about their ability to ensure fair and transparent processes and promote genuine reconciliation among communities. Similarly, in Colombia, the implementation of the peace agreement and transitional justice mechanisms has faced political obstacles and practical challenges. Balancing justice for victims with the need to promote long-term stability and reconciliation is a central theme that emerges from both examples.

In conclusion, the examples of Rwanda and Colombia highlight how the pursuit of social justice can be a challenging yet vital path to building fairer and more balanced societies. Both countries have confronted situations of intense inequality, violence, and divisions, but have demonstrated that through a commitment to justice, reconciliation, and the construction of strong institutions, it is possible to initiate paths to address challenges and create a better future. It is also clear that the path toward social justice is complex and requires lasting attention, adaptability, and collaboration among governments, civil society, and local communities. Only through collective effort and enduring commitment can the goal of a fair, inclusive, and equitable society be achieved.

In pursuing peace, justice, and strong institutions, it is crucial to understand the specific obstacles that can undermine the achievement of such goals. To this end, a detailed examination of concrete contexts can offer an illuminating perspective on how these challenges manifest and what strategies can be adopted to address them.

One of the most widespread obstacles to achieving SDG 16 is corruption. Countries around the world grapple with various forms of corruption that undermine trust in governance and compromise the equitable allocation of resources. For example, Nigeria, despite being one of the world's major oil producers, has faced widespread political and economic corruption that has hindered the transformation of oil wealth into sustainable development (Hope, 2017). Resources that should benefit the entire population are often siphoned off by corrupt elites, leaving the country in a state of persistent inequality and poverty. An effective and forceful fight against corruption requires promoting transparency, accountability, and citizen participation in political and economic decisions. The creation of strong institutions and the adoption of robust anti-corruption laws can help limit the scope of corruption and ensure a more equitable use of resources.

The lack of respect for human rights constitutes another crucial obstacle to achieving SDG 16. In many contexts, citizens are deprived of their fundamental rights, including freedom of expression, association, and political participation. In countries like China, North Korea, and Russia, governments often suppress dissenting voices and limit freedom of the press and expression, undermining the vitality of civil societies (Biddulph, 2015; Fahy, 2019; Nathan, 2015). These attacks on human rights not only threaten the well-being of citizens but also weaken the possibility of building strong and inclusive institutions. Addressing this challenge requires a steadfast commitment to the protection and promotion of human rights, both at the national and international levels. Respect for fundamental rights must be placed at the core of public policies and government actions to create an environment in which all people can fully participate in social, economic, and political life.

The presence of criminal groups and the lack of intervention by law enforcement represent two elements that inevitably push the achievement of SDG 16 further. This situation describes certain areas of Mexico. The Fray Bartolomé de las Casas Human Rights Center published a report titled "Chiapas: A Disaster" (Frayba, 2023), portraying the country as in disarray, as it is plagued by violence. In 2023, the conflict between criminal groups intensified, terrorizing the population in a strip of land along the border between the Mexican state of Chiapas and Guatemala. Due to clashes between rival factions, hundreds of residents were forced to leave their homes in the ejidos, which are communal agricultural lands managed by the government in the municipality of Frontera Comalapa, north of Tapachula. The Fray Bartolomé de las Casas Human Rights Center reported that cartels are forcing young people from these communities to join their ranks, under threat of death. Videos recorded by residents of the municipality vividly depict the effects of the wave of violence. One video shows dozens of people walking quickly, apparently fleeing from criminal groups. Another recording shows trucks with handmade armor, commonly known in the region as "monsters." Similar trucks have been seen in Michoacán and Tamaulipas in recent years and are used by armed bandits to carry out raids. The recent increase in violence along the border adds to the conflicts that other areas of Chiapas have been experiencing for years. For instance, in Ocozocoautla, a small corner of the southernmost Mexican state of Chiapas characterized by its impressive waterfalls, sparkling rivers, mountains, and forests – all rich in biodiversity – a criminal group kidnapped 16 public officials on the road leading to the town, where roadblocks set up by organized crime are frequent. Just a few months later, in San Cristóbal de las Casas, a shootout occurred on the street. Jerónimo Ruiz, an artisan and leader of the Association of Tenants of the Traditional Chiapas Market, was assassinated. The escalation of deaths and disappearances in the state, along with the silent response of the authorities, has led to denunciations even from religious authorities. Bishop Luis Manuel López Alfaro of the Diocese of San Cristóbal de las Casas described in a public interview the situation in Chiapas as a "silent war," while the Diocesan Justice and Peace Commission released a document in which it detailed the cases of 53 people murdered in the state between January and April 2023.

It is clear that achieving SDG 16's aim of promoting peace, justice, and strong institutions in such environments is an arduous task. The presence of criminal organizations, which often operate with impunity, undermines the ability of governments to establish and maintain effective institutions that can provide security and uphold the rule of law. In places where criminal groups hold significant power, their influence can infiltrate political, economic, and social spheres, making it challenging to establish the conditions for peace and justice to thrive.

In many cases, these criminal organizations exploit existing social and economic vulnerabilities, capitalizing on high levels of poverty, inequality, and lack of access to basic services. For example, in parts of Central and South America, drug cartels and criminal gangs often target at marginalized communities where residents lack economic opportunities and are susceptible to recruitment (Decker & Pyrooz, 2015). The promise of financial gain and protection can seduce young individuals into criminal activities, perpetuating cycles of violence and hindering the development of just and equitable societies.

To sum up, the attainment of SDG 16 stands as a crucial pillar for a more accountable and inclusive world, pushing the preservation and enhancement of territorial identity. SDG 16, with its focus on promoting social justice, ensuring access to fair governance, and preventing violence, emerges as a beacon of hope for nurturing the diverse cultural landscapes that comprise the world. The pursuit of peace and conflict resolution not only quells the disruptive forces that threaten to fracture cultural traditions but also cultivates an environment where heritage can flourish unimpeded. By advocating for access to justice, protection of cultural rights, and empowerment of marginalized communities, SDG 16 champions the very elements that underpin the richness of territorial identity. The imperative remains clear: The successful realization of SDG 16 offers a compass for cultivating societies where every voice is heard, every heritage is celebrated, and every identity contributes to a tapestry of unity in diversity.

References

Biddulph, S. (2015). *The stability imperative: Human rights and law in China*. UBC Press.
Clark, P. (2010). *The Gacaca courts, post-genocide justice and reconciliation in Rwanda: Justice without lawyers*. Cambridge University Press.
Cossa, J. (2021). Modernity's university, social justice, and social responsibility: A Cosmo-Ubuntu critique. *Educação, Sociedade & Culturas, 58*, 33–50.
Dahrendorf, R. (1957). *Soziale Klassen und Klassenkonflikt in der industriellen Gesellschaft*. Stuttgart.
Decker, S. H., & Pyrooz, D. C. (Eds.). (2015). *The handbook of gangs*. John Wiley & Sons.
Fahy, S. (2019). *Dying for rights: Putting North Korea's human rights abuses on the record*. Columbia University Press.
Frayba (Fray Bartolomé de las Casas). (2023). *Chiapas: A disaster*. Fray Bartolomé de las Casas.
Hope Sr, K. R. (2017). *Corruption and governance in Africa: Swaziland, Kenya, Nigeria*. Springer.
Maher, D., & Thomson, A. (2018). A precarious peace? The threat of paramilitary violence to the peace process in Colombia. *Third World Quarterly, 39*(11), 2142–2172.

Marx, K. (1867). *Das Kapital: Kritik der politischen Oekonomie. Vol. 1: Der Produktionsprozess des Kapitals* (1st ed.). Verlag von Otto Meissner.
Nathan, A. J. (2015). China's challenge. *Journal of Democracy, 26*, 156–163.
Nozick, R. (1974). *Anarchy, state, and Utopia*. Basic Books.
Nussbaum, N. (1999). *Sex & social justice*. Oxford University Press.
Nyiransabimana, V. (2018). Gender equality-key challenges and practical solutions to women participation in local governance in Rwanda. *African Journal of Public Affairs, 10*(3), 1–22.
Pérez-Garzón, C. A. (2018). Unveiling the meaning of social justice in Colombia. *Mexican Law Review, 10*(2), 27–66.
Rawls, J. (1971). *A theory of justice*. Belknap Press.
Sandel, N. (1998). *Liberalism and the limits of justice*. Cambridge University Press.
Weber, M. (1922). *Wirtschaft und Gesellschaft*. Tübingen.

Chapter 17

SDG 17. Strengthen the Means of Implementation and Revitalize the Global Partnership for Sustainable Development

Abstract

The chapter highlights the role of cooperation as a conduit through which diverse territorial identities can harmoniously contribute to realizing the SDGs. By embracing the principles of meaningful engagement, shared purpose, equality, and formalization, cooperative initiatives metamorphose into catalysts for fostering sustainable transformation. In this context, cooperation assumes a focal role in bridging gaps, nurturing comprehension, and establishing a fertile ground where collective aspirations converge. This convergence results in outcomes that not only propel developmental objectives forward but also pay homage to and elevate the distinctive identities that render each territory a crucial participant in the global quest for a sustainable future. Territorial identities encompass the cultural, social, and historical facets that delineate and distinguish specific regions or communities. These facets exert potent influence in shaping viewpoints, values, and conduct, deeply embedded in the shared consciousness. When interwoven with collaborative undertakings, territorial identities not only enrich the cooperative process but also imbue it with genuineness and significance.

SDG 17 acknowledges the crucial necessity for effective and inclusive collaboration among diverse actors to address the complex challenges characterizing the contemporary world. In its entirety, the 2030 Agenda for Sustainable Development represents an ambitious and interconnected vision to create a better world for present and future generations, with SDG 17 serving as the glue that holds this vision together. It promotes strategic partnerships on international, national, and local levels to achieve the established objectives. The very essence of SDG 17

Identity, Territories, and Sustainability: Challenges and Opportunities for Achieving the UN Sustainable Development Goals, 167–175
Copyright © 2024 by Salvatore Monaco
Published under exclusive licence by Emerald Publishing Limited
doi:10.1108/978-1-83797-549-520241018

reflects a central concept in the current socio-political and economic discourse: The need to overcome divisions and work together to address global challenges. The goal recognizes the fact that current issues cannot be solved by individual actors, nations, or sectors alone, but require a synergy of joint efforts and teamwork. This involves robust and multilateral partnerships between countries, international organizations, the private sector, civil society, and other stakeholders to successfully achieve the other 16 DSGs.

While the conventional emphasis of the SDGs has predominantly centered around economic, social, and environmental dimensions, it is essential to recognize that the underlying essence of global partnership for sustainable development inherently encompasses the recognition and amplification of territorial identity.

Firstly, it fosters a profound appreciation for the diversity and uniqueness that each territory contributes to the global mosaic. Appreciating and respecting territorial identity, the partnership embraces the multifaceted nature of human existence and reinforces the principle that sustainable development must be contextually grounded to be truly efficacious. Moreover, the incorporation of territorial identity into the realm of global partnership serves as a catalyst for collaboration and mutual learning. Territories, whether they be local communities, regions, or entire nations, possess a reservoir of localized knowledge, expertise, and insights that can profoundly influence the trajectory of sustainable development. When these diverse entities come together in a spirit of cooperation, they can leverage their distinct strengths to address complex challenges that transcend geographic boundaries. This collaboration not only fosters innovative solutions but also nurtures a sense of shared responsibility and involvement in the pursuit of common goals. Furthermore, the global partnership's recognition of territorial identity serves as a powerful driver for equitable development. In many instances, territories facing similar challenges can draw solace and inspiration from another's experiences, creating a sense of solidarity that transcends geopolitical divides. By acknowledging the nuances of territorial identity, the partnership underscores the importance of tailoring development interventions to cater to the specific needs and aspirations of each territory. This approach is inherently inclusive, ensuring that no territory is left behind and that the benefits of sustainable development are distributed equitably across diverse landscapes. The integration of territorial identity within the global partnership framework also underlines the role of local agencies in shaping sustainable development outcomes. Communities and regions possess an inherent understanding of their landscapes, resources, and vulnerabilities. Their intimate connection to their territories positions them as natural stewards of their environments and champions of sustainable practices. By elevating territorial identity, the partnership empowers local actors to actively participate in decision-making processes, design interventions that resonate with their unique contexts, and drive meaningful change from the grassroots level upwards.

A typical example of how SDG 17 embraces territorial identity and global collaboration is the approach to combating climate change (Nordhaus, 2019; Sabel & Victor, 2017). Climate change transcends borders, affecting every corner of the globe. Addressing this challenge requires a collective commitment to reduce greenhouse gas emissions, adapt to climate impacts, and promote sustainable technologies and practices. Cooperation between nations together with the sharing of best practices plays a crucial role. For instance, the Paris Agreement on climate change represents a global work to limit the rise in global temperatures. This commitment was also underscored in the final agreement of COP28, which not only obligates signatory countries to limit their emissions but also calls them upon to actively contribute to the global transition effort toward sustainable development. This approach emphasizes collaborative efforts rather than placing the sole burden of such transformative changes on individual nations. On one hand, this collaboration reflects a sense of belonging to a global community and a shared commitment to safeguard the planet. On the other hand, each territory, with its unique identity, has the opportunity to play a significant role in this fight, integrating traditional solutions and sharing specific knowledge that can contribute to the well-being of the planet. This cooperation amplifies the effectiveness of the undertaken actions, fostering the appreciation of and giving full play to local traditions and skills. The unique contribution of each territory represents a distinctive and proud trait that strengthens the sense of belonging and territorial identity within a broader collaboration framework.

A crucial aspect of SDG 17 is the encouragement of international cooperation, both among industrialized countries, and among them and developing countries (Imaz & Eizagirre, 2020; Prashantham & Birkinshaw, 2020). This implies promoting fair and beneficial exchanges, sharing technologies and expertise, ensuring access to markets, and providing financial support to struggling countries. For example, the World Bank and the International Monetary Fund (IMF) have built a strong collaboration over the years to address socio-economic challenges affecting developing nations (Reinhart & Trebesch, 2016). Through their joint commitment, they have helped mitigate the devastating effects of debt and promote sustainable economic development in many parts of the world. The Heavily Indebted Poor Countries (HIPC) international program is a concrete response to the challenge of excessive debt that has burdened many low-income countries. Launched in 1996, this initiative aimed to reduce the burden of foreign debt on heavily indebted countries, allowing them to free up financial resources for investments in crucial sectors such as education, health, and infrastructure (Siddique et al., 2016). To date, nearly 40 nations have received funds under the program, totaling over $100 billion. The HIPC approach involved a range of measures, including debt restructuring, concessional loans, and technical support to ensure sustainable financial management. IMF, on the other hand, played a key role in facilitating the debt reduction process through structural adjustment programs and financial assistance. The goal was to create favorable conditions for economic growth and institution strengthening in beneficiary countries. The program, which underwent review and reforms in 1999, identified 38 particularly needy nations, with 32 in sub-Saharan Africa. Countries like Ghana, Tanzania, and Uganda benefited from funds to reduce their external debt while implementing structural reforms that contributed to improving their economic prospects. For instance, the HIPC program allowed Ghana to make significant strides toward sustainable development (Opoku, 2010). Ghana initiated the HIPC program in 2001 in response to the overwhelming burden of foreign debt that had constrained its ability to invest in crucial areas such as education, healthcare, and infrastructure. The initial impact of the HIPC program was evident in the early years of implementation. The reduction in public debt allowed the Ghanaian government to redirect its financial resources toward programs and projects that directly improved citizens' lives. Investments in education led to increased access to basic education, with a particular focus on girls' education. This not only improved learning opportunities but also promoted gender equality, strengthening territorial identity through a more equitable and inclusive society. Healthcare was another priority area for investments resulting from the HIPC program. Funds freed up through debt reduction facilitated the enhancement of healthcare infrastructure, access to quality medical care, and the prevention of deadly diseases. These efforts contributed to improving the health of the Ghanaian population. In addition to the direct impacts on education and healthcare, the HIPC program also supported infrastructure expansion and overall economic development. The promotion of public and private investments contributed to the growth of productive sectors, fostering job creation, and improving the economic conditions of local communities. A crucial aspect of the HIPC program was the promotion of active participation by civil society and local communities in decisions regarding resource allocation. Furthermore, Ghana leveraged the opportunity provided by the HIPC program to strengthen its presence and influence internationally. Collaboration with international organizations like the IMF and the World Bank opened doors to increased cooperation and knowledge exchange. Such collaboration contributed to reinforcing Ghana's territorial identity as a global actor committed to pursuing sustainable development goals and promoting social justice on an international level. This kind of engagement, which is not merely assistance-based, helped enhance people's sense of pride and belonging to their country. Territorial identity was further strengthened through citizens' involvement in shaping public policies and implementing projects.

Another demonstration of the effectiveness of these partnerships occurred in Latin America. Emblematic countries like Brazil and Ecuador embarked on significant and collaborative commitments within the framework of HIPC to address debt challenges and promote structural reforms that would foster inclusive and sustainable economic growth. Over the years, this collaboration has demonstrated a profound impact on strengthening the territorial identity of both countries, shaping the path toward a fairer and more prosperous development. Brazil faced severe issues of indebtedness and economic instability, which intensified especially during the 1990s and early 2000s (Oliveira et al., 2013). Active participation by Brazil in the HIPC Initiative enabled the country to negotiate debt restructuring plans and implement economic policies aimed at stimulating growth and stability. These efforts contributed to establishing the foundations for increased investor confidence, promoting the attraction of foreign and national capital necessary for sustainable development. The implementation of structural reforms helped improve the business environment, enhancing competitiveness and driving economic growth. The combined effect of these initiatives was a tangible improvement in the living conditions of Brazilian citizens. Access to essential social services such as education and healthcare expanded, thus promoting greater social inclusion, and contributing to the fight against extreme poverty. In this context, Brazil's territorial identity was strengthened through the creation of a more just and equitable society in which citizens felt involved and valued. The promotion of a sustainable economy also contributed to preserving the country's natural and cultural resources, enriching territorial identity with an awareness of its wealth, and diversity.

SDG 17 also focuses on promoting the capacity of developing countries to implement sustainable policies and programs through knowledge sharing, training, and technical assistance. This emphasis on enhancing the developmental capabilities highlights a profound recognition of the vital importance of territorial identity in shaping effective and contextually relevant strategies for sustainable development. This recognition within the framework of SDG 17 is not merely a symbolic gesture, but a pragmatic acknowledgment of the role that local cultures, traditions, and knowledge systems play in shaping sustainable development outcomes. For instance, a developing nation with a strong cultural tradition of community-based resource management may find greater success in implementing sustainable natural resource management practices that align with its cultural values. In such a scenario, the integration of traditional knowledge and practices can contribute to more effective and lasting outcomes, as the community's inherent connection to its land and resources drives responsible stewardship.

The acknowledgment of territorial identity within SDG 17 underscores the importance of a bottom-up approach to sustainable development. This approach not only ensures that policies are better aligned with local needs but also empowers communities to take ownership of their development trajectories. By engaging communities as equal partners in the decision-making process, a sense of agency and responsibility is nurtured, contributing to the strengthening of territorial identity as people become active participants in shaping their own future.

One illustrative example of international partnership under the umbrella of SDG 17 is represented by the initiative "Ending the AIDS Epidemic by 2030," launched by the United Nations in 2016 (Harries et al., 2016; Lamontagne et al., 2019). This initiative aims to combat HIV/AIDS through a series of interventions that include prevention, treatment, and support for individuals affected by the virus. An integral part of this initiative is the promotion of collaboration among countries, international organizations, civil society, and the private sector to ensure universal access to HIV/AIDS prevention and care services. The goal is to end the AIDS epidemic by 2030, demonstrating how international cooperation can make a difference in promoting global health and implementing the SDG agenda.

In the field of education, the Global Partnership for Education (GPE) is a concrete example of how SDG 17 has been translated into action to promote access to quality education for all (Menashy, 2016). Launched in 2002, the GPE has become a catalyst for education financing in low-income and developing countries. In 2018, the GPE mobilized over $2 billion in education funding, contributing to improving access and quality of education in many parts of the world.

Another initiative that illustrates the potential of SDG 17 is the partnership for maternal and child health launched in 2015, known as "Every Woman Every Child." This global partnership aims to improve the health of women and children through accelerated investments and actions at both national and international levels. The initiative promotes collaboration among governments, international organizations, civil society, and the private sector to address challenges related to maternal and child health, improving access to basic health services and reducing maternal and child mortality (Ateva et al., 2018).

Furthermore, the financial sector has played a key role in implementing the SDGs by introducing innovative financing mechanisms and developing tools. For example, the microfinance sector has significantly contributed to promoting entrepreneurship and access to credit for marginalized and low-income communities, thus fostering inclusive economic growth, especially in the world's most vulnerable and marginalized countries. The introduction of innovative financial instruments has created new opportunities for funding projects and initiatives related to environmental sustainability, paving the way for a significant evolution in the global financial landscape. Among these instruments, "green bonds" have emerged as one of the most promising and influential, providing an effective means to mobilize capital for projects aimed at mitigating climate change, promoting energy efficiency, preserving biodiversity, and addressing other pressing environmental challenges (Bhutta et al., 2022). "Green bonds" are debt securities issued by public or private entities to finance low-impact environmental projects and promote sustainability. This means that the capital raised through the issuance of these bonds is directed toward initiatives that have a positive impact on the environment and contribute to sustainable development goals. The issuance of "green bonds" is managed by established guidelines and standards, such as the Green Bond Principles (GBP), which set criteria for identifying eligible projects and ensuring transparency and integrity in the process.

An exemplary instance showcasing the efficacy of "green bonds" is evident through the endeavors of Stockholm, the capital city of Sweden (Maltais & Nykvist, 2020). The issuance of Stockholm's inaugural green bond marked a watershed moment, with a lot of resources dedicated to propelling transformative sustainable mobility projects. The resonance of this initiative extended far beyond the confines of traditional fiscal mechanisms. It epitomized the fusion of financial innovation with environmental stewardship, echoing the profound sentiments of global partnership for sustainable development. The synergy between local actions and global aspirations signifies the embodiment of the principle that sustainable development transcends geographic boundaries, beckoning for collaboration that embraces territorial identities. The issuance of green bonds encouraged cooperation in the pursuit of sustainable development. Several national and international investors, recognizing the profound impact of sustainable mobility on the trajectory of urban evolution, found resonance with Stockholm's vision.

This alignment of purpose fostered a unique brand of partnership that enriched the discourse with shared commitment and cooperative ambition. While the enhancement of air quality and the reduction of greenhouse gas emissions undeniably exemplify the tangible benefits of Stockholm's initiative, the intangible dimensions of success are manifested through the fostering of a palpable spirit of cooperation respectful of the territorial identities of all involved partners. The convergence of territorial identities, as encapsulated by the inhabitants of Stockholm, investors, and the global community, is an ode to the synergistic potential of partnerships rooted in shared purpose and mutual respect.

Equally significant is the case of the International Finance Corporation (IFC), the leading global development institution promoting the private sector in developing countries. The IFC has issued numerous "green bonds" to finance projects addressing environmental challenges in different regions of the world. For example, in 2017, the IFC issued a $1 billion "green bond" to finance renewable energy projects, including wind and solar parks, in developing countries. This initiative contributed to increasing renewable energy production capacity in these regions while simultaneously reducing CO_2 emissions and promoting sustainable economic growth.

Another effective example of "green bond" utilization comes from the European Investment Bank (EIB), which issued green bonds to finance projects in the renewable energy, energy efficiency, sustainable transportation, and climate adaptation sectors. In 2019, the EIB launched a "Sustainable Awareness Bond," raising over €2 billion to finance projects that promote the transition to a low-carbon economy (Igbudu et al., 2018). Thus, the introduction of "green bonds" has opened new horizons in the global financial context, offering an innovative and potentially transformative perspective to address the urgent challenges of environmental and social sustainability. These financial instruments are not merely vehicles for capital raising. They play a crucial role in directing financial resources toward projects that promote environmental protection and improve the living conditions of communities. The emergence of "green bonds" embodies the idea that the financial sector can become a positive actor in pursuing sustainable development goals, aligning profit with the common good and public interest (Ahmad & Mokhchy, 2023).

In conclusion, cooperation emerges as a potent and indispensable instrument in the pursuit of realizing the SDGs. While cooperation holds immense value, it does not possess a universal profile. Its effectiveness hinges upon a nuanced and comprehensive assessment of a multitude of factors. First, mere contact among partners cannot be deemed sufficient. On the contrary, certain circumstances may give rise to interactions escalating into conflicts, exacerbating hostilities, or further widening existing disparities. Thus, the efficacy of cooperation is intricately intertwined with the context within which it unfolds. Second, genuinely catalyze sustainable development through cooperative initiatives, the quality of relationships plays a decisive role. In this regard, the depth of these relationships proves to be of paramount significance. Superficial or sporadic interactions, while facilitating a nominal connection, fail to yield the substantial outcomes required for meaningful progress. Cooperative engagements should be characterized by a sense of continuity, involving frequent interactions of substantial duration and meaningful depth. It is within these prolonged interactions that the exchange of ideas, perspectives, and insights can occur, nurturing a deeper understanding and appreciation of diverse viewpoints. Furthermore, the cultivation of a shared sense of purpose emerges as an indispensable cornerstone for successful cooperation. The pursuit of a common goal not only serves as a unifying force but also contributes to dismantling barriers and nurturing a collaborative favorable environment for mutual growth and achievement. This shared purpose not only bridges differences but also provides a framework for setting collective targets, guiding joint efforts, and fostering a sense of belonging and commitment among cooperating entities. The alignment of motivations and collective aspirations within the framework of a shared purpose amplifies the potential for meaningful impact. Equally crucial is maintaining equal status among partners in any cooperation. Hierarchical relationships must be avoided, ensuring that no single actor holds undue influence over others. This principle of equality extends beyond the realm of power dynamics, encompassing the respectful recognition and valorization of all territorial identities involved in the cooperative process. Each partner's unique cultural, social, and historical context contributes to the collective endeavor's richness and potential, underscoring the importance of inclusivity and active participation in sustainable development. In light of the above, the formalization of cooperation through well-structured agreements and frameworks enhances its efficacy. These agreements serve as binding commitments that outline roles, responsibilities, objectives, and mechanisms for conflict resolution and respect for territorial specificities. They provide a clear roadmap for collaborative action, ensuring that cooperation remains focused, organized, and accountable. This formalization also underscores the seriousness and commitment of all parties involved, fostering an environment of trust and shared accountability.

References

Ahmad, S., & Mokhchy, J. (2023). Corporate social responsibilities, sustainable investment, and the future of green bond market: Evidence from renewable energy projects in Morocco. *Environmental Science and Pollution Research*, *30*(6), 15186–15197.

Ateva, E., Blencowe, H., Castillo, T., Dev, A., Farmer, M., Kinney, M., Mishra, S. K., Hopkins Leisher, S., Maloney, S., Ponce Hardy, V., Quigley, P., Ruidiaz, J., Siassakos, D., Stoner, J. E., Storey, C., & Tejada de Rivero Sawers, M. L. (2018). Every woman, every child's progress in partnership for stillbirths: A commentary by the stillbirth advocacy working group. *BJOG: An International Journal of Obstetrics and Gynaecology*, *125*(9), 1058–1060.

Bhutta, U. S., Tariq, A., Farrukh, M., Raza, A., & Iqbal, M. K. (2022). Green bonds for sustainable development: Review of literature on development and impact of green bonds. *Technological Forecasting and Social Change*, *175*, 121378.

Harries, A. D., Suthar, A. B., Takarinda, K. C., Tweya, H., Kyaw, N. T. T., Tayler-Smith, K., & Zachariah, R. (2016). Ending the HIV/AIDS epidemic in low- and middle-income countries by 2030: Is it possible? *F1000Research*, 5–10.

Igbudu, N., Garanti, Z., & Popoola, T. (2018). Enhancing bank loyalty through sustainable banking practices: The mediating effect of corporate image. *Sustainability, 10*(11), 4050.

Imaz, O., & Eizagirre, A. (2020). Responsible innovation for sustainable development goals in business: An agenda for cooperative firms. *Sustainability, 12*(17), 6948.

Lamontagne, E., Over, M., & Stover, J. (2019). The economic returns of ending the AIDS epidemic as a public health threat. *Health Policy, 123*(1), 104–108.

Maltais, A., & Nykvist, B. (2020). Understanding the role of green bonds in advancing sustainability. *Journal of Sustainable Finance & Investment, 1*, 1–20.

Menashy, F. (2016). Understanding the roles of non-state actors in global governance: Evidence from the global partnership for education. *Journal of Education Policy, 31*(1), 98–118.

Nordhaus, W. (2019). Climate change: The ultimate challenge for economics. *American Economic Review, 109*(6), 1991–2014.

Oliveira, G. R., Tabak, B. M., de Lara Resende, J. G., & Cajueiro, D. O. (2013). Determinants of the level of indebtedness for Brazilian firms: A quantile regression approach. *Economia, 14*(3-4), 123–138.

Opoku, D. K. (2010). From a 'success' story to a highly indebted poor country: Ghana and neoliberal reforms. *Journal of Contemporary African Studies, 28*(2), 155–175.

Prashantham, S., & Birkinshaw, J. (2020). MNE–SME cooperation: An integrative framework. *Journal of International Business Studies, 51*, 1161–1175.

Reinhart, C. M., & Trebesch, C. (2016). The international monetary fund: 70 years of reinvention. *Journal of Economic Perspectives, 30*(1), 3–28.

Sabel, C. F., & Victor, D. G. (2017). Governing global problems under uncertainty: Making bottom-up climate policy work. *Climatic Change, 144*, 15–27.

Siddique, A., Selvanathan, E. A., & Selvanathan, S. (2016). The impact of external debt on growth: Evidence from highly indebted poor countries. *Journal of Policy Modeling, 38*(5), 874–894.

Conclusions: Moving Forward with Territorial Identities – Concluding Perspectives

Abstract

The concluding chapter illuminates the path toward a harmonious integration of territorial identities within the realm of sustainable development. The analysis delves into both direct and subtle connections, demonstrating how sustainable development strategies that honor and leverage territorial identities can yield profound positive impacts. The conclusions address the challenges inherent in this endeavor, including balancing local identities with broader development goals, guarding against external appropriation, and fostering education and awareness. As the chapter asserts, navigating these challenges with respect and collaboration can transform territorial identities into catalysts for positive change, ushering in a future where sustainable development and identity preservation intertwine seamlessly, leading to a more equitable, inclusive, and prosperous world.

This volume has reviewed various initiatives that have been implemented in recent years to address the numerous global challenges threatening both human well-being and the health of the planet. These solutions have been driven by the principles of sustainability, which have emerged as a guiding ethos in the contemporary world, encompassing environmental, economic, and social considerations. Both political agendas and the scientific community now concur that the pursuit of sustainability entails reconciling the needs of present and future generations, ensuring the preservation of natural resources, promoting social equity, and fostering long-term economic prosperity through locally and globally realized policies, initiatives, and practices.

The environmental dimension of sustainability is still the central focus of many initiatives aimed at sustainable development. It pertains to the safeguarding and responsible management of natural resources, as well as the preservation of ecosystems that sustain life on Earth (UNEP, 2019). This involves the reduction of greenhouse gas emissions, sustainable water resource management, biodiversity conservation, and pollution prevention. In accordance with the agreements reached during COP28, all countries will transition their energy systems away from fossil fuels by 2050 in a fair and orderly manner. Additionally, countries are urged to contribute to the global transition effort rather than being solely responsible for such a change. The approved agreement contains various calls related to the energy transition, including an invitation to triple renewable energy capacities and double the pace of energy efficiency improvements by 2030. The agreement also commits to accelerating "zero carbon" and "low carbon" technologies, encompassing nuclear energy, low-carbon hydrogen, and emerging carbon capture and storage.

The conservation of ecosystems, such as forests, oceans, and wetlands, is vital for preserving biodiversity, maintaining the balance of the world, and ensuring essential ecosystem services for humanity, including climate regulation, water purification, and soil fertility. In recent years, youth movements, such as Fridays for Future and Extinction Rebellion (XR), have played a significant role in drawing public and governmental attention to the urgent need to address environmental challenges (Hannigan, 2022). Fridays for Future, initiated by young Swedish activist Greta Thunberg, marked a significant turning point in public awareness of the urgency to combat climate change. What began as a solitary protest quickly transformed into a mass movement involving thousands of students worldwide, organizing Friday protests to demand concrete actions from governments and institutions to address the climate crisis. Greta Thunberg's presence, along with her speech at the United Nations in September 2019, captured the attention of media and people worldwide. She questioned the ability of global leaders to effectively address climate change and called for immediate action to ensure a sustainable future for generations to come. The movement has not been without criticism, particularly regarding the vagueness of the demands without concrete proposals to address climate change. Despite these criticisms, peaceful demonstrations and student strikes captured the attention of governments and institutions, compelling them to address the demands of young activists. In many countries, politicians had to review their policies and commit to more decisive measures to reduce greenhouse gas emissions and address the effects of climate change. In Europe, following Fridays for Future protests, the German government announced a climate package in 2019, aiming to reduce the country's greenhouse gas emissions by 55% by 2030 compared to levels in 1990. Additionally, initiatives to promote renewable energy and reduce coal usage were launched. Similarly, in the United Kingdom, the Fridays for Future movement helped raise awareness about the climate crisis and prompted the government to declare a climate emergency in May 2019. This led to the adoption of more ambitious policies to reduce greenhouse gas emissions, with the goal of achieving climate neutrality by 2050. In Canada as well, the Fridays for Future movement had a significant impact. Several Canadian politicians expressed support for the movement and committed to stronger measures to address climate change, such as the ban on single-use plastics and the introduction of a range of policies aimed at reducing greenhouse gas emissions. In response to Fridays for Future protests, the New Zealand government introduced a climate change law in 2019, with the goal of achieving climate neutrality by 2050. The law also established the creation of an independent Climate Change Commission to monitor progress and provide recommendations to the government. The influence of the movement also extended to international institutions, such as the European Union, which intensified efforts to achieve the goals of the Paris Agreement.

XR is a global movement that rapidly gained popularity in recent years, focusing on environmental protection and the fight against the climate crisis. It adopts a non-violent civil disobedience approach as a tool to draw public and governmental attention to the dangers humanity faces due to climate change (Gardner et al, 2022). XR's protest actions are characterized by roadblocks, building occupations, and other forms of civil disobedience aimed at disrupting normal daily activities to draw attention to environmental issues. These provocative actions captured media attention and contributed to intense public debate about the climate crisis and the necessary policies to address it. One of XR's main goals is to achieve an immediate reduction in greenhouse gas emissions to ensure the survival of the planet and future generations. The movement also calls for a transition to a sustainable society that is socially and ecologically equitable. XR emphasizes the need for a paradigm shift in how societies produce and manage energy, advocating for the adoption of global ecological and sustainable solutions. Its approach has sparked debates both within and outside the movement itself. Some argue that the movement's civil disobedience tactics may alienate the public and compromise support for environmental causes. On the contrary, XR supporters argue that the provocative nature of the actions is necessary to catalyze change and push governments and institutions to take decisive actions to address the climate crisis (Sauerborn, 2022). XR's actions and media presence have influenced political debate and the formulation of environmental policies in many countries. For example, in Australia, the movement pushed the government to consider more ambitious policies for transitioning to renewable energy sources and reducing greenhouse gas emissions.

To ensure an equitable ecological future, the significance of the transition to a sustainable economy is undoubted. Kate Raworth (2017) introduced the concept of "doughnut economics," which is built upon the idea of meeting basic human needs without surpassing critical planetary limits. This approach recognizes the importance of an economy that meets the needs of all individuals, reduces inequalities, and ensures equitable distribution of resources. On the same matter, Jeffrey Sachs (2015) emphasized the need for inclusive and sustainable economic policies that promote dignified employment, poverty reduction, and equitable access to economic opportunities. This covets also incorporates the proposals for transitioning to a circular economy, which highlights waste elimination and resource optimization, promoting reuse, recycling, and materials restoration (Geissdoerfer et al., 2017). The circular economy concept is grounded in the principle that waste can be considered valuable resources, and they can be reused in a continuous cycle of production and consumption. This paradigm shift contrasts with the traditional linear "take, make, dispose" economic model. The circular economy promotes responsible resource extraction, durable and repairable product design, object reuse, and material recycling (Ghisellini et al., 2016). The circular economy approach is recognized as an effective way to address challenges related to natural resource depletion and environmental pollution. Promoting waste reduction and efficient resource utilization, the circular economy can contribute to mitigating the environmental impact of human activities (Murray et al., 2017). Numerous studies have already highlighted the economic benefits arising from adopting a circular economy. A World Economic Forum report (WEF, 2019) estimated that transitioning to a circular economy could generate an economic value of $4.5 trillion by 2030. This brings about more job creation opportunities, technological innovation, and reduced costs associated with extracting new resources. The economic dimension of sustainability also necessitates a revision of economic success assessment models. In this regard, the ecological economy approach (Costanza et al., 1997) argues that traditional indicators such as GDP do not account for negative externalities and environmental costs of economic activities. Therefore, new indicators need to be developed that also consider the environmental and social impact of economic activities to evaluate the progress and effectiveness of sustainable development policies more accurately.

In the same vein, it is imperative to highlight the importance of a social perspective in sustainability too. Anthony Giddens (1990) argued that sustainability requires a radical social transformation that encompasses both institutional changes and alterations in how individuals' daily lives. This perspective implies the promotion of greater democratic participation, equitable access to resources and opportunities, and the protection of fundamental human rights. Furthermore, Amartya Sen (2000) stated that the promotion of human rights is also a key element of the social dimension of sustainability, emphasizing the importance of a social justice perspective. He asserted that sustainability entails eliminating inequalities, ensuring equitable resource access, eradicating poverty, and promoting development opportunities for all. This perspective involves strengthening social capital, enhancing community cohesion, and valuing sharing and cooperation practices (Kim, 2018). To achieve social sustainability, increased public awareness and participation are also crucial (Talan et al., 2020). People need to be engaged in the decision-making process and encouraged to adopt sustainable behaviors at both individual and collective levels, as active engagement in environmental protection can lead to a society in harmony with the environment.

Drawing on these insights, the SDGs aspire to drive a transformative global change by urging collective action focused on environmental and economic concerns, also directed toward rectifying social inequalities (Arora-Jonsson et al., 2023).

The comprehensive analysis presented within this text has not only deepened understanding but has also expanded the scope of the SDGs. It infuses their inherent significance with a strong connection to territorial identities. This perspective underscores how each SDG, be it in a direct or indirect manner, is intricately connected with specific facets that shape and nurture a place's identity. With this newfound awareness, it is possible to dismantle some conceptual barriers that may have previously constrained conventional interpretations of the SDGs.

Through a series of in-depth case studies, the analysis allows to affirm that the pursuit of a specific SDG can have positive or negative implications for territorial identity, depending on the ability of public and private actors engaged in the territory to adopt a perspective that recognizes the specificities of the place and the interconnection among its foundational factors.

SDG 1, "No Poverty," aims to end poverty in all its forms and dimensions by 2030. This goal can contribute to the respect of territorial identity when poverty eradication initiatives consider the cultural, historical, and economic specificities of the place. In situations where efforts to reduce poverty are developed uniformly without considering territorial nuances, there is a risk of neglecting the specific needs and realities of different communities, undermining local identity, and potentially generating inequalities.

SDG 2, "Zero Hunger," commits to ending hunger, achieving food security, improving nutrition, and promoting sustainable agriculture. Respect for territorial identity can emerge when food security policies consider traditional farming practices and local knowledge. Sustainable agriculture can be developed in harmony with the specific characteristics of the territories, ensuring the conservation of natural resources and the respect of socio-cultural dynamics.

SDG 3, "Good Health and Well-being," aims to ensure healthy lives and promote well-being for people of all ages. When initiatives for improving health take into account the specific cultures of different communities within a territory, territorial identity is respected. This can include actively involving local populations in defining health programs.

SDG 4, "Quality Education," aims to ensure inclusive, equitable, and quality education for all. Including content related to local history, traditions, and realities in the curriculum can help preserve territorial identity, supporting a sense of belonging. Conversely, if educational curricula ignore local cultures or promote a homogenized view of education, the identity and self-esteem of the new generations might be compromised.

The aim of SDG 5, "Gender Equality," is to bridge the gender gap, promoting the empowerment of women. In this framework, it is important to recognize and support grassroots initiatives for women's empowerment and change, actively involving women in decisions concerning their lives. When these initiatives are rooted in the local reality and respond to the needs and aspirations of women, territorial identity is valued. However, there can be situations where SDG 5 risks not fully respecting territorial identity. This could happen when policies do not consider the cultural and social specificities of the female population. In some contexts, there might be tension between women's empowerment initiatives and deeply rooted cultural traditions.

SDG 6, "Clean Water and Sanitation," endeavors to ensure the sustainable management of water resources. Ensuring access to safe drinking water and sustainable water resource management undoubtedly constitutes a cornerstone of development. Nevertheless, a potential pitfall lies in fixating solely on this aspect, thereby potentially neglecting the complex relationship that water shares with other components of territorial identity. Beyond its role as a vital natural resource, water is entwined with human history, religion, cultural practices, and societal dynamics. Initiatives focusing exclusively on the functional dimensions of water risk to disregard its cultural and symbolic significance, and by extension, underrate a crucial facet of territorial identity.

SDG 7, "Affordable and Clean Energy," advocates for the transition toward sustainable energy sources. When this transition is guided by the consideration of territorial specificities, it respects the identity of the place. However, if energy policies are "eco-blinded" and fail to account for local conditions, they may overlook the significance of energy to community identity and the cultural nuances tied to traditional energy practices.

Similarly, sustainable infrastructures, as envisioned by SDG 8, "Industry, Innovation, and Infrastructure," can also fall victim to being "eco-blinded." This occurs when development projects prioritize immediate environmental goals without fully comprehending the interconnected socio-cultural and economic elements that shape territorial identity. Consequently, they could inadvertently diminish the overall desirability of the territory. On the contrary, when infrastructural projects respect local characteristics and traditional architecture, they contribute to preserving territorial identity.

SDG 9, "Decent Work and Economic Growth," underscores the importance of creating sustainable jobs and promoting economic prosperity. When these foster local industries or artisanal traditions they also reinforce the identity of a place. Nonetheless, economic development policies solely focused on quantitative growth or environmental impact might neglect the qualitative aspects of territorial identity, such as the enhancement of local skills and the preservation of traditional practices.

SDG 10, "Reduced Inequality," seeks to remove disparities and promote inclusivity within societies. Embracing diversity, including the rights and inclusion of LGBTQ+ individuals, becomes an integral part of a territory's identity tapestry. Pride Parades, as a powerful visual representation of the celebration of identity and the integration of LGBTQ+ narratives into a place's essence, embody the spirit of inclusivity that resonates with territorial identity. Fostering a sense of belonging and acceptance, these events contribute to the richness of a place's identity. On the opposite side, forms of discrimination and exclusion, such as the establishment of "LGBT-free zones" and the imposition of restrictive legislations in certain countries, starkly oppose the trajectory of inclusivity. These actions not only undermine the principles of equality and human rights but also detract from the comprehensive identity of a region. When a territory fails to uphold the values of inclusiveness and respect for diversity, it erodes the very foundations that contribute to its distinctive identity.

SDG 11, "Sustainable Cities and Communities," holds the promise of creating urban environments that are both desirable and sustainable. This goal explicitly acknowledges the paramount importance of cultural heritage through Target 11.4, emphasizing the value of safeguarding tangible and intangible heritage assets that serve as custodians of a group or society's identity (Hosagrahar et al., 2016). The rapid urbanization of modern societies has prompted governments and civil society actors worldwide to explore innovative approaches to achieve these goals. In this context, the concept of U-Cities, or ubiquitous cities, has emerged as a promising model to seamlessly integrate cutting-edge technologies into urban scenarios while promoting social, economic, and environmental sustainability. This approach, when applied thoughtfully, can contribute to the preservation and enhancement of territorial identity. By leveraging technology to improve mobility, resource management, and citizen engagement, U-Cities offer the potential to enhance the overall quality of life while maintaining a strong sense of place, allowing residents to embrace modernity without forsaking their heritage. Alongside the potential benefits, U-Cities can also introduce challenges that could impact the respect for territorial identity. The concept of "digital divide" highlights the unequal access and usage of digital technologies among different segments of society. If left unaddressed, this divide can exacerbate the existing societal disparities and further marginalize certain communities, eroding the inclusivity and authenticity of a territory.

SDG 12, "Responsible Consumption and Production," signifies a crucial step toward integrating sustainable practices into daily life. When efforts to promote responsible consumption and production encourage local and traditional production methods, it can bolster economic resilience and maintain cultural authenticity. Conversely, a one-size-fits-all approach to sustainability may disregard the diverse fabric of territorial identity, leading to the erosion of local craftsmanship and heritage.

SDG 13, "Climate Action," envisions a world that mitigates the impacts of climate change. When climate action strategies incorporate traditional ecological knowledge, they also promote resilience by leveraging local wisdom to counteract environmental challenges. However, if climate policies neglect the unique vulnerabilities and strengths of a place, they might upset the balance of territorial identity.

SDG 14, "Life Below Water," centers on the protection of marine ecosystems. Coastal communities that integrate marine conservation into their practices contribute to sustainable development across social, economic, and environmental realms. Only when fisheries and aquatic resources are sustainably guided by local knowledge in mind, they can ensure a harmonious coexistence between humanity and the oceans for present and future generations.

SDG 15, "Life on Land" endeavors to safeguard and restore terrestrial ecosystems. While this goal acknowledges the central role of natural ecosystems in shaping territorial identity, it is imperative to recognize that such ecological preservation does not occur in isolation. The intricate interplay between ecosystems and the socio-cultural context is often underestimated. In safeguarding specific ecosystems, there might be instances where the cultural practices and historical bonds of local communities, intricately connected with these ecosystems, are inadvertently ignored. In addition, the analysis delves into the urgent task of combating desertification, exacerbated by climate change and unsustainable practices, with a particular emphasis on the challenges inherent in the realm of tourism. As underlined by John Urry (2015), in the contemporary world mass tourism is contributing to the pressure on natural habitats, with a negative impact on local communities in many tourist destinations. Consequently, he emphasized the need for more sustainable tourism management, promoting a more responsible utilization of local resources.

SDG 16, "Peace, Justice, and Strong Institutions," is aimed at creating societies that are peaceful, just, and inclusive. When efforts to establish peace and stability within territories address underlying grievances and include diverse voices, they can foster a sense of belonging and respect for territorial identity. Initiatives that prioritize conflict resolution and social cohesion acknowledge the multi-dimensional nature of identity and contribute to a more harmonious coexistence. On the contrary, when internal conflicts, insecurity, and instability persist, they can fracture the social structure of a territory, undermining the very foundation of its identity and leaving communities fractured.

SDG 17, "Partnerships for the Goals," underscores the importance of collaboration in achieving sustainability. Collaborative endeavors that build upon a region's strengths, resources, and cultural assets amplify the impact of development initiatives while preserving the essence of the territory. Conversely, partnerships driven solely by external interests, without sensitivity to local dynamics, may overlook the local identity, perpetuating imbalances in power and representation.

In light of the above, it is safe to argue that the specific individual activities, initiatives, or policies aimed at the pursuit of the SDGs cannot be definitively classified as aligned or misaligned with the preservation and enhancement of territorial identity in its entirety. When a comprehensive perspective is adopted, the dynamic interplay between SDGs and territorial identity unveils a landscape in which specific goals are seamlessly woven into the very fabric of a region's essence. In this view, territorial identity is not seen as a mere additive aspect, but rather as a fundamental context in which such objectives can be anchored and understood in their entire complexity. At the same time, when the approach is limited or blind to other needs not strictly tied to specific SDGs, the result can be partial and misaligned with territorial desirability. The achievement of the specific goal can be decisive and celebrated, but if this outcome does not consider the complexity of territorial identity as a whole, it risks being contradictory or even counterproductive. In this case, formal success is translated into substantial failure, as the achieved goal does not address the real needs, values, and dynamics of the territory. The consequences of such a limited approach can range from a lack of understanding of the subtle connections among the aspects that constitute territorial identity to a potential disconnect between the achieved objectives and the overall well-being of the community.

Accordingly, it is essential to carefully address a series of complex issues that may arise along the path toward sustainability. One central challenge is to balance the aspect of territorial identity with the broader needs and goals of development. Analyzing how the post-industrial society has generated new global threats and risks, such as climate change and nuclear safety, Ulrich Beck's work (1992) contributed to greater awareness of the interconnection between global challenges and the need for sustainable solutions at the local level. Each territory possesses a unique feature, and decisions to promote sustainable development must take these factors into account. This can present difficulties when local traditions conflict with the adoption of more sustainable practices advocated at a higher level. In such cases, finding compromises to address these challenges constructively is crucial, aiming to create synergies between the preservation of territorial identity and the adoption of new approaches.

Furthermore, it is important to promote education and awareness about the value of territorial identities, in order to foster greater understanding and collective commitment to their preservation and promotion.

Finally, there is a risk of undue appropriation of territorial identity by external actors. While the integration of territorial identities can enrich development strategies, it is important to avoid situations where these identities are exploited or manipulated for external interests. To mitigate this risk, an integrated approach involving active engagement of local communities, governmental institutions, non-governmental organizations, and other relevant local actors is necessary. As several successful case studies presented in the chapters of this volume have allowed to highlight, consultations and stakeholder participation are critical to ensuring that the integration of territorial identity into sustainable development occurs equitably and respectfully. In this scenario, eco-social work can stand out as an innovative and promising response to address the challenges related to sustainable innovation. Social workers, in this context, play a role as essential facilitators, possessing the skills and knowledge necessary to promote community-based initiatives and individual and collective empowerment (Beder, 2006; Gray et al., 2013; Hölscher et al., 2023). These professionals can act as mediators amongst various actors and interests within communities, promoting collaboration and social cohesion to achieve common sustainability and well-being goals. Eco-social work emphasizes the recognition of the interconnections among environmental, social, and economic sustainability and focuses on actions aimed at promoting a harmonious balance between people and their territory. Through this approach, social workers attempt to facilitate community empowerment, encouraging the active participation of individuals in defining their own solutions and strategies to address local challenges. A central aspect of eco-social work is the promotion of social justice, which entails addressing inequalities, injustices, and disparities within communities. Social workers are committed to strengthening the voices of marginalized and disadvantaged groups, working to create opportunities and equitable access to resources and services for all community members. As a result, through eco-social work, communities can become stronger and more resilient, as solid foundations are built to address future challenges. This type of work can help reinforce territorial identities and identify specific aspects of local culture that need to be preserved in the current transitioning scenario, in line with sustainability. A concrete example of how eco-social work can be effective is illustrated by local development initiatives and sustainability promotion implemented in various communities. In these initiatives, social workers collaborate with residents to identify community needs and challenges, and to develop targeted plans and strategies to promote collective well-being and environmental conservation. For instance, in a rural context, social workers can collaborate with farmers and local communities to promote sustainable agricultural practices that reduce environmental impact and preserve natural resources. This may involve promoting organic farming techniques, sustainable water resource management, and biodiversity conservation. In an urban context, eco-social work can aim to engage with vulnerable communities to address challenges such as environmental pollution, energy poverty, and lack of access to essential services. This could entail promoting innovative solutions for energy efficiency, supporting access to renewable energy sources, and actively involving people in defining strategies for adapting to climate change.

By approaching challenges with a constructive and respectful attitude, it is possible to harness territorial identities as drivers of positive change, pushing toward a future where sustainable development and the preservation of cultural roots seamlessly merge, forging a more just, inclusive, and prosperous future world.

References

Arora-Jonsson, S., McAreavey, R., Waldenström, C., Stiernström, A., Sandström, E., Asztalos Morell, I., Kuns, B., González-Hidalgo, M., Cras, P., & Alarcon-Ferrari, C. (2023). Multiple dimensions of sustainability: Towards new rural futures in Europe. *Sociologia Ruralis*, *63*(3), 379–389.

Beck, U. (1992). *Risk society: Towards a new modernity*. Sage.

Beder, S. (2006). *Environmental principles and policies: An interdisciplinary introduction*. Routledge.

Costanza, R., Perrings, C., & Cleveland, C. J. (Eds.). (1997). *The development of ecological economics*. Edward Elgar.

Gardner, P., Carvalho, T., & Valenstain, M. (2022). Spreading rebellion? The rise of extinction rebellion chapters across the world. *Environmental Sociology*, *8*(4), 424–435.

Geissdoerfer, M., Savaget, P., Bocken, N. M., & Hultink, E. J. (2017). The circular economy – A new sustainability paradigm? *Journal of Cleaner Production*, *143*, 757–768.

Ghisellini, P., Cialani, C., & Ulgiati, S. (2016). A review on circular economy: The expected transition to a balanced interplay of environmental and economic systems. *Journal of Cleaner Production*, *114*, 11–32.

Giddens, A. (1990). *The consequences of modernity*. Stanford University Press.

Gray, M., Coates, J., & Hetherington, T. (Eds.) (2013). *Environmental social work*. Routledge.

Hannigan, J. (2022). *Environmental sociology*. Taylor & Francis.

Hölscher, D., Hugman, R., & McAuliffe, D. (Eds.) (2023). *Social work theory and ethics: Ideas in practice*. Springer.

Hosagrahar, J., Soule, J., Girard, L. F., & Potts, A. (2016). Cultural heritage, the UN sustainable development goals, and the new urban agenda. *BDC. Bollettino Del Centro Calza Bini*, *16*(1), 37–54.

Kim, J. (2018). Social dimension of sustainability: From community to social capital. *Journal of Global Scholars of Marketing Science*, *28*(2), 175–181.

Murray, A., Skene, K., & Haynes, K. (2017). The circular economy: An interdisciplinary exploration of the concept and application in a global context. *Journal of Business Ethics*, *140*, 369–380.

Raworth, K. (2017). *Doughnut economics: Seven ways to think like a 21st-century economist*. Chelsea Green Publishing.

Sachs, J. D. (2015). *The age of sustainable development*. Columbia University Press

Sauerborn, E. (2022). The politicisation of secular mindfulness – Extinction Rebellion's emotive protest practices. *European Journal of Cultural and Political Sociology*, *9*(4), 451–474.

Sen, A. K. (2000). What is development about. *Frontiers of Development Economics: The Future in Perspective*, *1*, 506–513.

Talan, A., Tyagi, R. D., & Surampalli, R. Y. (2020). Social dimensions of sustainability. In *Sustainability: Fundamentals and applications* (pp. 183–206). John Wiley & Sons.
UNEP (United Nations Environment Programme). (2019). *Measuring progress: Towards achieving the environmental dimension of the SDGs*. United Nations Environment Programme.
Urry, J. (2015). Climate change and society. In J. Michie & C. L. Cooper (Eds.), *Why the social sciences matter* (pp. 45–59). Palgrave Macmillan.
WEF (World Economic Forum). (2019). *Making the $4.5 trillion circular economy opportunity a reality*. https://www.weforum.org/impact/helping-the-circular-economy-become-a-reality/

Index

2030 Agenda for Sustainable Development, 6, 47, 167
5G, 131

Accessibility, 104, 128, 129, 132, 137
Affordable and Clean Energy (SDG7), 71–78
Affordable Inputs Program (AIP), 28
Africa Health Strategy (2016–2030), 36–37
African Development Bank, 122
African Union (AU), 3, 36
  guidance of, 38
Agenda 5, 21
Air-to-water (WFA), 66
American Psychological Association (APA), 96
American school system, 44
Aquatic ecosystems, 68
Artificial intelligence (AI), 109, 131
Assimilation, 47
Augmented Reality (AR), 110
Automation, 83

Beetles, 146
Big data, 131
Biodiversity, 145–147
Bioenergy with carbon capture and storage (BECCS), 131
Biomedical model, 34
Blockchain technology, 131
Borehole drilling, 67
Brundtland Commission, 4
Butterflies, 146

Catastrophes, 25
Chinese Belt and Road Initiative (BRI), 88

Cholera, 64
Circular economy concept, 179–180
Clean Development Mechanism (CDM), 5
Clean Water and Sanitation (SDG6), 63–68
Climate Action (SDG13), 129–135
Climate change, 129–130
Collaborative approach, 29
Common Agricultural Policy (CAP), 149
Common Fisheries Policy (2015), 142
Communitarian approach, 159
Communities livelihoods, 65
Community Self-Sufficiency Initiative (CISER), 28
Computers, 112
Conference on Sustainable Development, 6
Conflict theory, 158
Conservation of ecosystems, 178
Construction process, 20
Convention on International Trade in Endangered Species of Wild Fauna and Flora (CITES), 4
Conventional emphasis of SDGs, 168
Cooperation, 173
Cooperative engagements, 174
Council of the European Union, the, 3
COVID-19 pandemic, 26, 111
Cultural capital concept, 17
Cultural homogenization, 46
Culture of consumerism, 117, 119
Cyclones, 25

Decent Work and Economic Growth (SDG9), 87–92
Decision-making process, 30, 135

Deforestation, 148
"Desert" ideology, 76
Desertification, 151
Detroit Future City, The (DFC), 91
Development policies, 30
Difference principle, 159
Differences, 95
Digital devices, 112
Digital divides, 112
Digital infrastructures, 131
Digital skills, 112
Direct Air Carbon Capture and Storage (DACCS), 131
Discrimination, 100
District Agriculture Office, The, 28
Doughnut economics, 179
Droughts, 25

Ebola, 37
Eco-blind
  infrastructures, 91
  projects, 75, 77
Economic institutions, 159
Education, 43–44
Educational policies, 46
Electrification of rural communities, 74
Endemism, 146
"Energy for All" initiative, 72
Energy poverty, 72
Environmental damage, 76
Environmental protection policies, 153
Environmental racism, 2
Environmental sociology, 118
Environmental sustainability, 109
Environmentalist movement, 2
European Commission, The, 3, 88
European Gender Equality Strategy (2020–2025), 59
European Parliament, the, 3
European Union (EU), 3, 179
European Union Joint Research Centre (EU-JRC), 68
Every Woman Treaty Association, 54
Extinction Rebellion (XR), 178–179

"Fair Trade" movement, 150
Female genital mutilation (FGM), 55
Feminist movement, 53
Financial sector, 172
Fishing, 139
Floods, 25
Food and Agriculture Organization of the United Nations (FAO), 142
Fridays for Future, 178
Friends of the Earth International (FOEI), 2
Functional analysis, 43

Ganges, The, 65
Gender, 17
  disparity, 51–52
Gender Equality and Empower All Women and Girls (SDG5), 51–60
Gentrification, 109
German environmentalist movement, The, 2
"Glass ceiling" phenomenon, 54
Global biodiversity, 148
Global Forest Watch satellite platform, 148
Global Fund, 38–39
Global Gateway initiative, The, 88
Global Gateway strategy, The, 88
Global Network Against Food Crises (GNAFC), 25
Global Partnership for Education (GPE), 172
Global sustainability, 2
Globalization, 117, 123–125
"Glocalization" concept, 125
Good Health and Well-being (SDG3), 33–40
Great Green Wall, 151
Green Bond Principles (GBP), 172
Green bonds, 172
  utilization, 173
Green economy, 82

Green grabbing concept, 91
Green revolution, 25, 30

Health, 33
Healthcare, 100
Heatwaves, 25
Heavily Indebted Poor Countries (HIPC), 169
"HeForShe" campaign, 56
Henrik Frode Obel Foundation, 90
Homophobia, 99
Hybrid Urbanism, 130

Income, 15
Indigenous communities, 47
Industrial sector, 67
Industry, Innovation, and Infrastructure (SDG8), 81–85
Inequality, 96
Infectious diseases, 37
Intensive agriculture, 149
International Conference on Population and Development (ICPD), 59
International cooperation, 142
International Finance Corporation (IFC), 173
International Labour Organization Convention, 76, 169
International Monetary Fund (IMF), 169
International organizations, 38
International Planned Parenthood Federation (IPPF), 59
International Union for Conservation of Nature (IUCN), 141
Internet of Things (IoT), 109

"Justice as fairness" concept, 159

Labor, 15
Land grabbing concept, 91
Languages Safeguarding Initiative (LSI), 48
Lesbian, gay, and bisexual (LGB) individuals, 96

"Let Girls Learn" program, 57–58
"LGBT-free zones", 100–101
Life Below Water (SDG14), 137–142
Life on Land (SDG15), 145–153
"Lighting Africa" project, 73–74
"Low carbon" technologies, 178

Mangroves, 141
Marine ecosystems, 138
Marine pollution, 138
Marine resources, 139
McDonaldization, 124
Medellín, 89
Millennium Development Goals (MDGs), 5–6
"More Water More Life" initiative, 68
Multicultural approach to education, 45
Multistakeholder platforms, 28

Nairobi Summit on ICPD25, The, 59
"National Centre for Truth and Reconciliation", 48
National Tuberculosis Control Program (PNCT), 39
Nature, 151
Neapolis, 140
Negative Emissions Technologies (NET), 131
Next Generation EU, 59
No Poverty (SDG1), 15–22
Noor Solar Power Complex project, 76
Nyngan Solar Plant project, 77

Obel Award, The, 90
Oceans, 137, 139
    acidification, 138
"One-size-fits-all" approach, 20–21
Open Working Group of UN, 6
Organic farming, 133
Organization of African Unity (OAU), 36
"Our Common Future", 2, 4

Paris Agreement, The, 5, 169
Participatory process, 38

Partners in Health (PIH), 35
Partnerships for the Goals (SDG17), 167–174
Pater familias, 52
Peace, Justice, and Strong Institutions (SDG16), 157–164
Political institutions, 158–159
Pollination, 146
Poverty, 16

Quality Education (SDG4), 43–48
Queer, 97

"Rainforest Alliance" label, 149–150
"Rationalization" concept, 158
Recycling, 120
Reduced Inequality (SDG10), 95–103
Reforestation, 148
Renewable energy sources, 75
Residential schools, 48
Responsible Consumption and Production (SDG12), 117–125
Revolutionary Armed Forces of Colombia (FARC), 161
Rio Earth Summit, 4
Roman patriarchal system, 52
Rural-urban migration, 108

Safe Childbirth Checklist, 59
"Safeguard Young People" program, 59
Second-level digital divide, 112
Sexuality, 115–118
Singaporean government, The, 111
Single-Use Plastics Directive (SUP Directive), 120
Smartphones, 112
Social cohesion, 28
Social justice, 157
Social sciences, 34
Social system, 34
Social well-being, 35
Social workers, 185
Sociology, 16

Special Criminal Court, 161–162
Stockholm Conference, The, 4
Subscription Economy, 121
Surveillance capitalism, 123
Sustainability, 1, 177
Sustainable agricultural practices, 133
Sustainable agricultural product certifications, 149
Sustainable agriculture, 133
Sustainable Cities and Communities (SDG11), 111–114
Sustainable consumption, 118
Sustainable development goal (SDG), 7
  SDG 1, 181
  SDG 2, 181
  SDG 3, 181
  SDG 4, 181
  SDG 5, 181–182
  SDG 6, 182
  SDG 7, 182
  SDG 8, 182
  SDG 9, 182
  SDG 10, 182–183
  SDG 11, 183
  SDG 12, 183
  SDG 13, 183
  SDG 14, 183
  SDG 15, 183–184
  SDG 16, 184
  SDG 17, 184
Sustainable development programs and initiatives, 72
Sustainable digitalization, 82
Sustainable energy economy, 77
Sustainable Energy for All (SE4ALL) initiative, 72
Symbolic policies, 102

Tarfaya Wind Farm, 74
Taxol, 146
Technological innovation, 84
Technological progress, 83
Technology, 88
"Territorial desirability" concept, 11
Territorial identity, 10

Territorial imagination, 9
Territorial trap, 8
Territory concept, 8
Tickbox approach, 7
Tourism, 79, 150, 159, 167, 169–171, 173, 174, 209
Transphobia, 99
Treadmill of production, 118
Triple oppression, 17
Truth Commission, 162
Typhoid fever, 64

Ubiquitous cities (U-cities), 109, 183
UN Conference on Sustainable Development, 4
UN Conference on the Human Environment, The, 3
UN Conferences on Climate Change (COP), 5
UNICEF, 39, 63
UNITAID, 39
United Nations Declaration on the Rights of Indigenous Peoples (2007), 19, 47
United Nations Educational, Scientific and Cultural Organization (UNESCO), 48
   Intergovernmental Oceanographic Commission, 141
   World Heritage, 147
United Nations Entity for Gender Equality and the Empowerment of Women, The (UN Women), 59–60
United Nations Environment Programme (UNEP), 3
United Nations Framework Convention on Climate Change, 4
United Nations Industrial Development Organization (UNIDO), 3

United Nations organization (UN organization), 3
   General Assembly, 6, 48
United Nations Population Fund (UNFPA), 59
United States Agency for International Development (USAID), 58
United States Environmental Protection Agency (EPA), 3
Universal Health Care (UHC), 36
Unsustainable fishing methods, 137
Urban Land Institute (ULI), 89
Urban revitalization, 109
Urbanization, 107–109, 149

Virtual Reality (VR), 110

Wall Street Journal (WSJ), 89
"Warka Tower" project, 66
Water, 63
   availability, 64
   resources, 64
Wealth, 15
Western agricultural technologies, 30
Whānau Ora community development program, 19
"White Wednesdays" protests, 57
Wildlife Corridor Action Plan, 150
World Bank, The, 68
World Economic Forum report (WEF), 180
World Health Organization (WHO), 34, 59, 63
World Health Statistics (2022), 36
World Resource Institute, 148

"Zero carbon" technologies, 178
"Zero deforestation", 148
Zero Hunger (SDG2), 25–30

Printed in the USA
CPSIA information can be obtained
at www.ICGtesting.com
JSHW011800031224
74704JS00004B/119